IRELAND

Scale 1:200 000
3.16 miles to 1 inch
2km to 1cm

Reprinted June 2005
Reprinted August 2004
Reprinted June 2004
1st edition April 2004

© Automobile Association Developments Limited 2005

This product includes mapping based upon data licensed from Ordnance Survey of Northern Ireland® reproduced by permission of the Chief Executive, acting on behalf of the Controller of Her Majesty's Stationery Office © Crown copyright 2005. Permit number 40457. This product includes RCDI by permission of Ordnance Survey of Northern Ireland on behalf of the Controller of Her Majesty's Stationery Office © Crown Copyright 2005.

Republic of Ireland mapping based on Ordnance Survey Ireland. Permit number 7954. © Ordnance Survey Ireland and Government of Ireland.

Many place names in the main-map section of this atlas are given in English and Irish. The names shown are those approved by the Ordnance Survey of Northern Ireland and Ordnance Survey Ireland.

The AA would like to acknowledge the following bodies and agencies for information used in the creation of this atlas:
The Environment & Heritage Service, Heritage of Ireland, RSPB, Department of Agriculture & Rural Development, Coillte Teoranta, The National Trust, An Taisce, Roads Service and The National Roads Authority. Relief map image supplied by Mountain High Maps ® Copyright © 1993 Digital Wisdom, Inc.

Published by AA Publishing (a trading name of Automobile Association Developments Limited, whose registered office (from 1st October 2005) will be Fanum House, Basing View, Basingstoke, Hampshire RG21 4EA, UK. Registered number 1878835)

Mapping produced by the Cartography Department of The Automobile Association (A02731).

ISBN 0 7495 3545 8

A CIP catalogue record for this book is available from The British Library.

Printed in Britain by Scotprint, Haddington, Scotland.

Atlas contents

Map pages	inside front cover
Route planning	**II-V**
Route planner	II
Ferry ports	III
Distance chart	IV
The shape of the land	V
Key to road maps	**VI-1**
Map pages	VI
Key to map symbols	1
Road maps 1:200 000 scale	**2-68**
Town plans	**69-75**
Key to town plans	69
Motorways	**76-80**
Key to motorway maps	76
Index to place names	**81-90**
County and administrative areas	81
Freshwater fishing	inside back cover

Route planner

Ferry ports

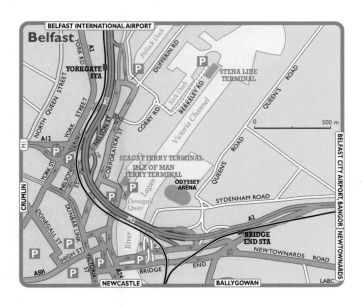

Belfast

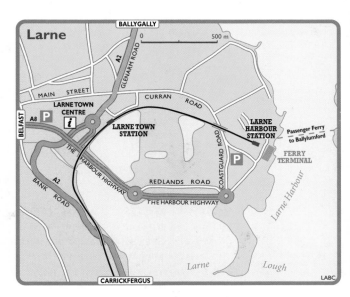

Larne

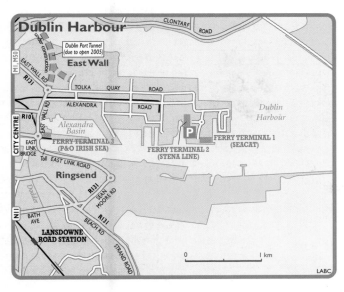

Dublin Harbour

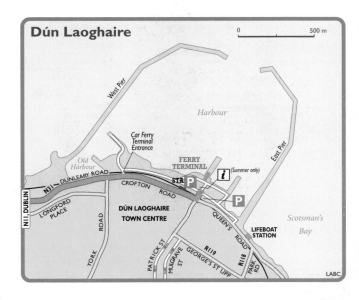

Dún Laoghaire

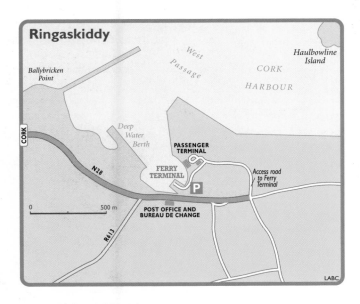

Ringaskiddy

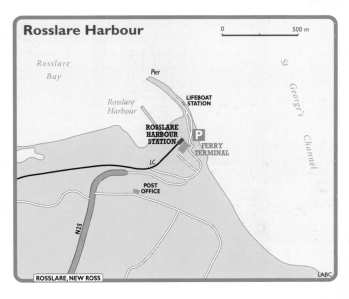

Rosslare Harbour

Distance chart

This chart shows distances, in both miles and kilometres, between two towns along AA-recommended routes. Using motorways and other main roads this is normally the fastest route, though not necessarily the shortest.

For example, the distance between Cork and Omagh is 395 kilometres or 245 miles (8 kilometres is approximately 5 miles).

To reflect the distances shown on road signs, distances shown on the road maps in this atlas are in miles in Northern Ireland and kilometres in the Republic of Ireland.

distances in miles

Cities (diagonal labels): Antrim, Armagh, Athlone, Ballina (Tipp.), Belfast, Belmullet, Bundoran, Carlow, Cavan, Clifden, Cork, Donegal, Downpatrick, Dublin, Dundalk, Dungloe, Ennis, Enniskillen, Galway, Glengariff, Kilkee, Kilkenny, Killarney, Larne, Limerick, Londonderry, Mallow, Mullingar, Omagh, Portlaoise, Portrush, Roscommon, Sligo, Tipperary, Tralee, Tullamore, Waterford, Waterville, Wexford, Wicklow

Upper triangle (distances in miles):

```
43 141 203 18 204 99 168 89 232 274 92 40 114 61 105 210 86 193 335 244 192 281 21 213 54 261 118 54 166 46 144 127 225 276 142 214 321 201 144
   99 161 41 168 83 140 47 196 246 84 47 86 33 96 167 50 150 277 202 164 239 62 171 71 233 85 37 138 68 101 92 197 235 109 186 280 173 116
      64 139 123 95 68 52 107 136 113 138 78 93 150 68 84 57 180 103 76 142 161 74 145 115 36 111 45 160 20 74 82 138 24 105 182 116 111
         193 157 157 81 115 104 78 175 186 114 142 212 32 147 55 121 67 71 83 214 15 207 57 84 173 58 223 84 135 38 79 59 91 124 129 141
            202 117 158 88 230 264 116 22 105 51 129 208 84 190 326 242 182 271 22 203 72 252 109 70 156 63 142 126 215 267 133 205 312 191 135
               98 192 148 91 231 116 212 189 195 153 144 118 111 140 144 169 199 103 76 191 232 147 229 277 239 222
                  164 65 126 230 18 127 132 96 55 144 33 110 274 178 172 236 120 166 63 209 106 45 141 100 75 22 191 232 120 201 276 212 168
                     116 165 116 184 152 52 107 222 114 147 116 177 148 24 145 180 91 197 103 69 163 23 221 89 142 70 155 44 47 196 47 52
                        160 187 69 94 68 61 106 121 32 103 231 155 121 193 109 125 93 166 44 59 90 109 55 70 133 189 68 162 233 161 104
                           177 144 240 185 201 181 91 146 50 221 125 154 183 251 113 189 156 143 172 142 227 98 104 138 179 125 184 224 202 218
                              248 257 162 213 285 87 219 129 62 94 92 56 286 64 279 22 154 245 108 326 156 208 64 76 129 80 99 118 160
                                 127 136 111 36 161 37 128 291 196 190 254 113 184 46 227 123 47 159 84 93 40 209 249 138 219 294 229 172
                                    98 44 139 207 95 196 319 242 175 264 44 196 93 245 102 80 149 85 146 136 208 260 126 198 305 184 128
                                       53 176 147 99 137 224 181 80 192 126 124 151 150 51 117 54 167 96 133 114 188 66 103 233 87 30
                                          124 163 64 152 274 197 130 220 73 152 99 200 57 65 105 113 102 105 164 216 81 153 260 140 83
                                             198 74 165 328 233 227 291 125 221 54 264 160 59 196 91 130 77 246 286 175 268 331 262 206
                                                153 42 130 34 98 92 230 23 207 66 106 179 91 229 86 122 47 88 87 101 133 139 174
                                                   114 263 187 153 225 106 157 61 198 76 27 122 98 65 41 165 221 100 193 265 192 135
                                                      172 76 105 134 212 64 173 107 94 141 93 210 49 88 89 129 75 135 174 153 169
                                                         101 154 38 347 107 323 67 200 289 169 339 200 252 125 58 175 142 56 179 222
                                                            132 63 264 57 241 73 140 214 125 263 121 156 82 43 121 135 96 173 208
                                                               121 203 75 220 80 77 186 31 244 96 150 51 139 51 30 172 48 77
                                                                  293 70 285 42 162 251 136 301 162 214 92 20 137 119 50 157 199
                                                                     225 75 273 130 75 178 55 164 147 237 288 154 226 333 213 156
                                                                        229 43 94 183 68 233 94 145 25 65 69 78 110 116 151
                                                                           259 137 34 183 40 126 85 226 281 161 243 326 237 180
                                                                              142 225 95 314 136 188 51 63 116 78 92 116 158
                                                                                 103 46 153 40 84 105 158 24 107 203 108 84
                                                                                    149 71 92 68 192 247 127 209 292 203 147
                                                                                       218 66 119 59 132 21 60 177 70 82
                                                                                          163 122 278 297 177 267 342 254 197
                                                                                             53 103 158 44 126 203 136 129
                                                                                                169 210 98 180 255 190 166
                                                                                                   88 80 53 133 91 133
                                                                                                      133 139 53 177 215
                                                                                                         81 178 91 93
                                                                                                            170 38 80
                                                                                                               208 250
                                                                                                                  59
```

Lower triangle (distances in kilometres):

```
69
227 159
326 259 102
29 66 224 310
328 270 198 253 324
160 134 154 252 188 158
271 226 109 130 256 308 264
144 75 84 184 141 238 104 186
373 315 171 167 370 147 203 265 257
441 396 218 125 425 371 371 188 300 286
148 135 182 281 187 187 29 296 111 232 399
64 76 221 299 35 342 205 243 151 387 414 204
184 139 125 183 169 305 212 90 109 299 261 219 157
98 53 150 228 83 314 155 171 99 323 342 179 71 85
168 155 242 340 207 246 88 356 171 291 459 58 224 283 199
338 269 110 52 335 232 231 183 194 146 139 260 333 236 262 319
138 81 135 236 135 189 53 236 52 235 352 60 152 159 102 119 245
310 241 91 88 307 179 176 185 166 80 206 205 315 219 244 265 67 184
540 446 289 195 524 441 440 287 371 356 99 469 513 360 441 529 210 423 277
393 324 165 107 390 287 287 238 249 202 152 315 389 291 318 375 55 301 123 162
302 257 122 114 287 321 277 39 195 249 148 305 282 123 204 365 158 246 170 247 213
452 385 228 134 436 380 380 235 310 295 90 408 425 309 354 468 149 362 216 61 101 195
34 100 259 345 36 359 193 289 175 404 460 182 71 203 117 202 369 170 341 559 425 327 471
342 276 119 25 327 268 268 146 201 184 103 296 315 199 244 356 37 252 104 173 92 121 112 362
87 114 233 333 115 259 101 316 149 305 449 74 150 242 159 87 333 98 278 542 388 354 481 120 369
421 376 185 91 405 338 337 167 268 253 35 366 394 241 322 425 106 319 174 107 118 129 67 440 69 417
190 137 58 136 175 226 170 111 71 231 248 199 164 82 92 258 170 122 152 322 225 124 261 210 152 220 228
87 60 178 279 112 232 73 262 95 277 395 75 129 188 104 95 288 43 227 466 344 300 405 120 295 55 362 165
267 222 73 93 251 272 227 37 145 229 173 256 240 87 168 315 146 197 150 273 202 49 219 286 110 294 153 75 240
74 109 258 359 101 319 162 355 175 365 525 135 136 268 183 147 369 158 338 546 424 393 485 89 375 64 505 245 115 351
232 163 32 136 229 166 121 142 88 157 251 150 235 155 164 209 139 105 78 322 194 155 261 263 152 202 219 65 148 106 262
205 147 118 217 202 123 35 229 112 168 335 64 219 214 169 123 196 67 141 405 252 241 344 236 233 137 302 135 110 192 197 86
362 317 133 61 347 308 307 113 215 223 102 336 335 183 263 396 76 266 144 202 132 82 148 381 40 364 82 169 309 95 447 166 272
445 378 221 127 429 374 373 249 303 289 122 418 418 302 347 461 142 355 209 94 22 223 464 105 452 99 254 398 212 478 254 338 141
229 176 38 95 214 237 321 70 109 201 207 221 202 131 281 140 161 122 282 195 83 221 248 111 259 189 39 204 34 284 71 158 128 214
346 301 170 147 330 369 324 76 262 296 129 353 320 167 248 413 162 313 217 228 218 48 192 366 126 392 125 171 338 97 431 203 289 86 224 130
517 451 294 200 502 446 445 316 376 361 159 474 490 374 419 533 214 427 282 90 154 277 82 536 177 525 148 327 470 285 550 327 410 214 85 286 273
324 279 186 207 308 385 341 75 260 327 189 370 297 140 225 423 223 310 247 289 278 78 253 343 186 382 187 174 327 113 408 219 305 147 285 147 61 334
232 187 178 227 217 357 270 83 166 352 257 276 206 48 134 331 280 217 273 357 335 124 231 251 243 290 254 134 331 131 317 207 267 215 346 150 129 402 95
```

The shape of the land

At a glance

Highest mountains
Carrauntoohil, Kerry	1038 m
Brandon Mountain, Kerry	950 m
Lugnaquilla Mountain, Wicklow	924 m
Galtymore Mountain, Lim/Tipp	919 m
Slieve Donard, Down, NI	850 m

★ World heritage sites
Boyne Valley Mounds, Meath
Giant's Causeway, Moyle, NI
Skellig Michael, Kerry

Highest cliff
Croaghaun, Achill Island, Mayo	668 m

Largest lake
Lough Neagh	147 sq miles

Longest river
Shannon	259 km

Highest waterfall
Powerscourt Falls, Wicklow	106 m

0	10	20	30	40	50 miles
0	20	40	60	80 km	

Map pages

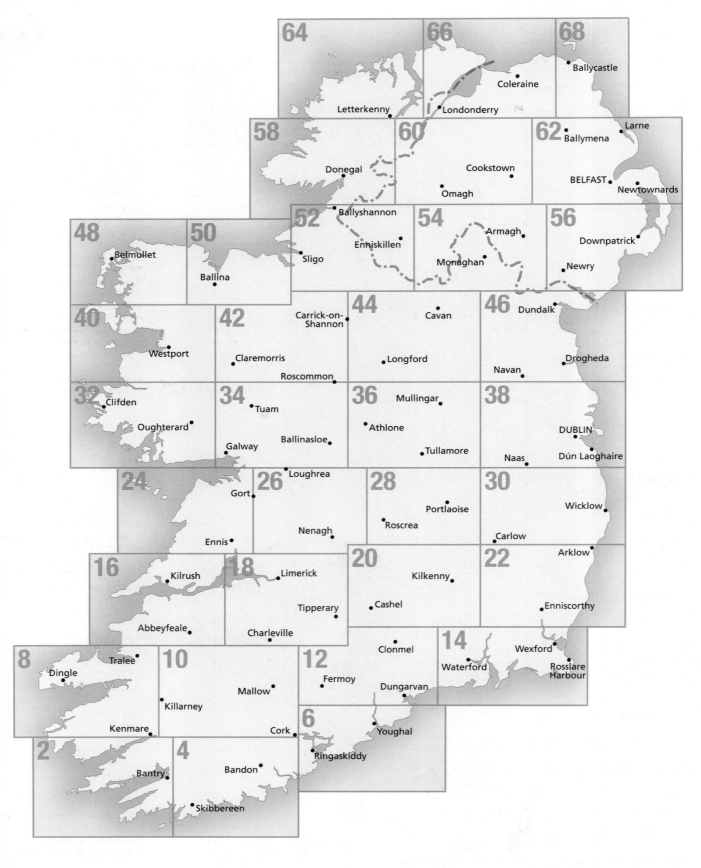

Key to map symbols
Eochair   Légende   Legende

Motoring information

Mótarbhealach saor in aisce / Autoroute gratuite	**M1**	**Toll-free motorway** / Mautfreie Autobahn
Mótarbhealach le híoc / Autoroute à péage	**M1 Toll**	**Toll motorway** / Mautpflichtige Autobahn
Acomhal lán, srianta / Échangeur partiel		**Full, restricted junction** / Vollwertige, eingeschränkte Anschlussstelle
Mótarbhealach á dhéanamh / Autoroute en construction		**Motorway under construction** / Autobahn in Bau
Carrbhealach dúbailte / Double voie		**Dual carriageway** / Straße mit getrennten Fahrbahnen
Carrbhealach singil / Une voie		**Single carriageway** / Straße mit einem Fahrstreifen
Bóthar á dhéanamh / Route en construction		**Road under construction** / Straße in Bau
Mionbhóthar / Route secondaire		**Minor road** / Nebenstraße
Droichead nó bóthar le híoc / Péage pont ou routier	Toll	**Bridge or road toll** / Brücken- oder Straßenmaut
Carrchaladh / Car-ferry		**Car ferry** / Autofähre
Carrchaladh catamaran / Catamaran-ferry		**Catamaran car ferry** / Katamaran-Autofähre
...*alach iarainn, stáisiún, crosaire comhréidh* / Voie de chemin de fergare, passage à niveau		**Railway, station, level crossing** / Eisenbahn, Bahnhof, Bahnübergang
Aerfort, aerpháirc / Aéroport, aérodrome	✈ ✈	**Airport, airfield** / Flughafen, Flugplatz
Cathair, baile mór, baile beag nó ceantar / Grande ville, ville, village ou localité		**City, town, village or locality** / Großstadt, Stadt, Dorf oder Ort
Airde i méadair, timpeall / Altitude en mètres, col	628 ▲	**Height in metres, pass** / Höhenangabe in Metern, Pass

Príomh cheann cúrsa (roghnaithe) / Destination primaire (sélectionnée)	**CORK**	**Primary destination (selected)** / Hauptziel (ausgewählt)
Bóthar príomha náisiúnta (IRL) / Route nationale (IRL)	**N17**	**National primary route (IRL)** / Nationalstraße erster Ordnung (IRL)
Bóthar tánaisteach náisiúnta (IRL) / Route départementale (IRL)	**N56**	**National secondary route (IRL)** / Nationalstraße zweiter Ordnung (IRL)
Bóthar réigiúnach (IRL) / Route communale (IRL)	**R182**	**Regional road (IRL)** / Regionalstraße (IRL)
Faid i gciliméadar (IRL) / Distance en kilomètres (IRL)	▽ 8 ▽	**Distance in kilometres (IRL)** / Entfernung in Kilometern (IRL)
Bóthar príomha (NI) / Route nationale (NI)	**A4**	**Primary route (NI)** / Straße erster Ordnung (NI)
Bóthar A (NI) / Catégorie A (NI)	**A21**	**A road (NI)** / Nationalstraße (NI)
Bóthar B (NI) / Catégorie B (NI)	**B75**	**B road (NI)** / Nebenstraße (NI)
Faid i mílte (NI) / Distance en miles (NI)	▽ 5 ▽	**Distance in miles (NI)** / Entfernung in Meilen (NI)
Tollán bóthair / Tunnel routier	======	**Road tunnel** / Straßentunnel
Teorainn idirnáisiúnta / Frontière internationale		**International boundary** / Staatsgrenze
Teorainn eile / Autre frontière		**Other boundary** / Andere Grenze
Trá, cladach eile / Plage, autre rivage		**Beach, other foreshore** / Strand, sonstige Uferbereiche
Abhainn, canáil, loch / Rivière, canal, lac		**River, canal, lough** / Fluss, Kanal, See
Uimhir leanúnach an leathanaigh / Numéro de continuation de page	**23**	**Page continuation number** / Nummer der Anschlussseite

Touring information

Ionad eolais turasóireachta / Office de tourisme	ℹ	**Tourist information** / Fremdenverkehrsamt
Ionad eolais turasóireachta (séasúrach) / Office de tourisme (saisonnier)	ℹ	**Tourist information (seasonal)** / Fremdenverkehrsamt (während der Saison)
Ionad cuartaíochta / Centre pour visiteurs	**V**	**Visitor centre** / Besucherzentrum
Láithreán campála AA / Terrain pour camping homologué AA		**AA approved campsite** / Mit AA ausgezeichneter Campingplatz
Láithreán carbhán eile / Autre terrain pour caravanes		**Other caravan site** / Sonstiger Wohnwagenplatz
Mainistir, ardeaglais nó prióireacht / Abbaye, cathédrale ou monastère		**Abbey, cathedral or priory** / Abtei, Kathedrale, Priorei
...*allóg mainistreach, ardeaglais nó prióireacht* / Ruines d'abbaye, de cathédrale ou de monastère		**Ruined abbey, cathedral or priory** / Abtei-, Kathedralen-, Priorei-Ruine
Caisleán, dún / Château, fortifications		**Castle, hill-fort** / Schloss, Festung
Iarsmalann nó dánlann / Musée ou galerie	Ⓜ	**Museum or gallery** / Museum oder Kunstgalerie
Gairdín, páirc tuaithe / Jardin, parc		**Garden, country park** / Garten, Landschaftspark
Zú, fiabheatha nó páirc éanlaithe / Zoo, réserve naturelle ou parc ornithologique		**Zoo, wildlife or bird park** / Zoo, Tier- oder Vogelpark
Dúlra, tearmann éin / Réserve naturelle, ornithologique	RSPB	**Nature, bird reserve** / Natur-, Vogelschutzgebiet
Slíbhealach le comharthaí / Promenade banalisée	— —	**Waymarked walk** / Ausgeschilderter Weg
Ionad dearctha, láithreán picnící / Panorama, aire de pique-nique		**Viewpoint, picnic site** / Aussichtspunkt, Picknick-Platz
Ar liosta AA, galfchúrsa eile / Terrain de golf homologué AA, non homologué AA		**AA listed, other golf course** / Mit AA ausgezeichneter, sonstiger Golfplatz

Bealach radharcach / Itinéraire pittoresque		**Scenic route** / Landschaftlich schöne Strecke
Rásaí capall, ciorcad rásaí cairr / Hippodrome, circuit automobile		**Horse racing, motor-racing circuit** / Pferde-, Motorrennbahn
Lúthchleasaíocht idirnáisiúnta, aontas rugbaí / Événements athlétiques internationaux, rugby		**International athletics, rugby union** / Internationale Leichtathletik-, Rugby-Union
Gníomhaíocht sciála, bádóireacht / Activités nautiques, ski		**Boating, skiing activities** / Wassersport, Ski
Áitreabh Taisce Náisiúnta / Propriété du National Trust	NT AT	**National Trust property** / Eigentum des National Trust
Teach nó foirgneamh stairiúil / Bâtiment ou maison historique		**Historic house or building** / Historisches Haus oder Gebäude
Páirc Náisiúnta / Parc national		**National Park** / Nationalpark
Páirc Foraoise / Parc forestier		**Forest Park** / Parkwald
Foraois / Forêt		**Woodland** / Wald
Leacht réamhstairiúil / Monument préhistorique		**Prehistoric monument** / Prähistorisches Denkmal
Suim tionsclaíoch / Point d'intérêt industriel		**Industrial interest** / Industriedenkmal
Láithreán catha le dáta / Champ de bataille avec date	✕ 1690	**Battle site with date** / Schlachtfeld mit Datum
Leacht, áit eile suimiúil / Monument, autre lieu d'intérêt	★	**Monument, other place of interest** / Denkmal, anderer interessanter Ort
Léiríonn comharthaí le boscaí tarraingtí laistigh de cheantair uirbeacha / Les symboles encadrés signalent un lieu d'attraction en zone urbaine	☐	**Boxed symbols indicate attractions within urban areas** / Eingerahmte Symbole bezeichnen Attraktionen innerhalb der Stadtgebiete

BRAY HEAD

Ⓐ Dromgour   Ⓑ   Ⓒ agh   Ⓓ   **8**   Ⓔ   Ⓕ   Ⓖ   Ⓗ

VALLENCIA ISLAND
Skellig Experience
Portmagee
An Caladh
Aghnagar Bridge
Failclogh
Dromaragh
Tooreenbog Lough
Knockmoyle
Derriana Lough
Lough Adoolig
676 ▲
Knocknagantee
R565
Derreen
N70
50
R565
20
Killoluaig
Emlaghmore
Muingydowda
Mastergeehy
Lough Namona
Cloonaghlin Lough
Tulla
Teeran
Cagh
Sallahig
Caherbarnagh
673 ▲
650 ▲
Coomcallee
Lomanagh
Ballynahow
R567
Killurly
R566
4
Puffin Island
ST FINAN'S BAY
Ballinskelligs
Baile an Sceilge
WATERVILLE
An Coireán
Ballybrack
LOUGH CURRANE
Iskanamacteery
Lough Iskanamacteery
377 ▲
Esknaloughoge
15
Derreenauliff
Pa
Horse Island
Ardkearagh
509 ▲
Mullaghbeg
542 ▲
Eagles Hill
The Kerry Way
Illaunleagh
Bunnow Harbour
Ducalla Head
409 ▲
Bolus
BALLINSKELLIGS BAY
N70
Cahernageeha Mountain
499 ▲
Castle Cove
N70
Illaundrane
BOLUS HEAD
Hog's Head
304 ▲
Beenarourke
Caherdaniel
Cathair Dónall
Nedanone
Daniel's Island
Dog's P
Sheehan's Point
Derrynane
KENMARE RIVER
Abbey Island
Derrynane Bay
Lamb's Head
Deenish Island
Ardgroom
Dhá Dhrom
Lough Fadda
19
Scariff Island
Kilcatherine Point
Inishfarnard
Gortgarriff
COULAGH BAY
R571
Eyeries
Na hAorai
Crumpan
Ardacluggin Point
Kealinch
Cod's Head
Urhin
Travara Bridge
6
19 R575
MOUNTAIN
Knocknagallaun
376 ▲
SLIEVE MISKISH
488 ▲ Knockgour
Baile Chaisleáin Bhearra
CA BE
Allihies
Na hAilichi
Ballydonegan
Gour Bridge
Garnish Point
Cable Car
Garnish Bay
Lackacroghan
260 ▲
R575
R572
Fair Head
DURSEY ISLAND
Ballynacallagh
The Béara Way
Firkeel
8
Cahermore
The Bull
Kilmichael
White Ball Head
Black Ball Head
The Cow
DURSEY HEAD
Crow Head
The Calf

A T L A N T I C   O C E A N

0 1 2 3 4 5 miles
0 1 2 3 4 5 6 7 8 km

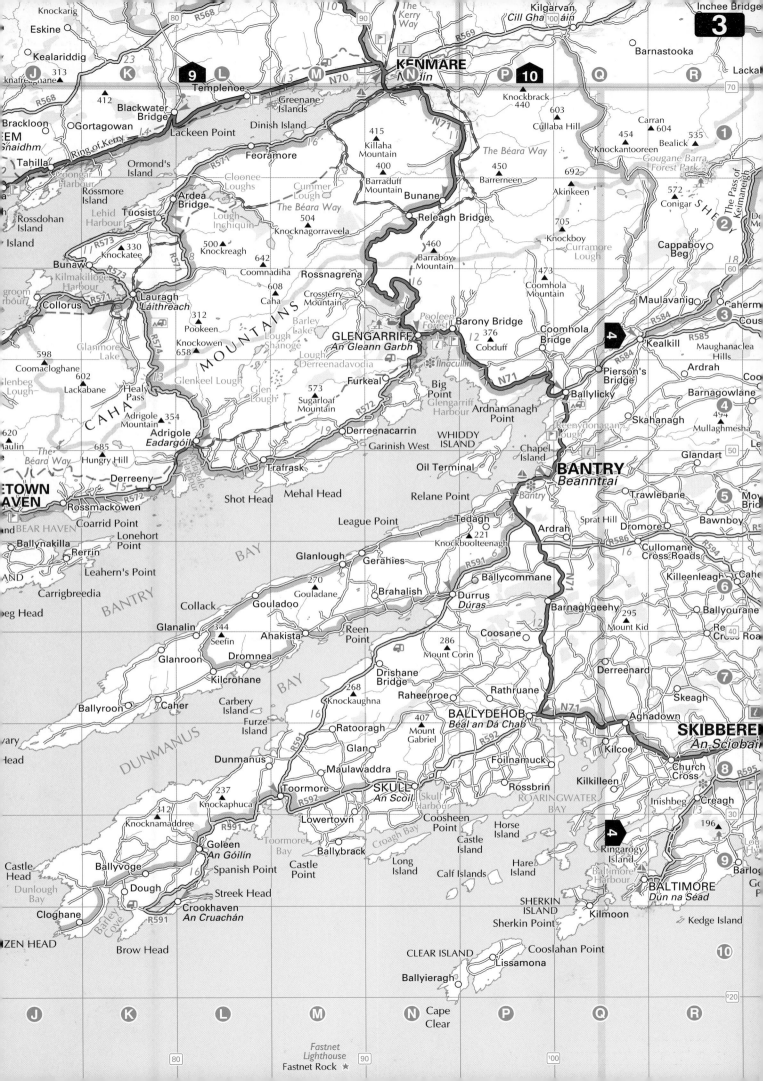

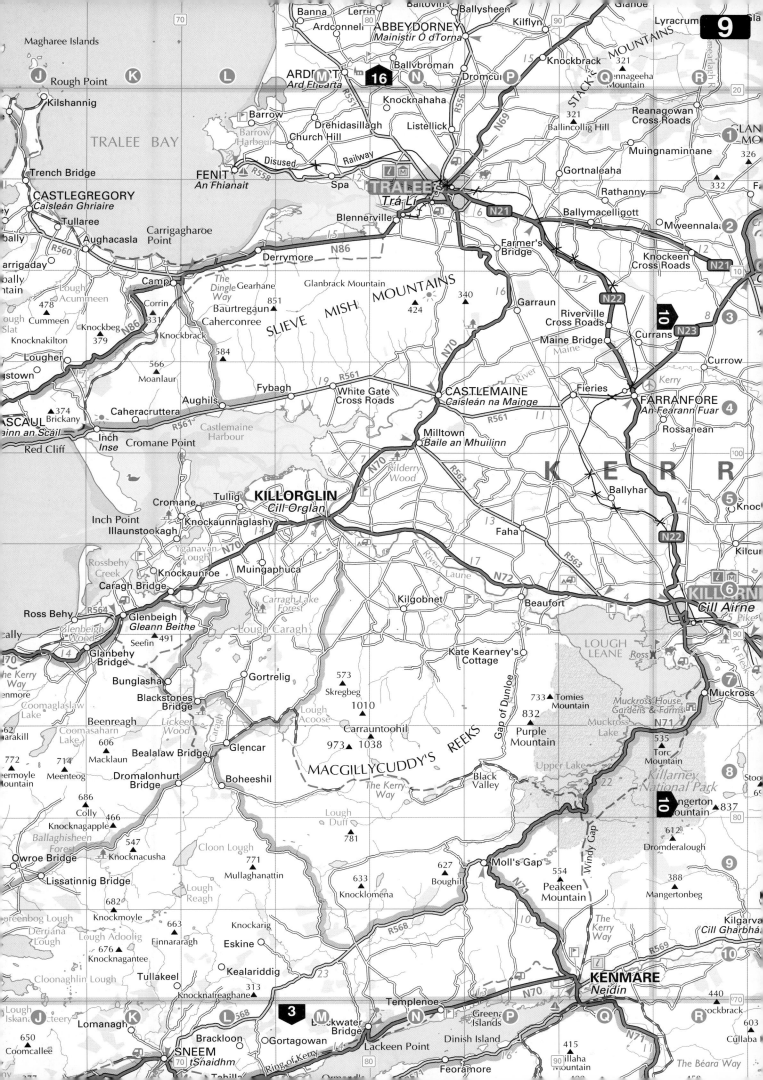

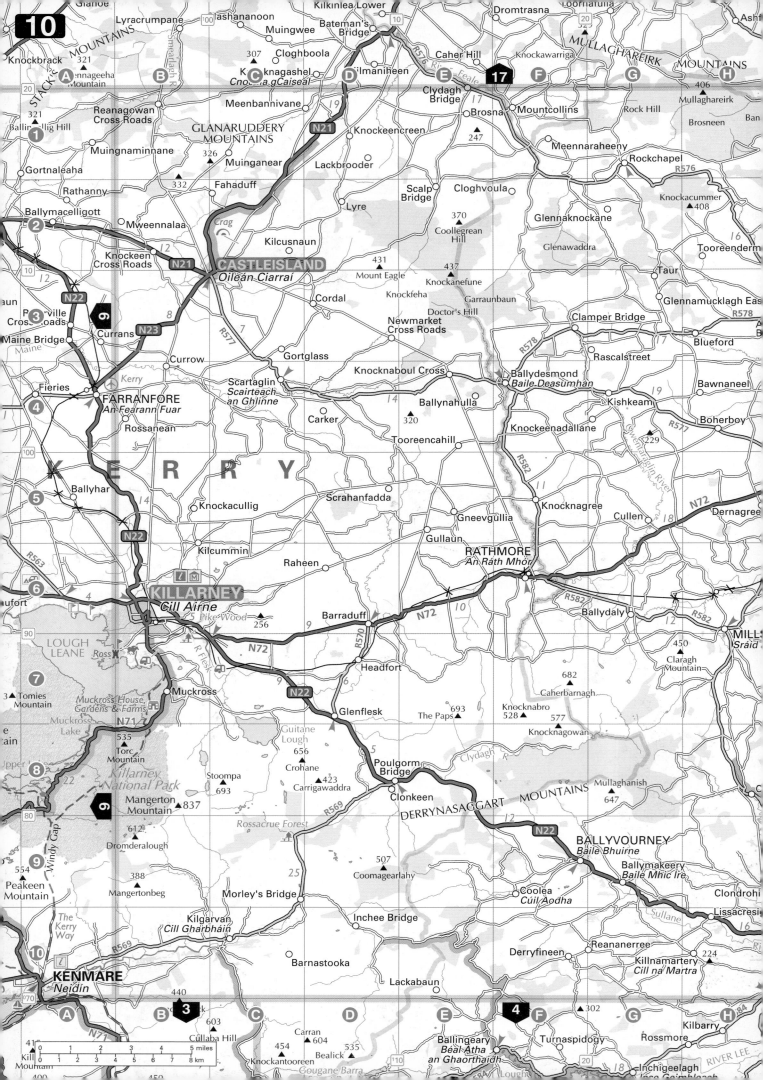

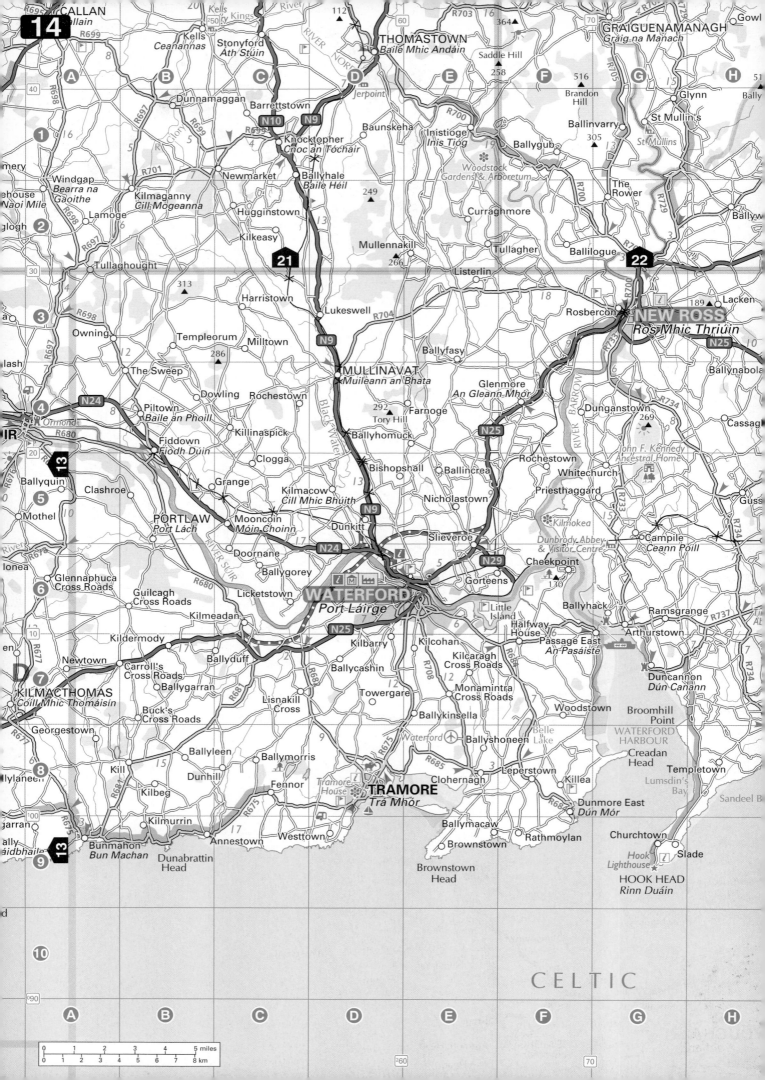

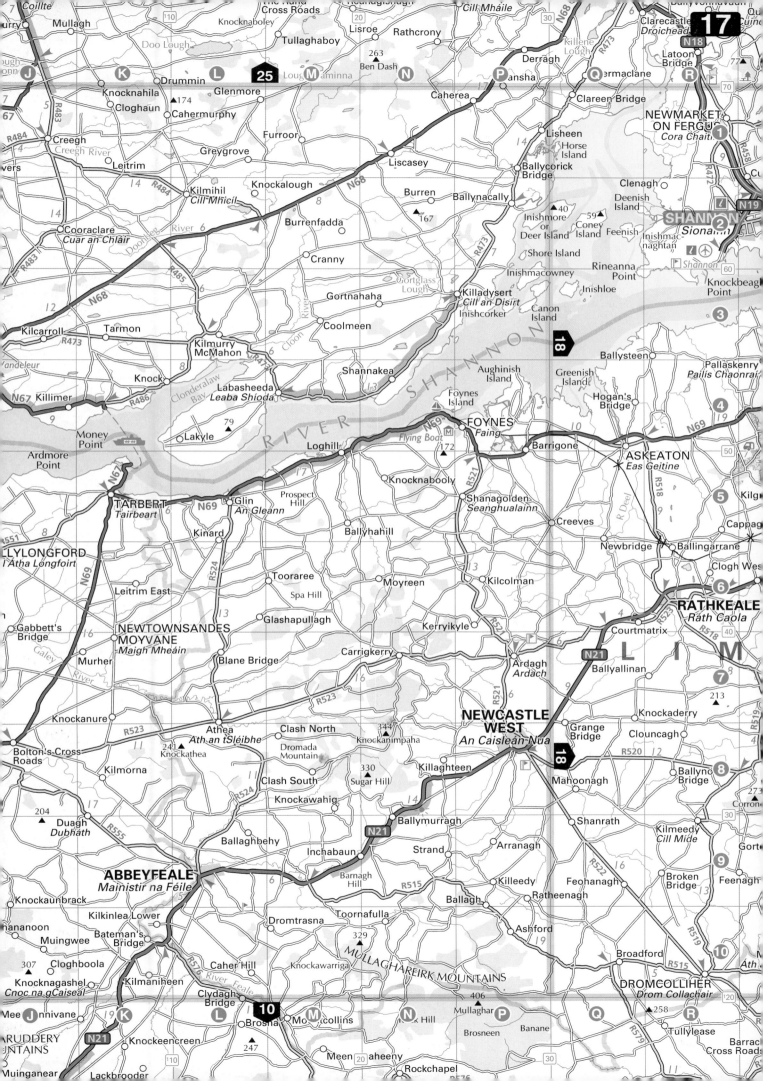

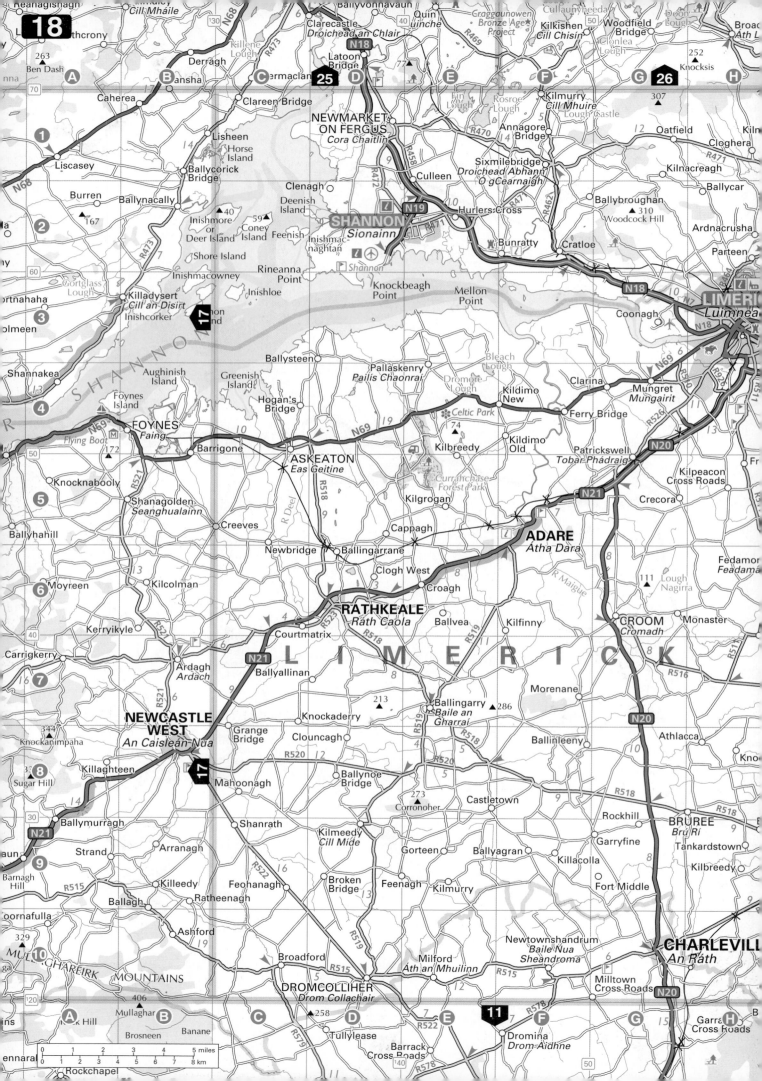

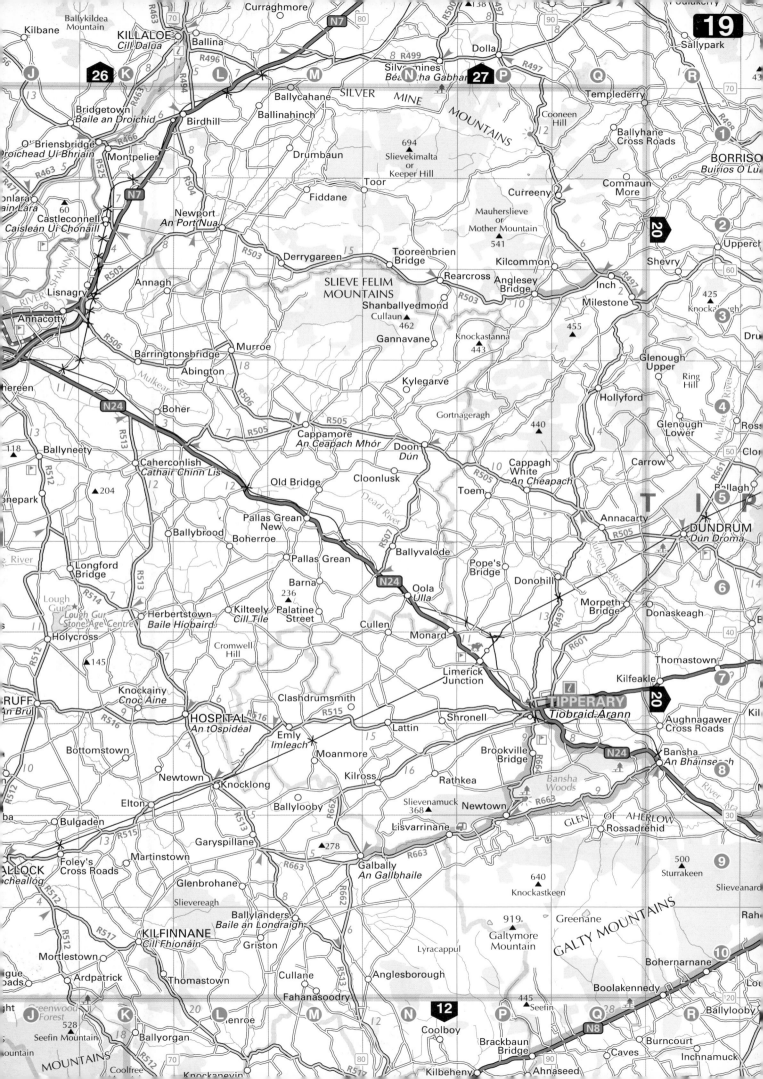

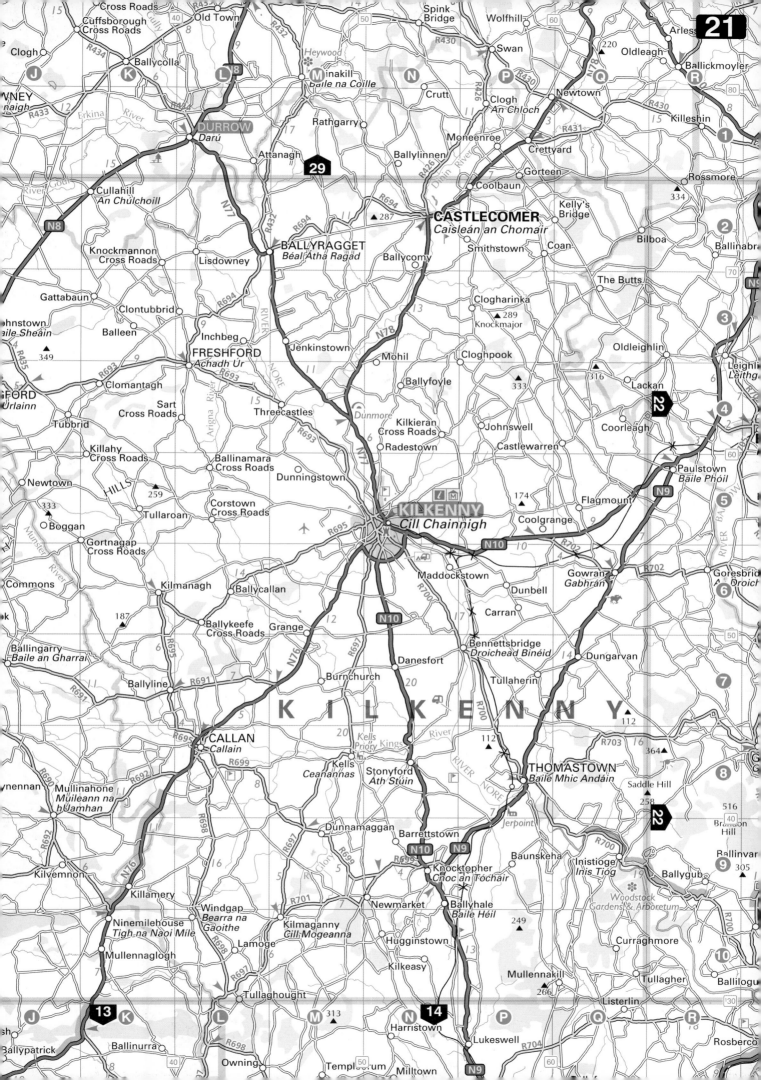

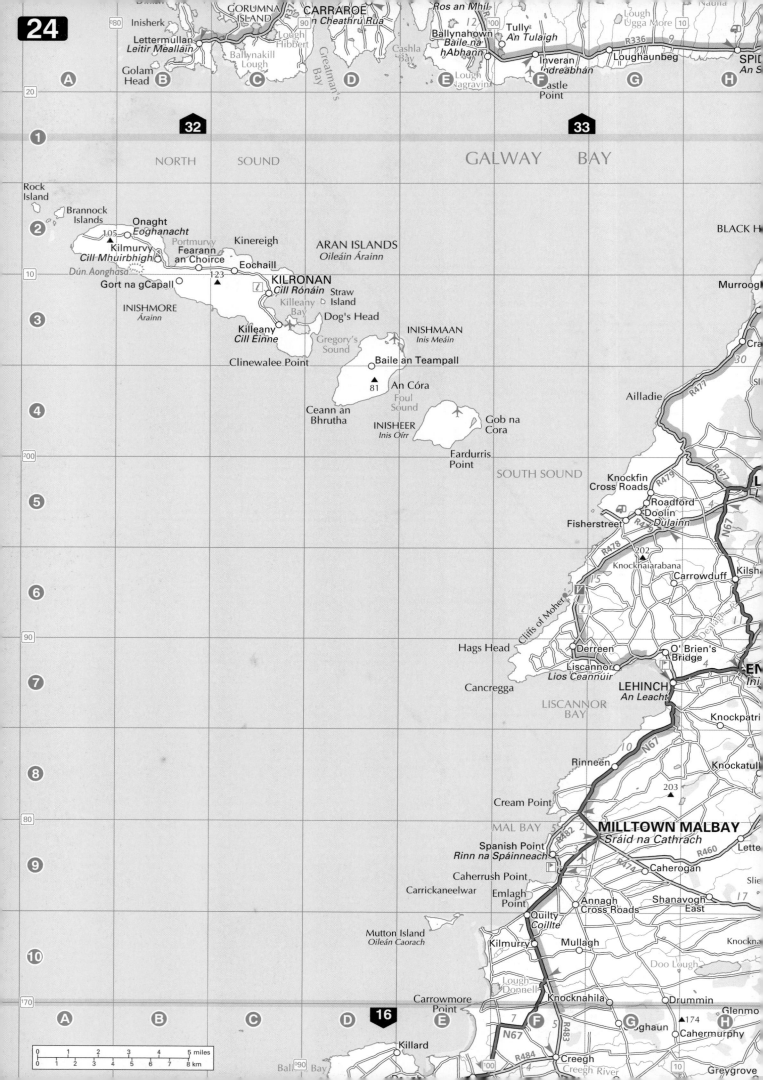

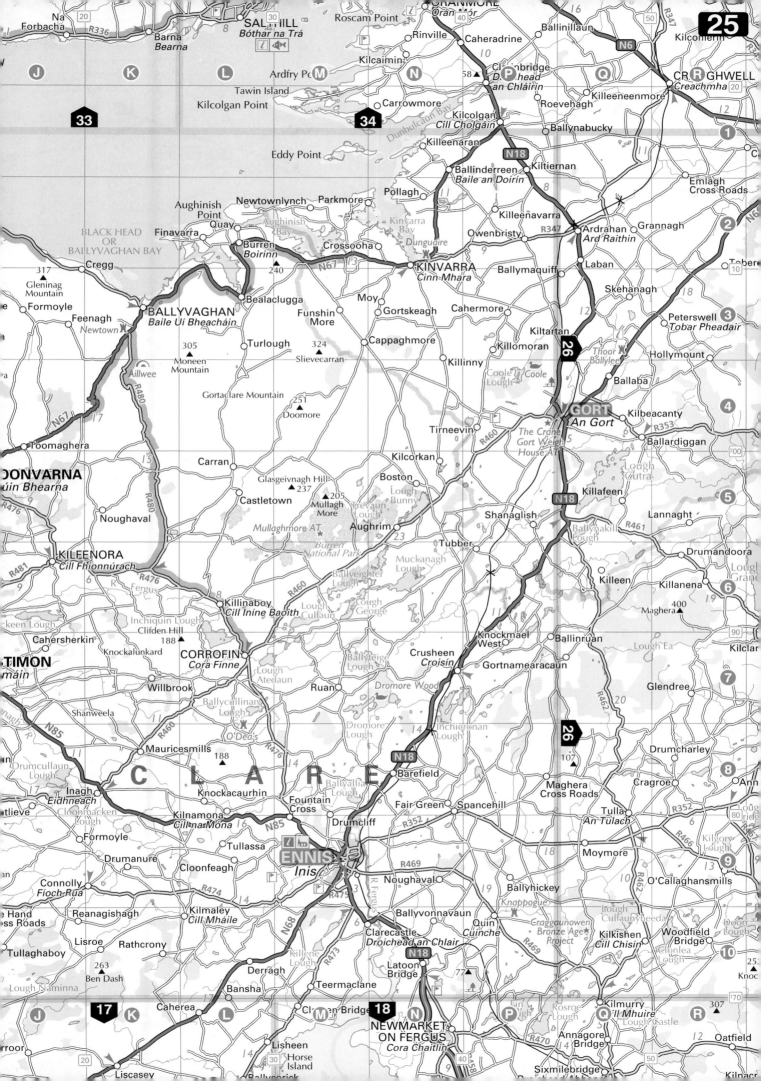

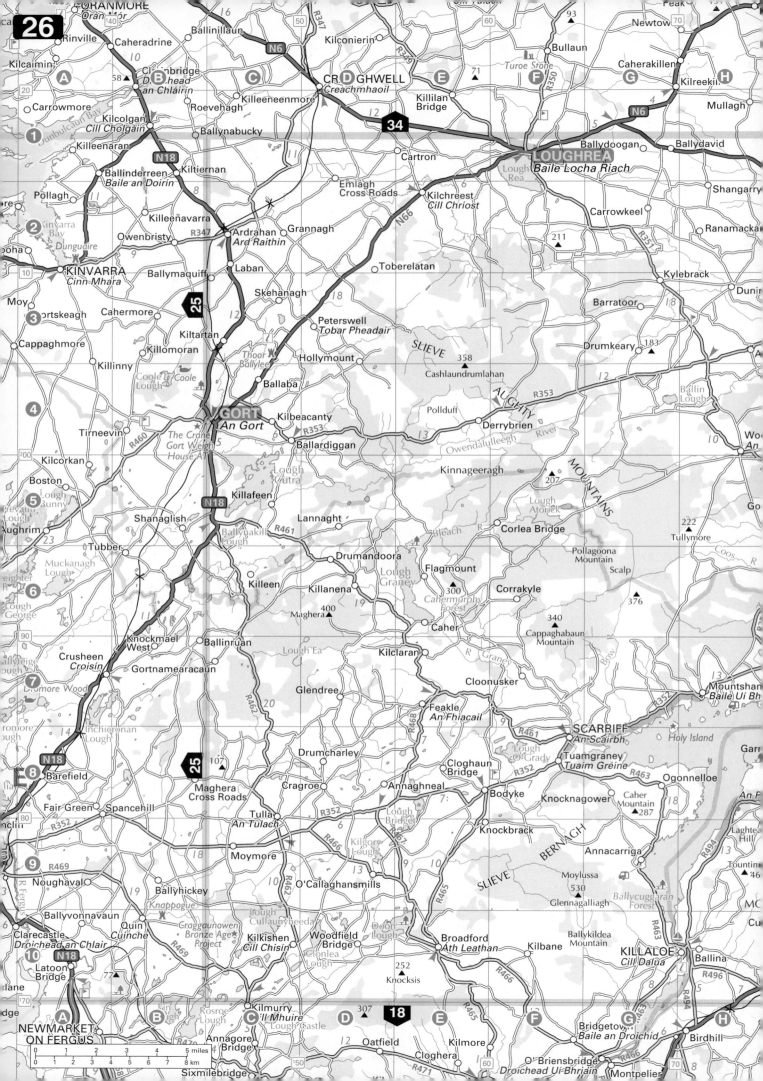

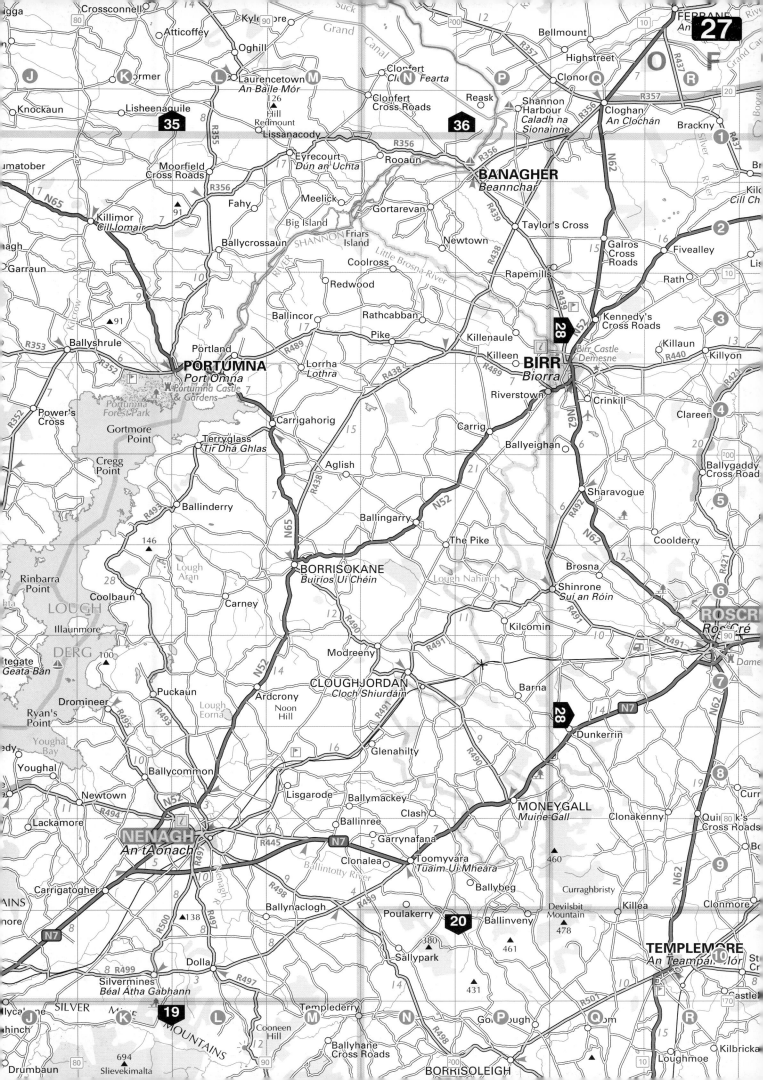

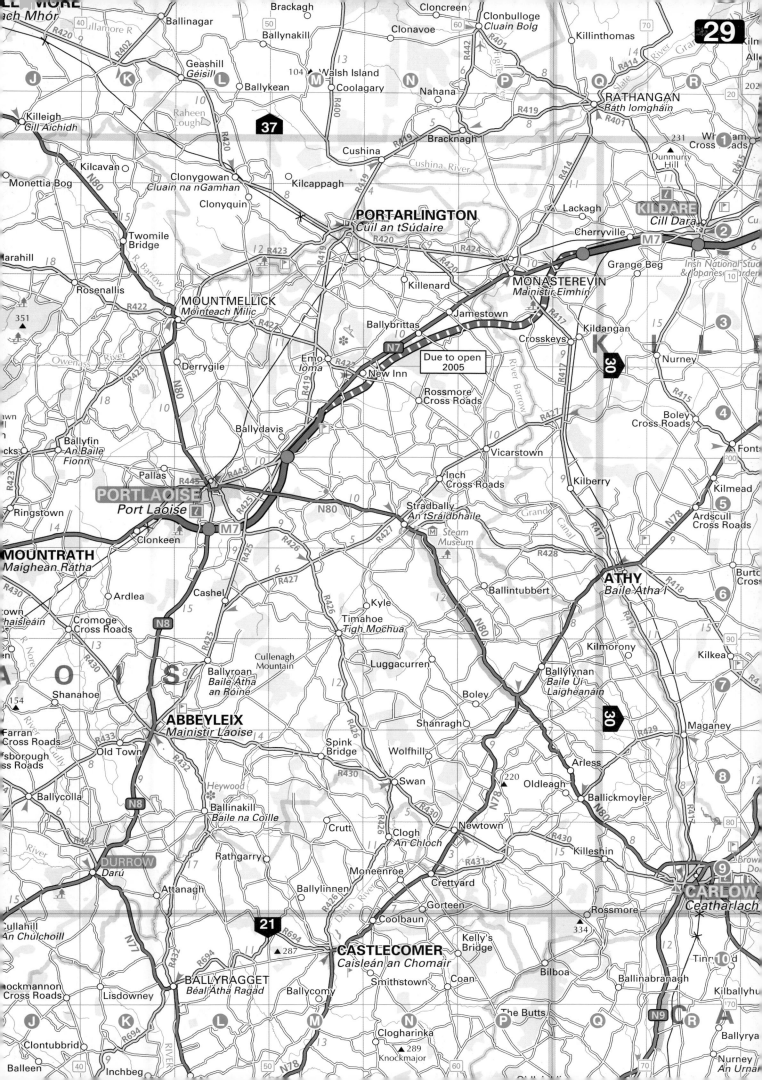

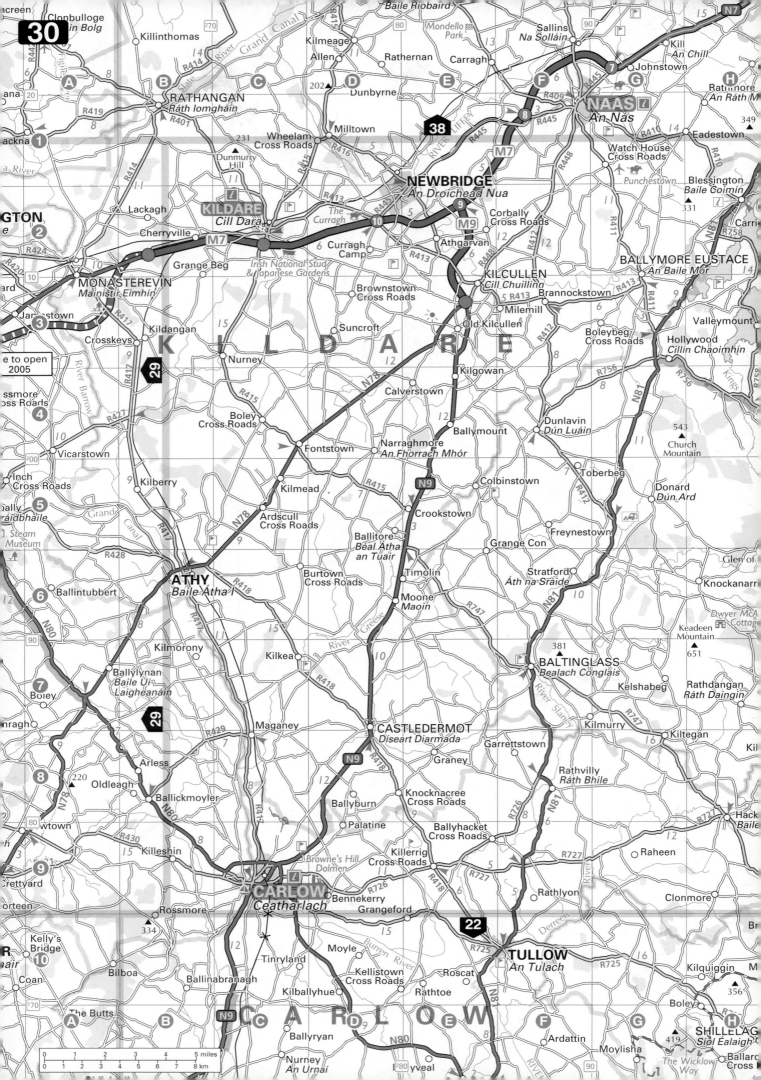

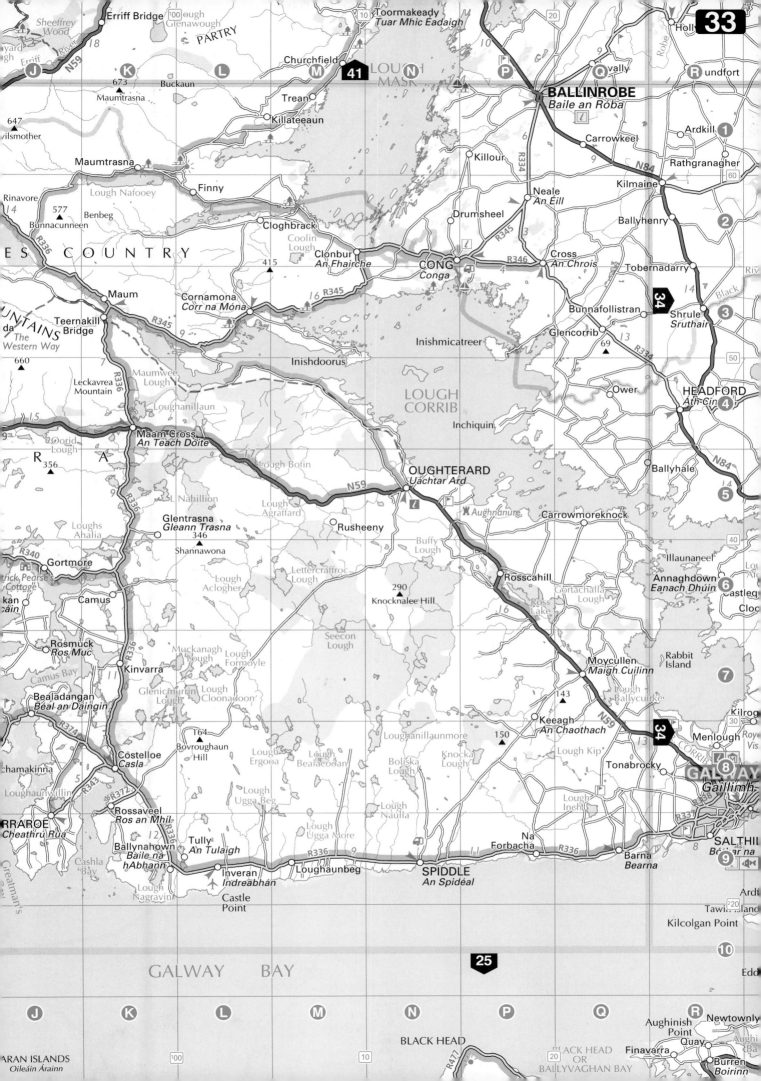

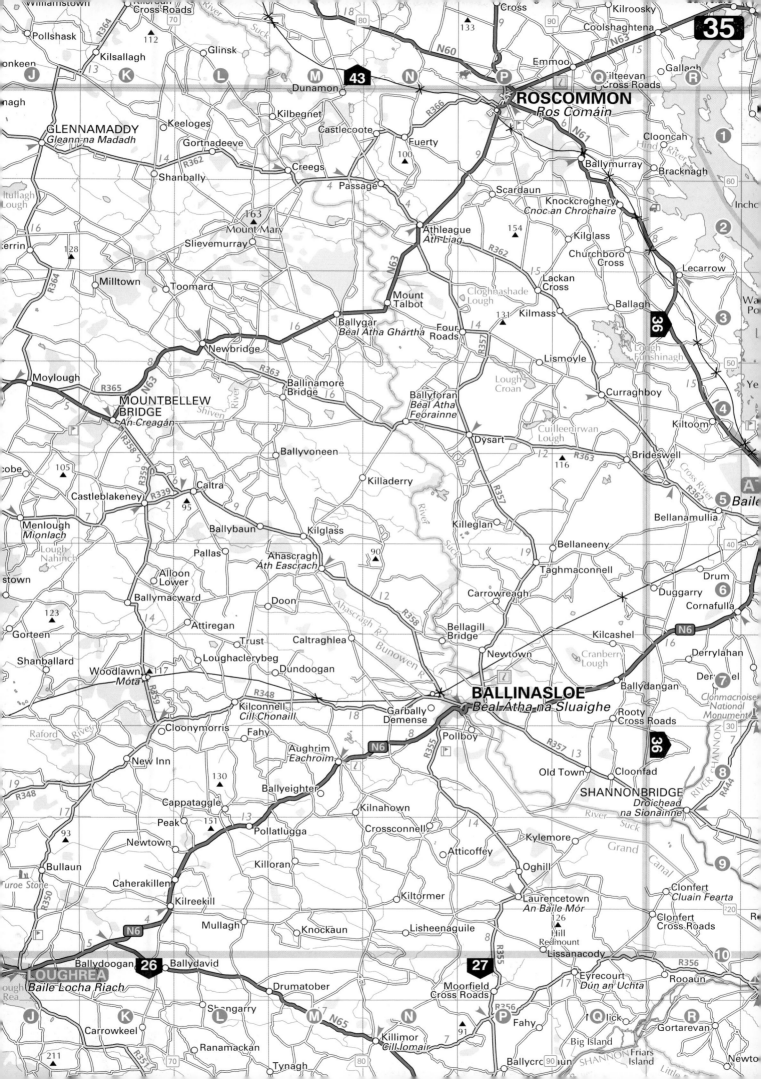

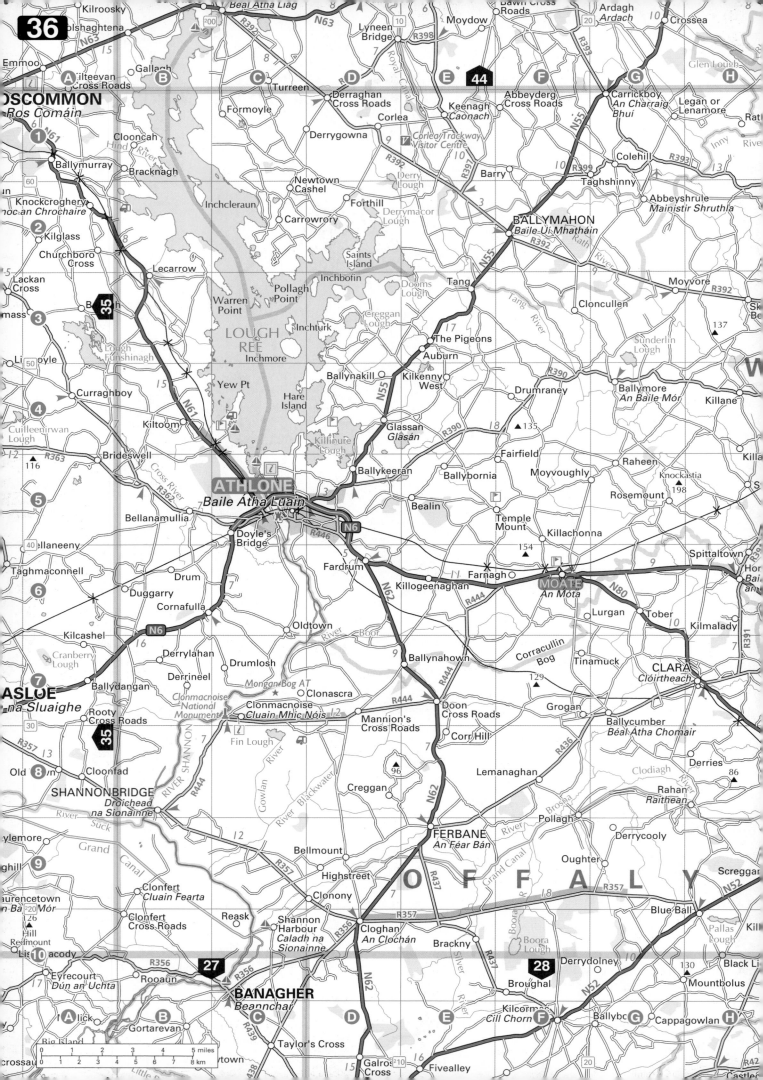

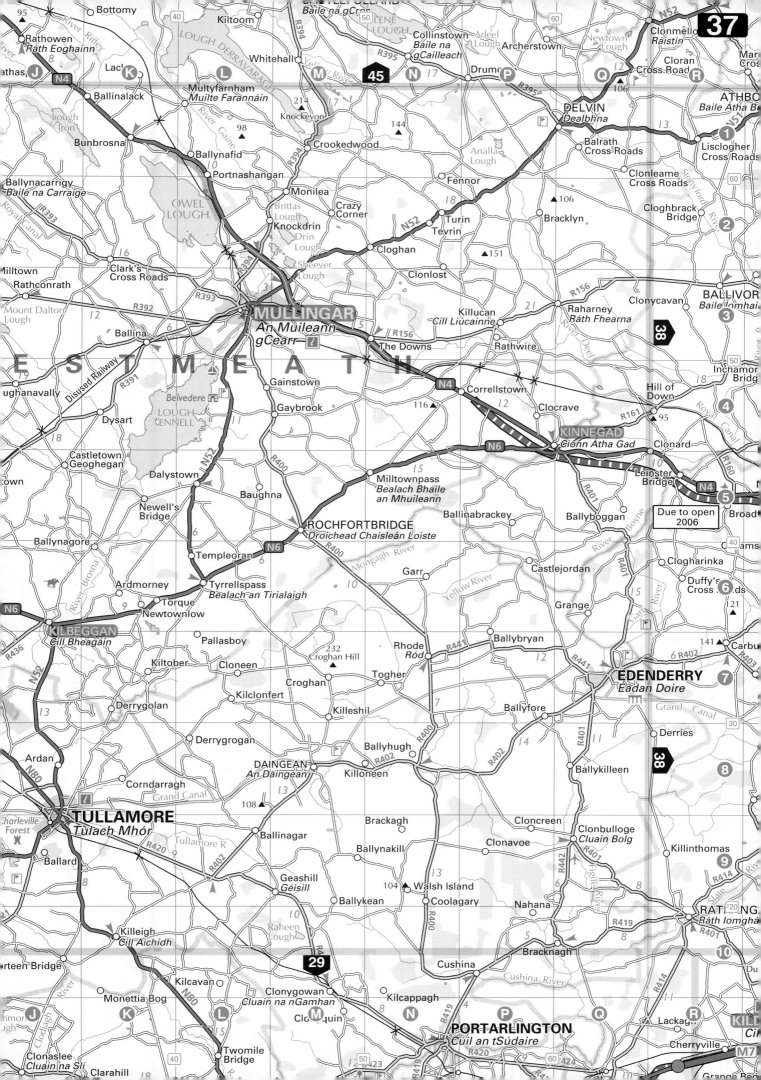

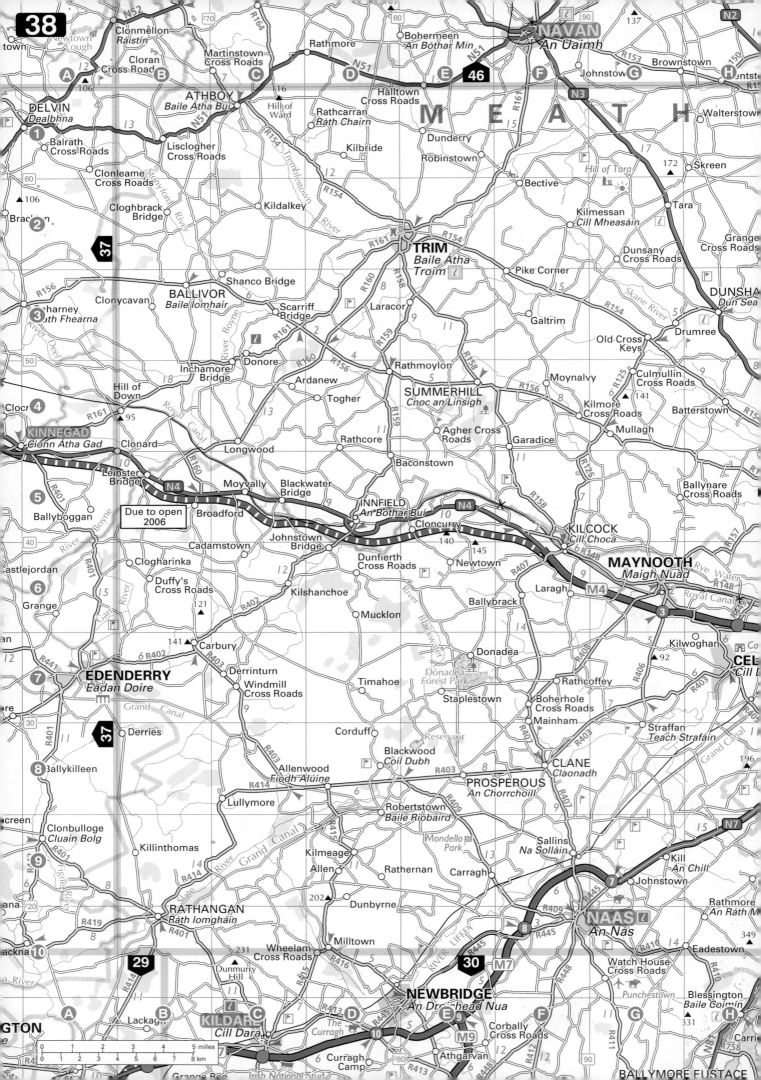

Inis Gé Theas
Termon
Hill
An Fód Dubh
Kanfinalt
Tullaghanduff
Rath Hill
61
Knocklettercus

Blacksod
Point

Doohooma

Srahnamanragh
Bridge

Duvillaun More

Duvillaun
Beg

BLACKSOD
BAY

Kinrovar

Doona

Fahy Lough

Ballycroy
Baile Chruaich

328
Slieve Alp

Ridge Point

ACHILL ISLAND
Acaill

Doogort
Dumha Goirt

Sruhill
Lough

Inishbiggle
Inis Bigil

Bellagarvaun

Saddle Head

671
Slievemore

48

Keel
Lough

Castlehill

ACHILL
HEAD

665
Croaghaun

Dooagh
Dumha Acha

Keel
An Caol

R319

Bunacurry
Bun an Churraigh

Annagh
Island

Claggan

Moyteóge
Head

Inishgalloon

Cashel

Tonregee

464

Mweelin

Achill Sound
Gob an Choire

380
Claggan
Mountain

Dooega
Head

Knockmore

Dooega
Dumha Éige

Sraheens Bridge

Corraun
Hill

540

Mallaranny
An Mhala Raithní

Portnahally or
Ashleam Bay

Derreen

Rosturk

Bills Rocks

Cloghmore

Corraun

Bolinglanna

Dooghbeg

Gubbaun
Point

Achillbeg
Island

Gubacarrigan

CLEW   BAY

Carrickfadda

Ballytoohy

Kinnacorra

462

Kinatevdilla

CLARE
ISLAND

Portnakilly

LOUISBURGH
Cluain Cearbán

Old Head

Kilsallagh

Aghany

Emlagh
Point

Mullagh

INISHTURK
Inis Toirc

Caher Island

Ballybeg
Island

Roonah L

Formoyle

Killeen

Dromore
Head

189

Inishdalla

Killadoon

Barnabaun
Point

270

Cregganbaun

Glenkeen
Bridge

SHEEFFRY

Kinnadoohy

761

INISHBOFIN
Inis Bó Finne

Tonakeera
Point

MWEELREA

Doo
Lough

86

Davillaun

Inishdegil More

817
Mweelrea

MOUNTAINS

Delphi

Ben Creggan

Inishgort

Inishbofin

Crump Island

32

Ben Gorm

Inishlyon

Cashleen

Rinvyle

Gowlaun

Garraun

LEENAUN
An Líonán

Tully Lough

Tully Mountain

Tully Cross

R335

0 1 2 3 4 5 miles
0 1 2 3 4 5 6 7 8 km

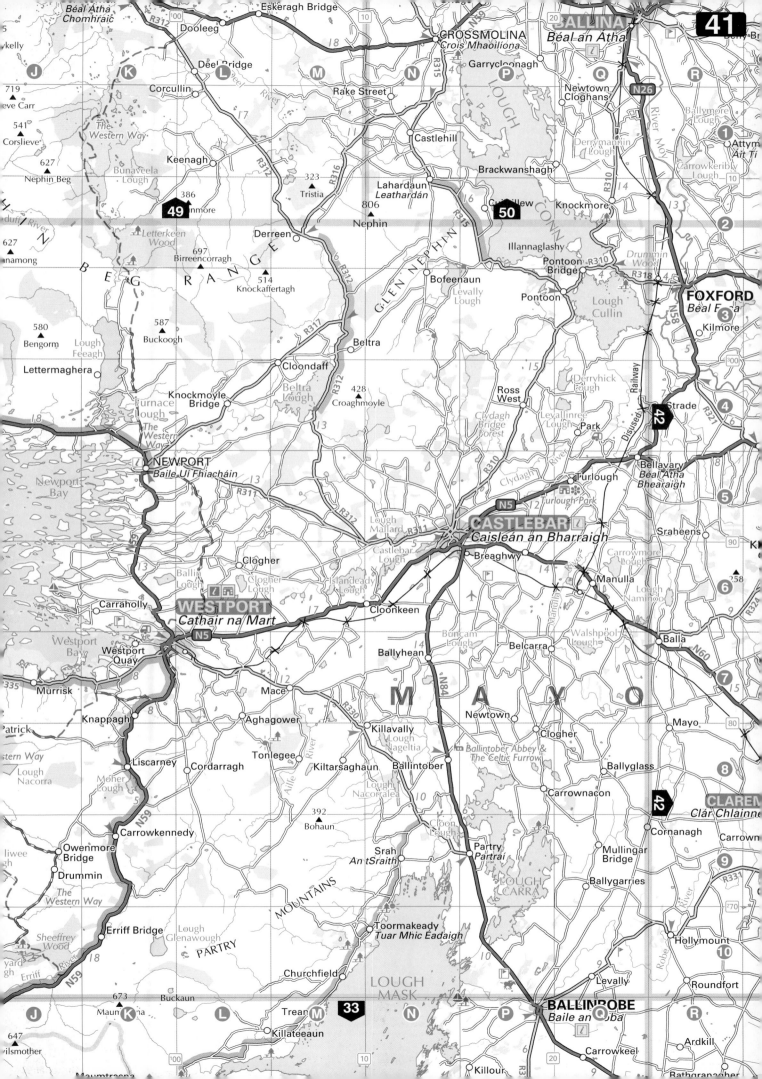

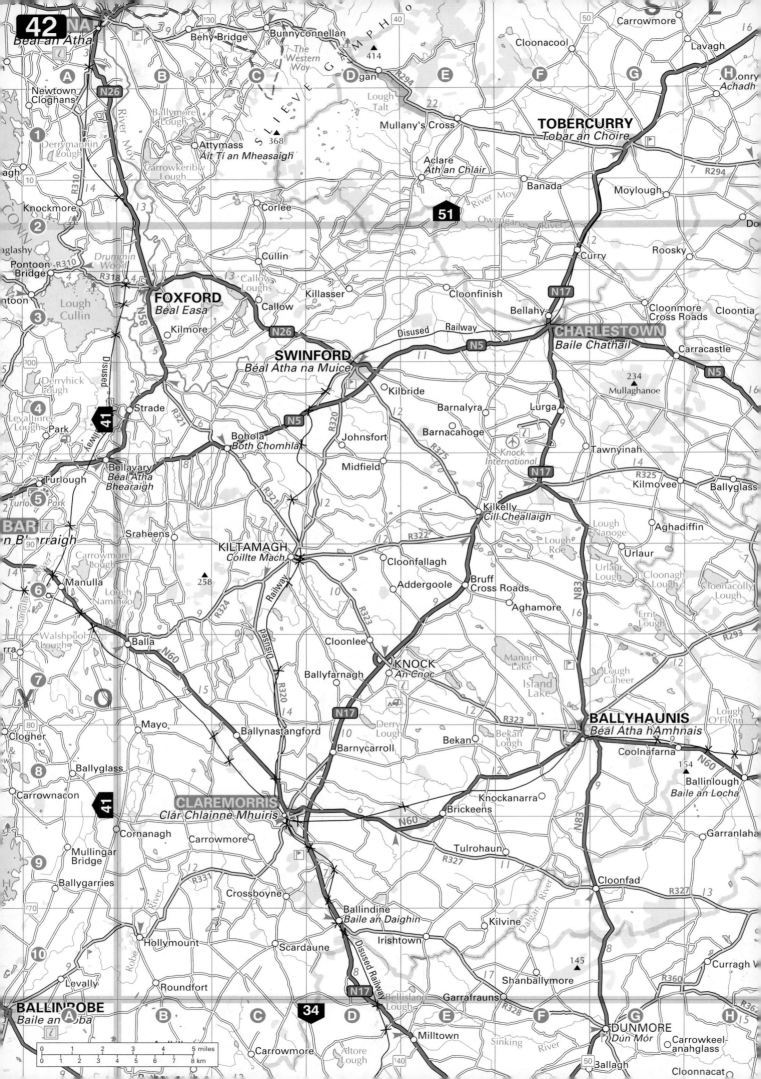

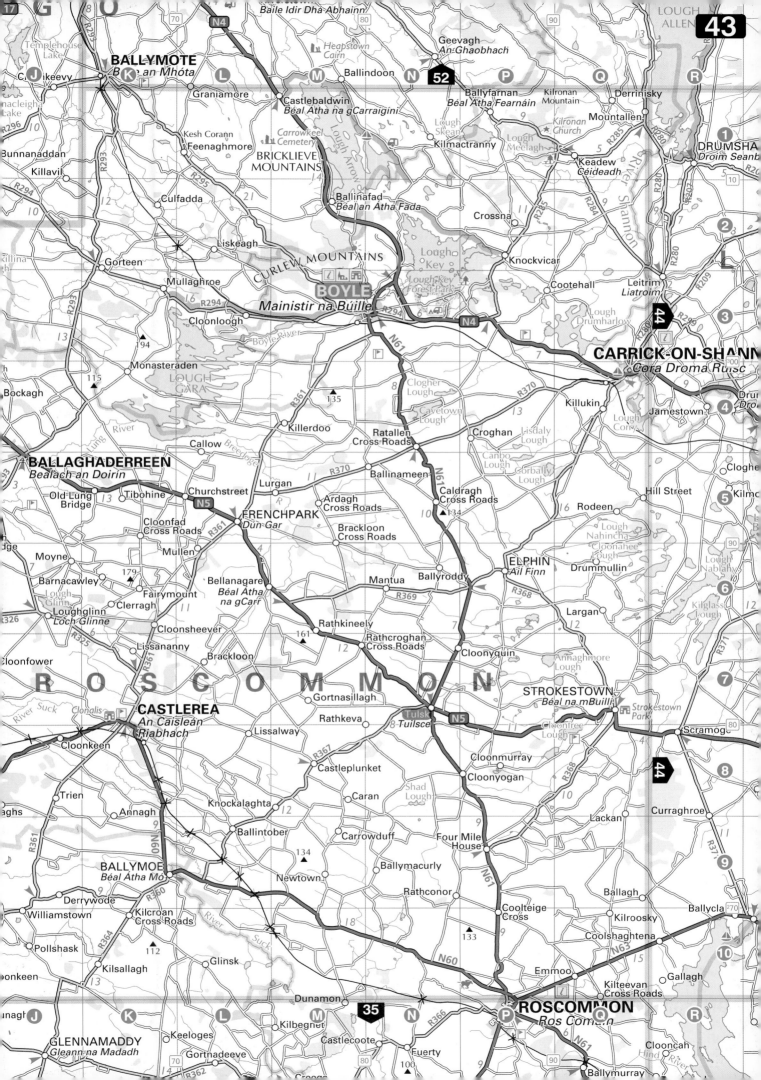

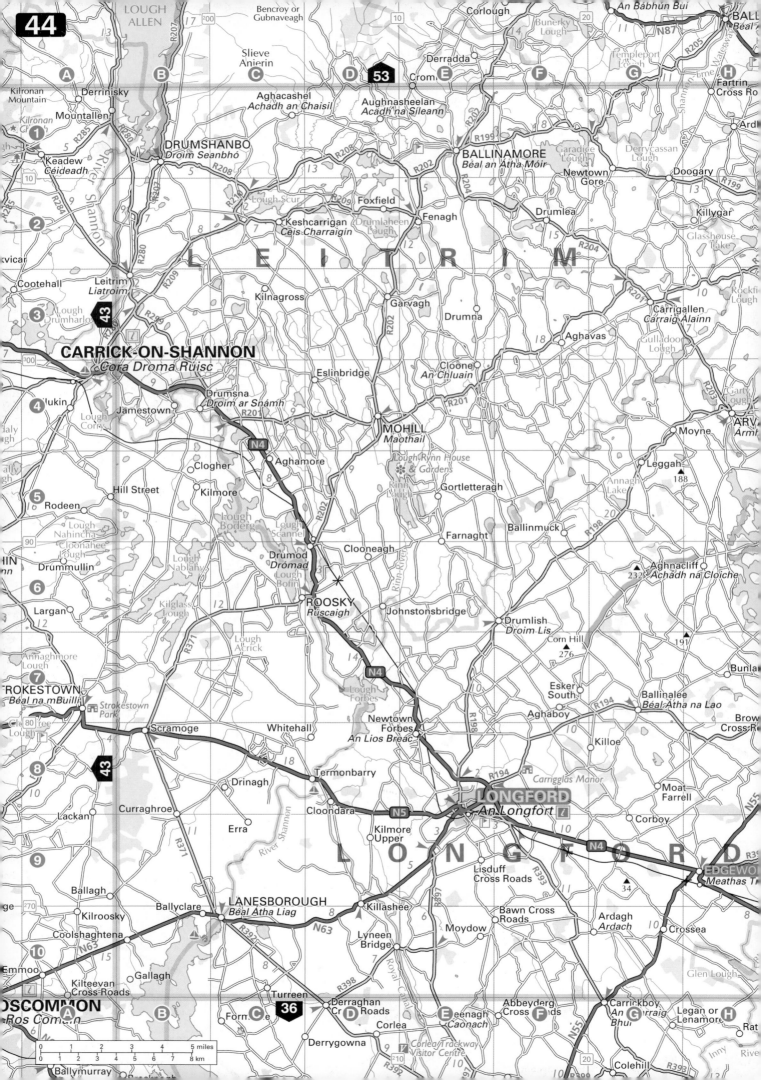

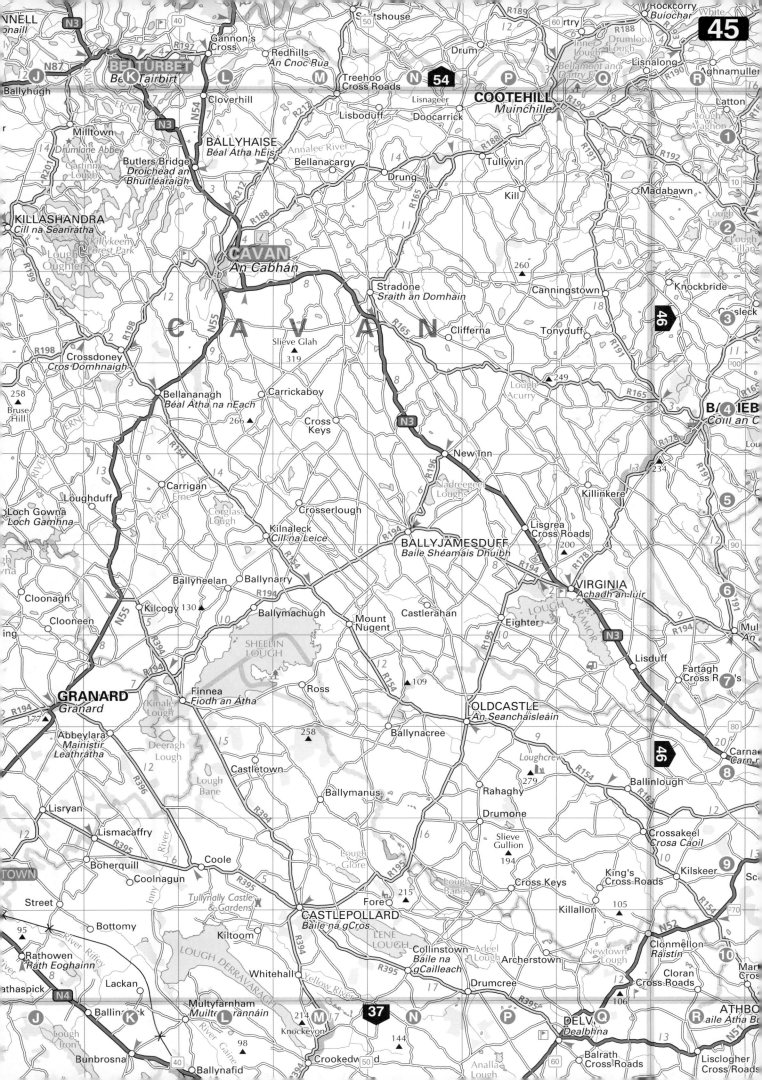

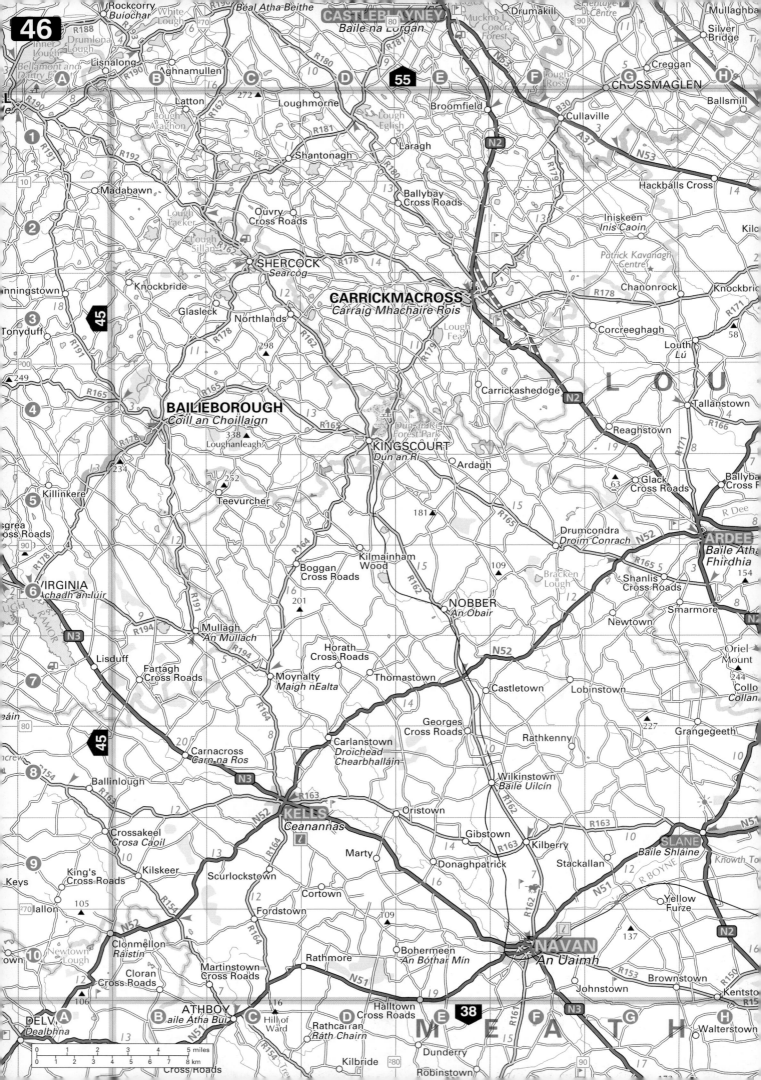

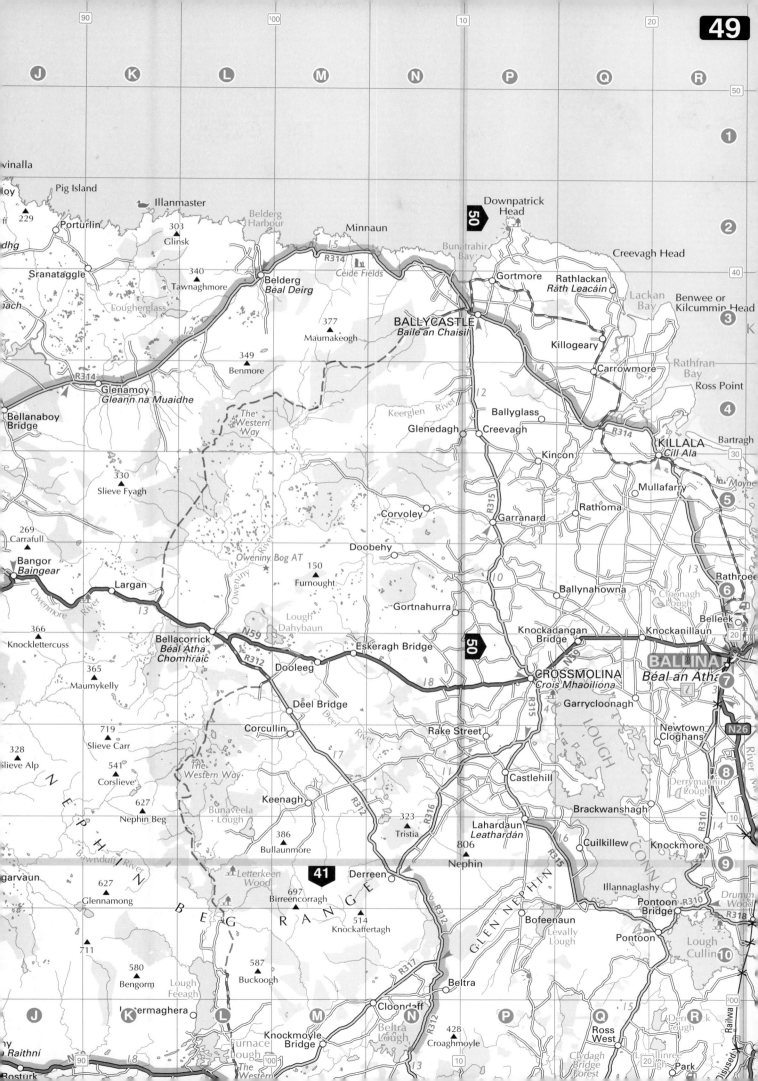

J   K   L   M   N   P   Q   R

229
Pig Island
Illanmaster
Porturlin
Minnaun
Downpatrick Head
50
Creevagh Head
Belderg Harbour
303
Glinsk
R314
Bunatrahir Bay
340
Sranataggle
Tawnaghmore
Belderg
Béal Deirg
Céide Fields
Gortmore
Rathlackan
Ráth Leacáin
Benwee or
Kilcummin Head
Lackan Bay
dhg
377
BALLYCASTLE
Baile an Chaisil
Lougherglass
Maumakeogh
Killogeary
Rathfran Bay
Glenamoy
Gleann na Muaidhe
349
Benmore
The Western Way
Carrowmore
Ross Point
R314
Bellanaboy Bridge
Keerglen River
Ballyglass
KILLALA
Cill Ala
Bartragh
Glenedagh
Creevagh
Moyne
330
Slieve Fyagh
Kincon
Rathoma
Mullafarry
269
Carrafull
Corvoley
R315
Garranard
Bangor
Baingear
Oweniny Bog AT
Doobehy
Rathroe
Largan
Owenmore River
150
Furnought
Gortnahurra
Ballynahowna
Cloonagh Lough
Belleek
366
Knocklettercuss
Lough Dahybaun
N59
Bellacorrick
Béal Átha Chomhraic
R312
Dooleeg
Eskeragh Bridge
Knockadangan Bridge
Knockanillaun
BALLINA
Béal an Átha
365
Maumykelly
Deel Bridge
CROSSMOLINA
Crois Mhaoilíona
Garrycloonagh
Newtown Cloghans
N26
719
Slieve Carr
Corcullin
Rake Street
R315
River N
328
Slieve Alp
541
Corslieve
The Western Way
Deel River
Castlehill
Brackwanshagh
Knockmore
R310
627
Nephin Beg
Bunaveela Lough
Keenagh
R312
323
Tristia
R316
Lahardaun
Leathardán
Cuilkillew
Illannaglashy
627
Glennamong
Bawnduff River
386
Bullaunmore
806
Nephin
Pontoon Bridge
R318
Drumm Wood
711
NEPHIN BEG RANGE
Letterkeen Wood
41
697
Birreencorragh
Derreen
GLEN NEPHIN
Bofeenaun
Levally Lough
Pontoon
Lough Cullin
580
Bengorm
587
Buckoogh
Lough Feeagh
514
Knockaffertagh
R317
Beltra
428
Croaghmoyle
Ross West
rmaghera
Knockmoyle Bridge
Cloondaff
Beltra Lough
Clydagh Bridge Forest
Park

J   K   L   M   N   P   Q   R

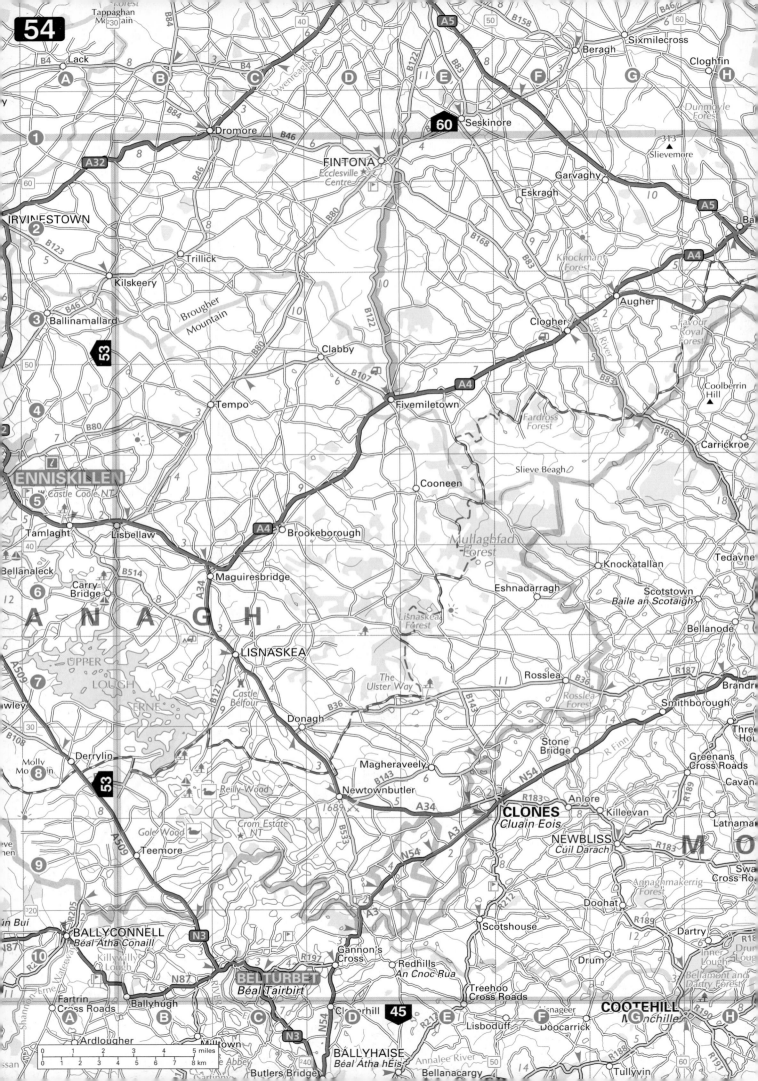

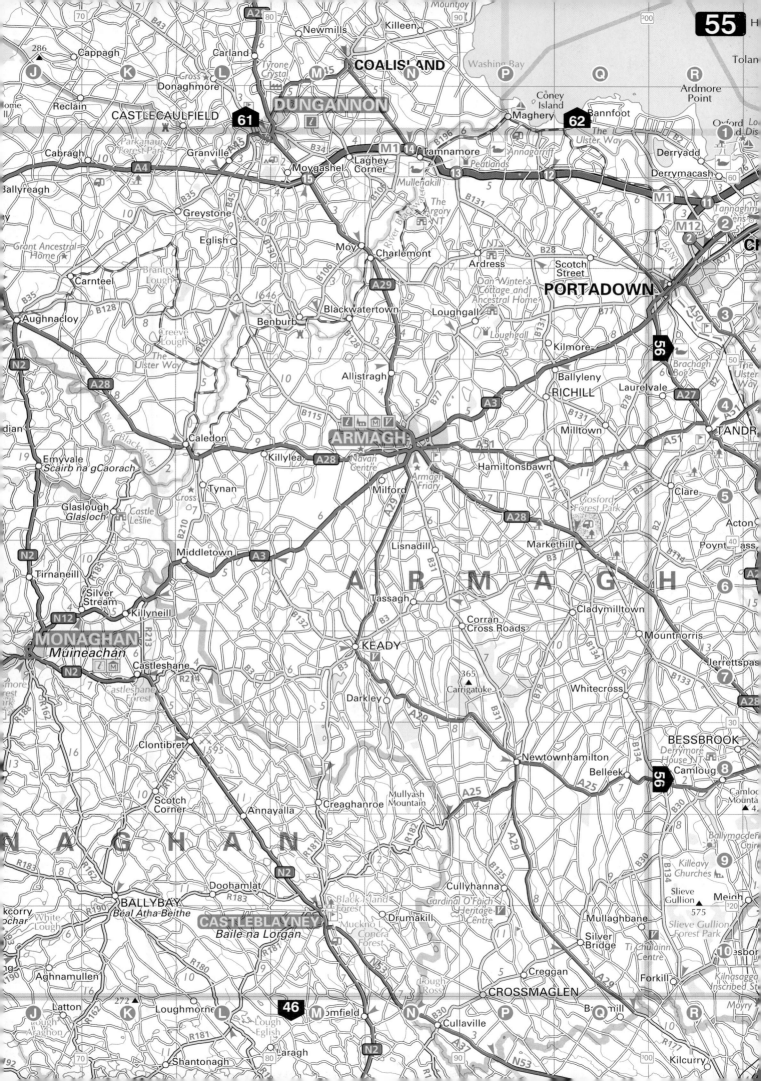

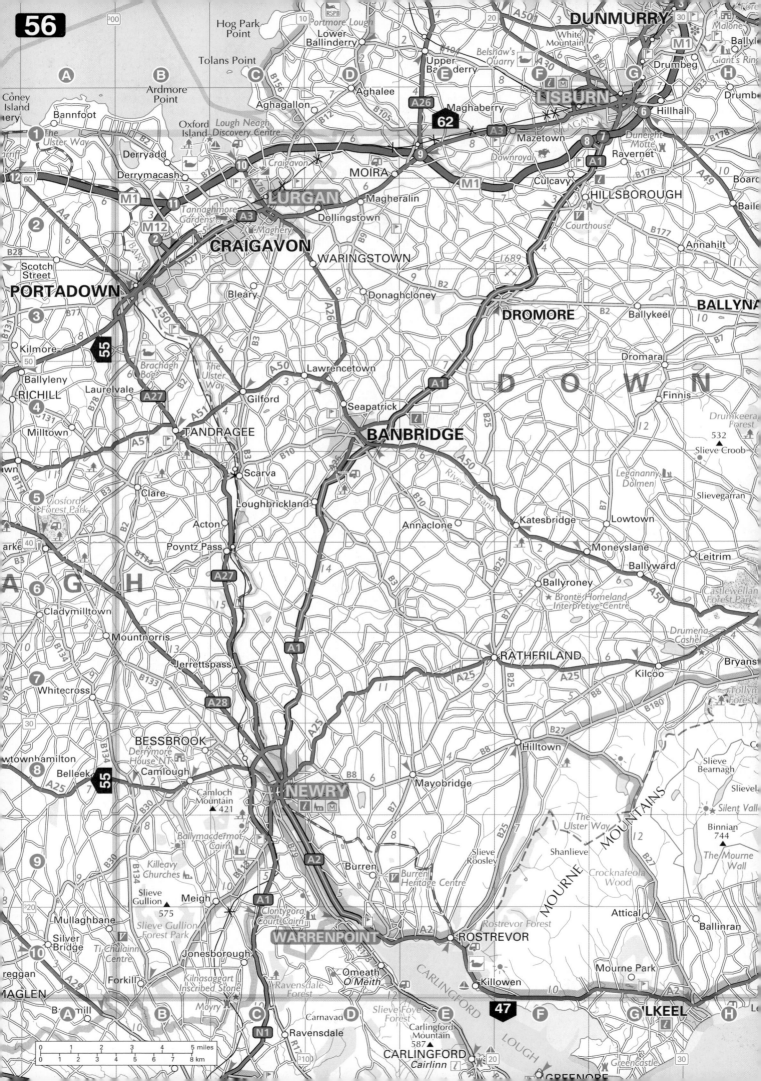

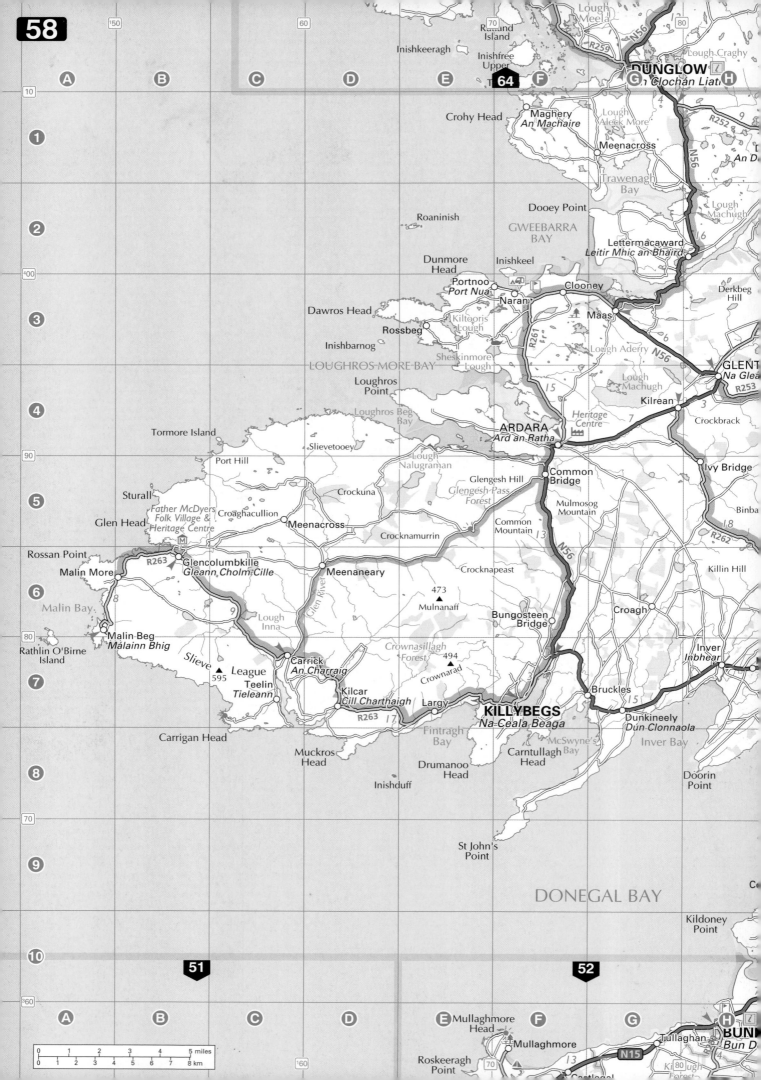

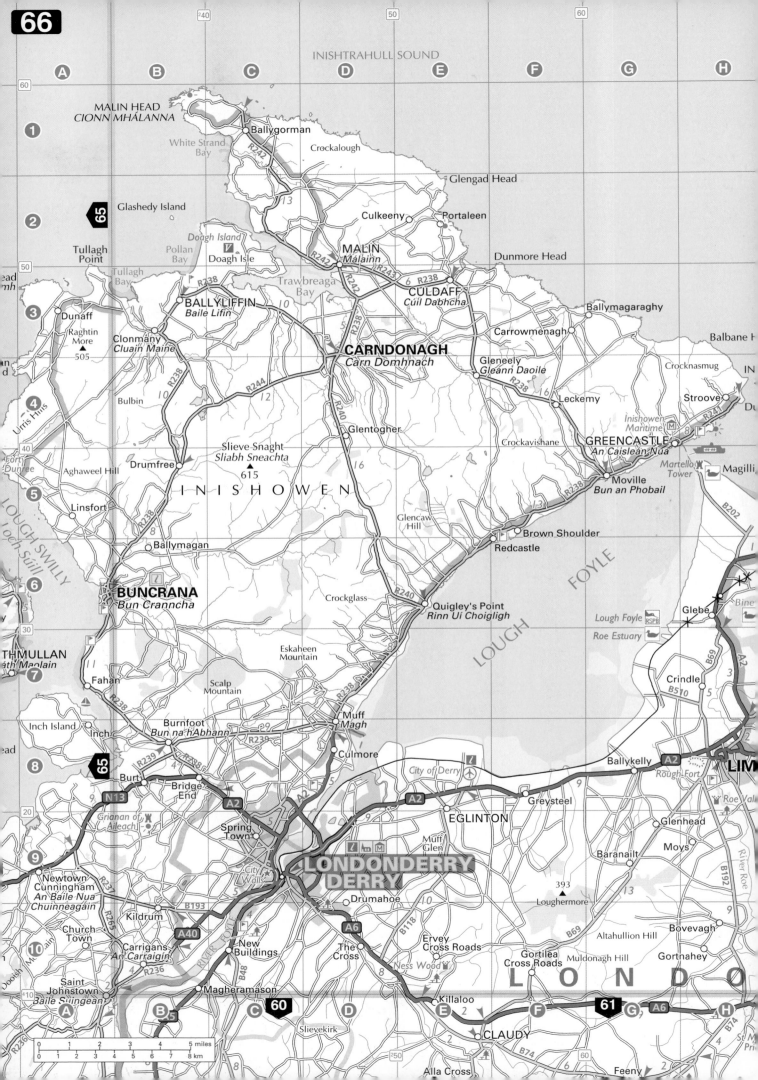

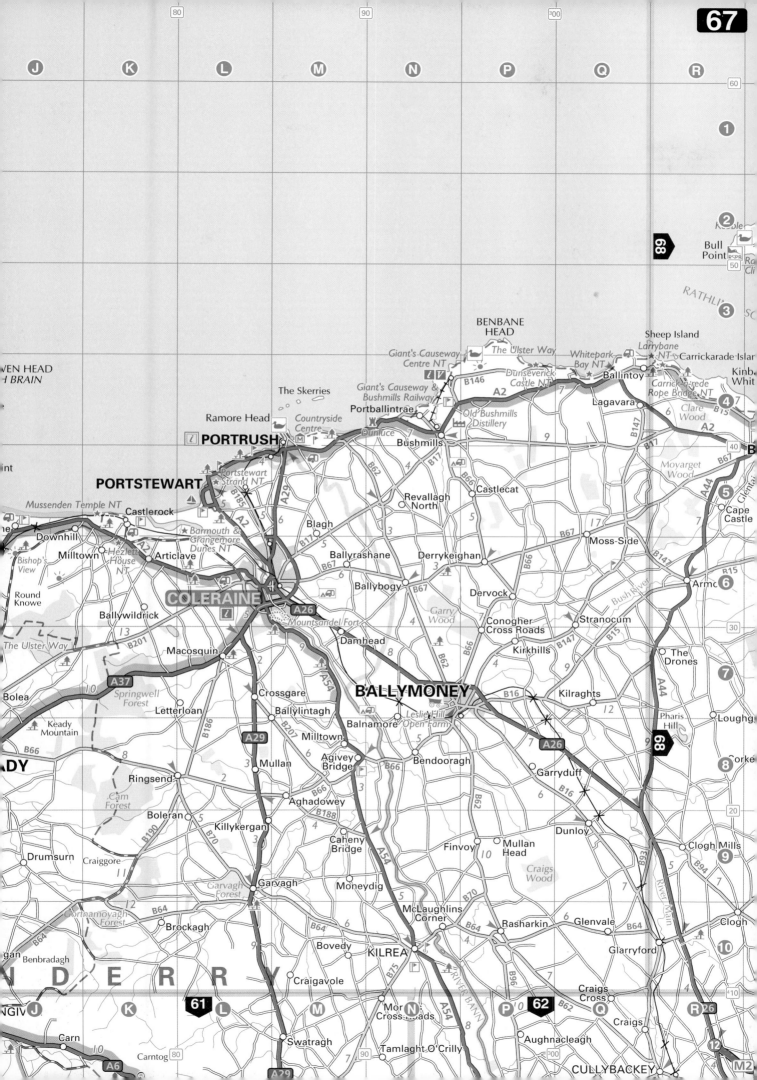

Town plans

Town plans

Page 70........... Belfast
71........... Cork
72........... Dublin
73........... Galway
73........... Kilkenny
73........... Killarney
74........... Limerick
74........... Londonderry
75........... Sligo
75........... Waterford

 Port plans

Page III........... Belfast
III........... Dublin Harbour
III........... Dún Laoghaire
III........... Larne
III........... Ringaskiddy
III........... Rosslare Harbour

Key to town plans
Eochair   Légende   Legende

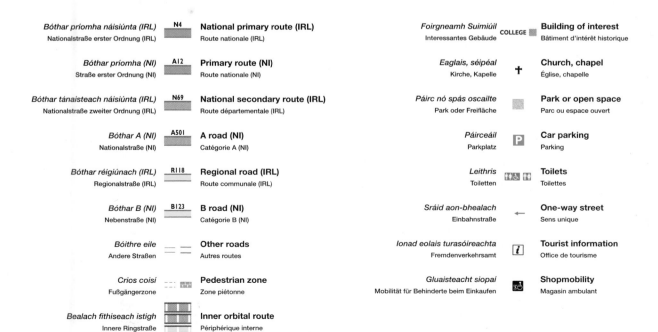

Bóthar príomha náisiúnta (IRL) / Nationalstraße erster Ordnung (IRL)	**N4**	**National primary route (IRL)** / Route nationale (IRL)
Bóthar príomha (NI) / Straße erster Ordnung (NI)	**A12**	**Primary route (NI)** / Route nationale (NI)
Bóthar tánaisteach náisiúnta (IRL) / Nationalstraße zweiter Ordnung (IRL)	**N69**	**National secondary route (IRL)** / Route départementale (IRL)
Bóthar A (NI) / Nationalstraße (NI)	**A501**	**A road (NI)** / Catégorie A (NI)
Bóthar réigiúnach (IRL) / Regionalstraße (IRL)	**R118**	**Regional road (IRL)** / Route communale (IRL)
Bóthar B (NI) / Nebenstraße (NI)	**B123**	**B road (NI)** / Catégorie B (NI)
Bóithre eile / Andere Straßen		**Other roads** / Autres routes
Crios coisí / Fußgängerzone		**Pedestrian zone** / Zone piétonne
Bealach fithiseach istigh / Innere Ringstraße		**Inner orbital route** / Périphérique interne

Foirgneamh Suimiúil / Interessantes Gebäude	COLLEGE	**Building of interest** / Bâtiment d'intérêt historique
Eaglais, séipéal / Kirche, Kapelle	✝	**Church, chapel** / Église, chapelle
Páirc nó spás oscailte / Park oder Freifläche		**Park or open space** / Parc ou espace ouvert
Páirceáil / Parkplatz	P	**Car parking** / Parking
Leithris / Toiletten		**Toilets** / Toilettes
Sráid aon-bhealach / Einbahnstraße	←	**One-way street** / Sens unique
Ionad eolais turasóireachta / Fremdenverkehrsamt	i	**Tourist information** / Office de tourisme
Gluaisteacht siopaí / Mobilität für Behinderte beim Einkaufen		**Shopmobility** / Magasin ambulant

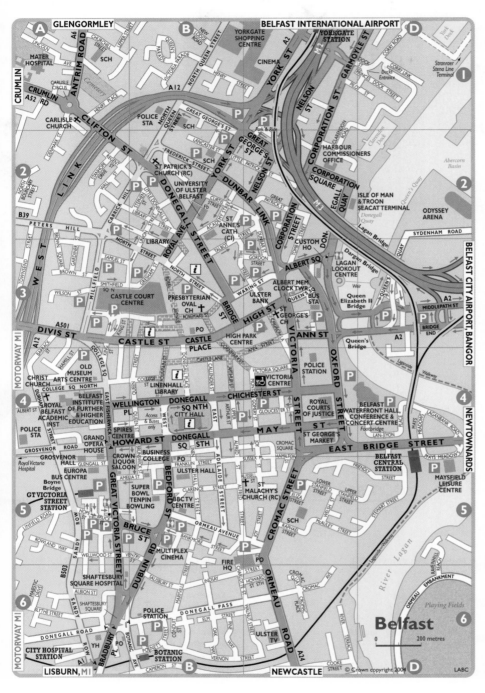

Belfast

Belfast is found on atlas page **63 J8**

B2	Academy Street
B5	Adelaide Street
C3	Albert Square
A4	Albert Street
A6	Albion Street
B5	Alfred Street
A5	Amelia Street
C3	Ann Street
A1	Antrim Road
B4	Arthur Street
B5	Bankmore Street
A4	Barrack Street

B5	Bedford Street
A6	Blythe Street
A6	Botanic Avenue
A6	Bradbury Place
D3	Bridge End
B3	Bridge Street
A3	Brown Square
A3	Brown Street
B5	Bruce Street
B4	Brunswick Street
B4	Callender Street
B6	Cameron Street

A1	Carlisle Circus
A2	Carrick Hill
B4	Castle Lane
B3	Castle Place
B3	Castle Street
B6	Charlotte Street
B4	Chichester Street
C3	Church Lane
A1	Churchill Street
B5	Clarence Street
C2	Clarendon Road
A1	Clifton Street

A4	College Square
A4	College Square North
B4	College Street
B6	Conduit Street
C6	Cooke Street
B4	Cornmarket
C2	Corporation Square
C2	Corporation Street
D1	Corry Link
D1	Corry Road
C6	Cromac Avenue
C6	Cromac Place

C6	Cromac Quay
C4	Cromac Square
C5	Cromac Street
A1	Crumlin Road
B2	Curtis Street
A2	Denmark Street
A3	Divis Street
D1	Dock Street
B6	Donegall Pass
B4	Donegall Place
C3	Donegall Quay
A6	Donegall Road
B4	Donegall Square East
B4	Donegall Square North
B4	Donegall Square South
B4	Donegall Square West
B2	Donegall Street
B2	Dunbar Link
C2	Dunbar Street
A4	Durham Street
C4	East Bridge Street
A4	East Fisherwick
C5	Eliza Street
B6	Elm Street
B4	Fountain Street
B5	Franklin Street
B2	Fredrick Street
D5	Friendly Street
B4	Gardiner Street
C1	Garmoyle Street
A5	Glengall Street
C4	Gloucester Street
C3	Gordon Street
B1	Great George's Street
C2	Great Patrick Street
A5	Great Victoria Street
B3	Gresham Street
A4	Grosvenor Road
A4	Hamill Street
C5	Hamilton Street
A1	Henry Place
B1	Henry Street
C3	High Street
B3	Hill Street
A5	Hope Street
A4	Howard Street
C6	Howard Street South
C4	Joy Street
A3	King Street
D4	Laganbank Road
B2	Lancaster Street
D4	Lanyon Place
A1	Lepper Street
B2	Library Street
A1	Lincoln Avenue
B6	Lindsay Street
B4	Linen Hall Street
A5	Linfield Road
B2	Little Donegall Street
C2	Little Patrick Street
C5	Lower Stanfield Street
A6	Majestic Drive
B6	Maryville Street
C4	May Street
D4	Mays Meadows
C5	McAuley Street
D3	Middlepath Street
A3	Millfield
C4	Montgomery Street
C2	Nelson Street
B1	New Lodge Road
A2	North Boundary Street
B1	North Queen Street
B3	North Street
B6	Oak Way
B5	Ormeau Avenue
D6	Ormeau Embankment
C6	Ormeau Road
C4	Oxford Street
A2	Peters Hill

C1	Pilot Street
B6	Pine Way
B6	Posnett Street
D1	Princes Dock Street
B4	Queen Street
B1	Queen's Parade
D3	Queen's Quay
C3	Queen's Square
C5	Raphael Street
D6	Ravenhill Reach
A2	Regent Street
C6	River Terrace
B3	Rosemary Street
A5	Rowland Way
B3	Royal Avenue
C5	Russell Street
B6	Salisbury Street
A3	Samuel Street
A6	Sandy Row
A6	Shaftesbury Square
A3	Smithfield Square North
A2	Stanhope Drive
B2	Stephen Street
D5	Stewart Street
C5	Sussex Place
D2	Sydenham Road
B3	Talbot Street
C3	Tomb Street
A3	Townsend Street
B2	Union Street
B4	Upper Arthur Street
C5	Upper Stanfield Street
B5	Ventry Street
B6	Vernon Street
B1	Victoria Parade
C4	Victoria Square
C3	Victoria Street
A2	Wall Street
C6	Walnut Street
C3	Waring Street
A4	Wellington Place
A5	Wellwood Street
C5	Welsh Street
A3	West Link
A3	Wilson Street
B2	York Street

Cork

Cork is found on atlas page **6 A5**

B5 Abbey Street
B3 Academy Street
A4 Adelaide Street
D4 Albert Quay
D3 Albert Road
D4 Albert Street
D1 Alexandra Road
D3 Alfred Street
C3 Anderson Quay
D4 Anglesea Street
B1 Assumption Road
B2 Audley Place
A4 Bachelor's Quay
D1 Ballyhooly New Road
A6 Bandon Road
B5 Barrack Street
C4 Beasly Street
C2 Bellevue Park
C2 Bellview Crescent
A5 Bishop Street
B1 Blackpool Bypass
A3 Blarney Street
B5 Bonaventure Place
B3 Camden Place
B3 Camden Quay
D6 Capwell Road
B3 Carrolls Quay
A3 Castle Market Avenue
B4 Castle Street
A2 Cathedral Road
A2 Cathedral Street
A2 Cathedral Walk
A3 Church Street
B3 Coal Quay
B3 Coburg Street
A5 College Road
C6 Congress Road
A5 Connaught Avenue
B4 Cook Street
C4 Copley Street
B3 Corn Market Street
B5 Cove Street
D6 Curragh Road
A5 Dean Street
B6 Deerpark Road
C6 Derrynane Road
B5 Desmond Square
B3 Dominick Street
C5 Douglas Street
C6 Doyle Road
C4 Dunbar Street
A4 Dyke Parade
B3 Eason's Hill
B3 Emmet Place
D6 Evergreen Road
B5 Evergreen Street
A3 Fair Street
C6 Father Mathew Road
B5 Fort Street
C4 Friar Matthew Quay
B5 Friar Street
C6 Friars Road
C6 Friars Walk
D1 Gardiners Hill
D4 Gas Works Road
C4 George's Quay
A2 Gerald Griffin Avenue
A2 Gerald Griffin Street
A5 Gill Abbey Street
D2 Glanmire Road
B1 Glen Avenue
A3 Glen Ryan Road
A6 Gould's Street
B4 Grand Parade
A4 Grattan Street
A1 Great William O'Brien
    Street
B6 Green Street
A6 Greenmount Avenue

A4 Greenville Place
A4 Hanover Street
A6 Hartlands Road
A4 Henry Street
D5 High Street
D3 Horgan's Quay
B5 Industry Street
B3 John Redmond Street
B2 John Street
B2 John Street Upper
B5 Kevin Street South
B3 Kyle Street
A3 Kyrl's Quay
A5 Lancaster Quay
D5 Langford Row
C3 Lapp's Quay
B3 Lavitt's Quay
B2 Leitrim Street
B4 Liberty Street
A6 Lough Road
A1 Lover's Walk
D2 Lower Glanmire Road
D2 Mahony's Avenue
B4 Marlborough Street
A3 Mary Aikenhead Place
C4 Mary Street
C3 Maylor Street
C3 McCurtain Street
C3 Merchants Quay
D2 Military Hill
C1 Military Road
A2 Monastery Road
C4 Morrison's Quay
B5 Mount Carmel Road
C6 Mount Pleasant
    Avenue
C6 Mount Pleasant Road
B5 Mount Sion Road
A3 Newsom's Quay
C5 Nicholas Road
A5 Noonan Road
A3 North Main Street
A3 North Mall
D6 O'Connell Avenue
A2 O'Connell Street
D5 Old Blackrock Road
A3 Old Market Place
D4 Old Station Road
B4 Oliver Plunkett Street
C3 Oliver Plunkett Street
    Lower
C3 Parnell Place
B4 Paul Street
C3 Penrose's Quay
B3 Pope's Quay
B1 Pope's Road
B6 Pouladuff Road
B5 Presentation Place
B4 Princess Street
B5 Proby's Quay
C5 Quaker Road
D3 Railway Street
B2 Rathmore Park
C1 Rathmore Road
A2 Redemption Road
B5 Reed Street
B2 Richmond Hill
D4 Rockborough Road
B2 Roman Street
A5 St Finbars Road
C5 Rutland Street
A5 Sharman Crawford
    Street

C4 Sawmill Street
A1 Seminary Road
A3 Shandon Street
A5 Sharman Crawford
    Street
A4 Sheares Street
C2 Sidney Park
C2 Smith Street
B4 South City Link Road
B4 South Main Street
C4 South Mall
C4 South Terrace

D5 Southern Road
B4 Sullivan's Quay
D2 Summer Hill
C5 Summer Hill South
B5 Tower Street
B5 Townsend Place
B4 Tuckey Street
C4 Union Quay
B5 Vicar Street
D3 Victoria Road
A4 Wandesford Quay
B4 Washington Street

A4 Washington Street West
B1 Watercourse Road
C2 Wellington Road
C5 White Street
D5 Windmill Road
A2 Wolfe Tone Street
A4 Woods Street
C3 York Street
C2 Youghal Old Road

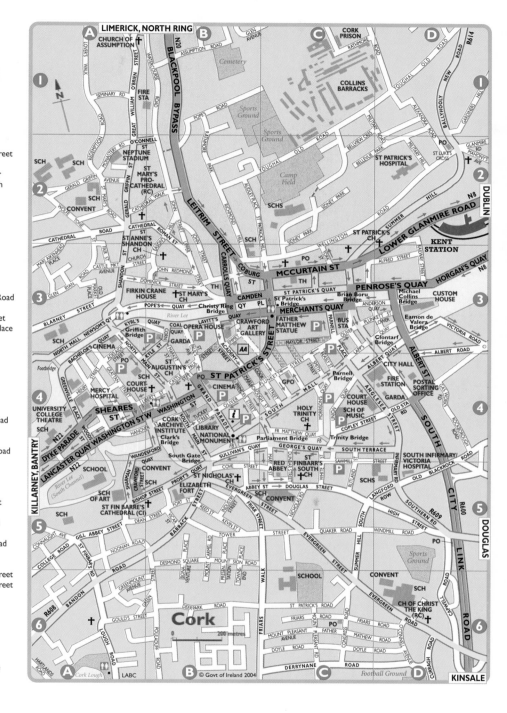

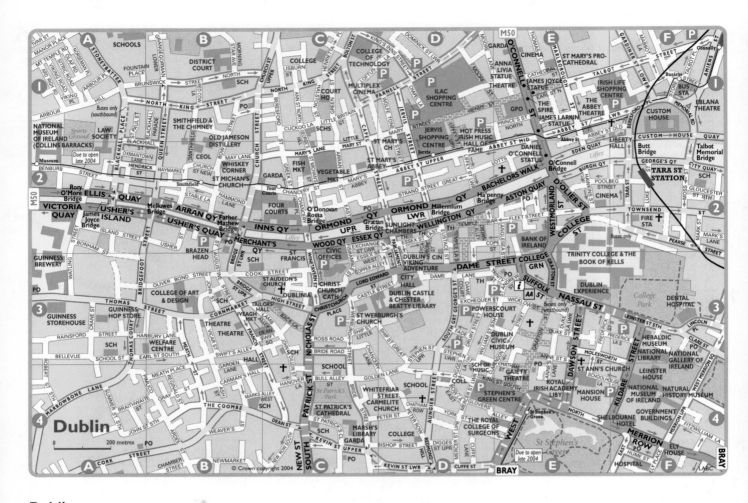

Dublin

Dublin is found on atlas page **39 M7**

E1 Abbey Street Lower	C3 Castle Street	B3 Earl Street South	D1 Jervis Street	B1 Morning Star Avenue	C3 Ship Street Little
E2 Abbey Street Middle	E1 Cathedral Street	E2 Eden Quay	C3 John Dillon Street	F2 Moss Street	A1 Sitric Road
E1 Abbey Street Old	B4 Chamber Street	A2 Ellis Quay	B3 John Street	A1 Mount Temple Road	B2 Smithfield
D2 Abbey Street Upper	C3 Chancery Lane	F4 Ely Place	A4 John Street South	E3 Nassau Street	D3 South Great George's Street
F1 Amiens Street	C2 Chancery Place	C2 Essex Quay	D4 Kevin Street Lower	C4 New Row South	B2 Stable Lane
E2 Anglesea Street	C2 Chancery Street	D2 Essex Street East	C4 Kevin Street Upper	C4 New Street South	D3 Stephen Street Lower
C1 Ann Street North	D1 Chapel Lane	C3 Essex Street West	F4 Kildare Street	B4 Newmarket	D3 Stephen Street Upper
E3 Anne Street South	D4 Chatham Row	D2 Eustace Street	D4 King Street South	C3 Nicholas Street	A1 Stoneybatter
E4 Anne's Lane	E4 Chatham Street	C2 Exchange Street Lower	C1 King's Inns Street	A1 Norseman Place	F1 Store Street
A1 Arbour Hill	E3 Christchurch Place	D3 Exchequer Street	C3 Lamb Alley	B1 North King Street	D2 Strand Street Great
A1 Arbour Place	B2 Church Street	D3 Fade Street	F3 Leinster Street South	E1 O'Connell Street	E3 Suffolk Street
A1 Ard Right Road	B2 Church Street New	C2 Fishamble Street	D2 Liffey Street Lower	A1 Olaf Road	A4 Summer Street South
B4 Ardee Street	C1 Church Street Upper	F4 Fitzwilliam Lane	D1 Liffey Street Upper	B1 Oliver Bond Street	B3 Swift's Alley
B2 Arran Quay	F2 City Quay	E2 Fleet Street	F3 Lincoln Place	D2 Ormond Quay Lower	D2 Sycamore Street
C2 Arran Street East	F3 Clare Street	A1 Fountain Place	C1 Lisburn Street	C2 Ormond Quay Upper	F1 Talbot Place
B4 Ash Street	E3 Clarendon Street	B3 Francis Street	C1 Little Britain Street	A2 Oxmantown Lane	E1 Talbot Street
E2 Aston Quay	E3 College Green	F3 Frederick Lane South	D1 Little Mary Street	D2 Parliament Street	F2 Tara Street
D4 Aungier street	E2 College Street	E3 Frederick Street South	C1 Loftus Lane	D1 Parnell Street	D2 Temple Bar
D2 Bachelors Walk	B3 Cook Street	B4 Garden Lane	C3 Lord Edward Street	C4 Patrick Street	D2 Temple Lane South
C3 Back Lane	D2 Cope Street	F1 Gardiner Street Lower	E2 Lotts	F2 Pearse Street	B4 The Coombe
A3 Bellevue	C3 Copper Alley	C1 George's Hill	F2 Luke Street	D4 Peter Row	A3 Thomas Court
A2 Benburb Street	A4 Cork Street	F2 George's Quay	F1 Mabbot Lane	B4 Peter Street	E1 Thomas Lane
F1 Beresford Place	B3 Cornmarket	F2 Gloucester Street South	A1 Manor Place	B4 Pimlico	A3 Thomas Street
C1 Beresford Street	A3 Crane Lane	D4 Glovers Alley	F2 Mark Street	E1 Prince's Street North	F2 Townsend Street
D4 Bishop Street	D2 Crown Alley	C4 Golden Lane	F2 Marks Alley West	B2 Queen Street	E3 Trinity Street
B1 Blackhall Parade	C1 Cuckoo Lane	E3 Grafton Street	A4 Marrowbone Lane	A3 Rainsford Street	B2 Usher Street
A2 Blackhall Place	D4 Cuffe Lane	B1 Grangegorman Lower	D1 Mary Lane	B1 Red Cow Lane	A2 Usher's Island
B2 Blackhall Street	D4 Cuffe Street	B4 Gray Street	C2 Mary's Abbey	D4 Redmond Hill	B2 Usher's Quay
C1 Bolton Street	F1 Custom House Quay	C2 Greek Street	C2 Mary's Lane	B4 Reginald Street	B3 Vicar Street
A2 Bonham Street	D3 Dame Court	C1 Green Street	B2 May Lane	A4 Robert Street South	A2 Victoria Quay
D4 Bow Lane East	D3 Dame Lane	C1 Halston Street	B4 Meath Place	C3 Ross Road	A1 Viking Place
B2 Bow Street	D3 Dame Street	B2 Hammond Lane	B3 Meath Street	E3 St Andrew Street	A1 Viking Road
A4 Braithwaite Street	E4 Dawson Street	A3 Hanbury Lane	F1 Memorial Road	C2 St Augustine Street	A3 Watling Street
C3 Bride Road	C3 Dean Street	C4 Hanover Lane	D4 Mercer Street Lower	B2 St Michan's Street	B4 Weaver's Street
C4 Bride Street	C3 Dean Swift Square	E2 Hawkins Street	D4 Mercer Street Upper	C4 St Patrick's Close	D2 Wellington Quay
B3 Bridge Street Lower	D4 Digges Lane	B2 Haymarket	B2 Merchant's Quay	A1 St Paul Street	C3 Werburgh Street
B3 Bridge Street Upper	D4 Digges Street Upper	C1 Hendrick Street	F4 Merrion Row	F4 St Stephen's Green East	E2 Westmorland Street
A3 Bridgefoot Street	D1 Dominick Street Lower	D1 Henrietta Place	F4 Merrion Row Upper	E4 St Stephen's Green North	E3 Wicklow Street
A1 Brunswick Street North	D3 Drury Street	D1 Henry Street	E3 Molesworth Street	E4 St Stephen's Green West	D3 William Street South
C4 Bull Alley Street	E3 Duke Lane Lower	C3 High Street	D1 Moore Lane	A3 School Street	C3 Winetavern Street
E2 Burgh Quay	E3 Duke Street	F4 Hume Street	D1 Moore Street	E4 Schoolhouse Lane	D1 Wolfe Tone Street
C1 Capel Street	E1 Earl Street North	C2 Inns Quay		D3 Ship Street Great	C2 Wood Quay
B4 Carman's Hall		A2 Island Street		C3 Ship Street Great	D4 York Street

Galway

Galway is found on atlas page **34 C8**

C2	Abbey Gate Street	B3	Munster Avenue
A1	Ash Road	C3	New Dock Street
D2	Bótha Na Mban	B2	New Road
B2	Bóthar Einde	B1	Newcastle Avenue
D2	Bothar Irwin	B2	Newcastle Road
A1	Bóthar Phadraic UI Chonnaire	C2	Newtown Smith
		B2	Nun's Island Street
C3	Bridge Street	A1	O'Flaherty Road
B2	Canal Road Lower	A2	Palmyra Avenue
B1	Canal Road Upper	B2	Presentation Road
B3	Claddagh Quay	D2	Prospect Hill
A1	Colmcillie Road	C3	Quay Street
A1	Costello Road	D3	Queen Street
A1	Davis Road	A2	Raleigh Row
C3	Dock Road	C3	St Augustine Street
C3	Dock Street	C2	St Brendan's Avenue
B3	Dominick Street	D1	St Bridget's Place
D1	Dyke Road	C2	St Francis Street
C2	Eglinton Street	B2	St Helen's Street
D2	Eyre Square	A2	St Mary's Park
C2	Eyre Street	A2	St Mary's Road
B3	Father Burke Road	C2	St Vincent's Avenue
A3	Father Griffin Avenue	A3	Sea Road
A3	Father Griffin Road	A1	Shantalla Road
D2	Forster Street	C2	Shop Street
A1	Fursey Road	D2	Station Road
D1	Headford Road	A2	Taylor's Hill Road
B2	Henry Street	A3	The Crescent
C3	High Street	C3	The Long Walk
D3	Lough Atalia Road	B1	University Road
C2	Market Street	D1	Water Lane
A1	McDara Road	C1	Waterside
C3	Merchants Road	A3	Whitestrand Road
C3	Middle Street	C2	William Street
B2	Mill Street	B3	William Street West

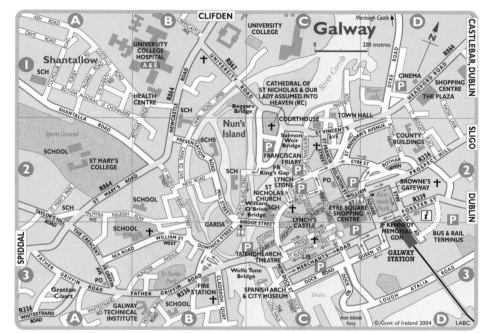

Kilkenny

Kilkenny is found on atlas page **21 N5**

A2	Abbey Street
B1	Ballybought Street
B1	Barrack Street
A2	Bateman's Quay
A2	Canal Square
B3	Castle Road
B1	Castlecomer Road
A3	College Road
A1	Dean Street
B2	Dublin Road
A2	Evan's Lane
B3	Father Hayden Road
A3	Friary Street
A3	Gaol Road
A1	Green Street
A1	Green's Hill
A1	Greensbridge Street
B1	Hebron Road
A2	High Street
A2	Irish Town
A2	James's Street
B2	John Street Lower
B2	John Street Upper
B2	John's Green
A2	John's Quay
A3	Lower New Street
B2	Maudlin Street
A2	Michael Street
A2	New Building Lane
A1	New Road
A3	Ormonde Street
A2	Parliament Street
A2	Parnell Street
A3	Patrick Street
A2	Rose Inn Street
A2	St Kiernan's Street
A3	The Parade
A2	Tilbury Place
A1	Vicar Street
A3	Walkin Street
B1	Wolfe Tone Street

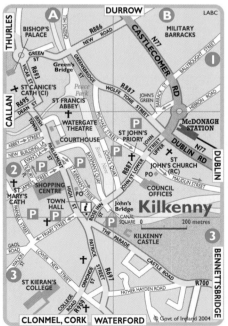

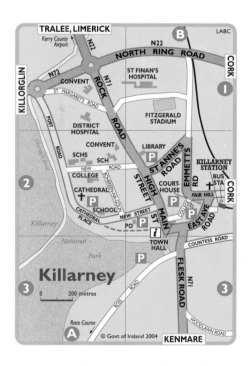

Killarney

Killarney is found on atlas page **10 B6**

A2	Bohereen-na-Goun	A2	New Road
A2	Cathedral Place	B2	New Street
B2	College Street	A1	North Ring Road
B3	Countess Road	A1	Port Road
B2	East Avenue Road	A1	Rock Road
B2	Emmetts Road	A3	Ross Road
B2	Fair Hill	B2	St Anne's Road
B3	Flesk Road	A1	St Margaret's Road
B2	High Street	B3	Woodlawn Road
B2	Main Street		

Limerick

Limerick is found on atlas page **18 H3**

B3	Anne Street
B2	Arthurs Quay
C1	Athlunkard Street
B1	Bank Place
B2	Bedford Row
A1	Belfield Gardens
C1	Bishop's Street
D3	Blackboy Road
C2	Brennans Row
B1	Bridge Street
C2	Broad Street
B1	Castle Street
C3	Cathedral Place
B3	Catherine Street
B3	Cecil Street
C1	Charlotte's Quay
B1	Clancy's Strand
D2	Clare Street
A1	Clareview Avenue
B3	Davis Street
B2	Denmark Street
A3	Dock Road
B3	Dominick Street
D2	Downey Street
B2	Ellen Street
A1	Ennis Road
A1	Farranshone Road
D2	Flood Street
B2	Francis Street
C1	Gaol Lane
D3	Garryowen
C1	George's Quay
D3	Geraldine Terrace
A3	Glentworth Street
A1	Glenview Gardens
C2	Grattan Street
D3	Greenhill Road
A3	Hartstonge Street
A2	Harvey's Quay
A3	Henry Street
C2	High Street

B2	Honans Quay
A2	Howley's Quay
C2	John Square
C2	John's Street
D2	Keane Street
D2	Keating Street
C1	Lock Quay
A2	Lower Cecil Street
C3	Lower Gerald Griffin Street
A3	Lower Mallow Street
B3	Mallow Street
C2	Market Street
C1	Mary Street
B2	Michael Street
C2	Milk Street
A3	Mount Kennett Place
C2	Mungret Street
C3	Musgrave Street
C2	New Road
A3	Newenham Street
B1	Nicholas Street
A2	North Circular Road
D2	North Claughaun Road
A2	O'Callaghan's Strand
A3	O'Connell Street
A3	O'Curry Street
C2	Old Clare Street
C2	Old Francis Street
B3	Parnell Street
B2	Patrick Street
D2	Pennywell
D2	Pennywell Lane
B3	Pery Square
B3	Pery Street
D3	Pike Avenue
B1	Priory Park
B3	Roche's Street
A1	Rockspring Gardens
C3	Rossa Avenue

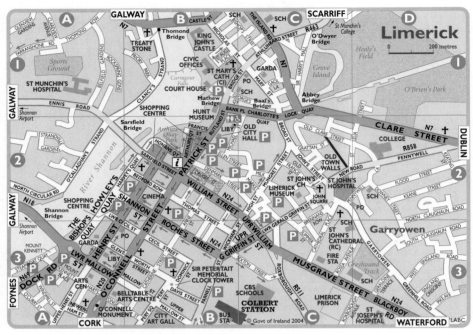

C3	Roxborough Avenue	B2	Shannon Street	A3	The Bishop's Quay	C3	Upper William Street
C3	Roxborough Road	D3	Singland Crescent	C1	The Island Road	D3	West Singland Road
B2	Rutland Street	C1	Sir Harry's Mall	A1	Thomond Row	B3	Wickham Street
B1	St Augustine Place	D3	South Claughaun Road	B2	Thomas Street	B2	William Street
D2	St Lelia Street	A3	Steamboat Quay	B3	Upper Gerald Griffin Street	A3	Windmill Street
B2	Sarsfield Street	A2	Strandville Gardens				
C3	Sexton Street	C3	Summer Street	A3	Upper Henry Street		

Londonderry

Londonderry is found on atlas page **66 C9**

B1	Abbey Street
B3	Abercorn Road
A3	Anne Street
C2	Artillery Street
C1	Bank Place
B3	Barrack Street
A1	Beechwood Avenue
A2	Beechwood Street
D3	Benvarden Avenue
A3	Bishop Street
A2	Bligh's Lane
A1	Blucher Street
A3	Bluebell Hill Gardens
D2	Bond's Hill
D1	Bond's Street
A3	Brandywell Road
C2	Bridge Street
B2	Butchers Street
A2	Cable Street
C3	Carlisle Road
A3	Carrigans Lane
C1	Castle Street
B1	Chamberlain Street
D3	Chapel Road
D2	Clooney Terrace
B3	Cooke Street
B1	Creggan Street
A2	Dove Gardens
D3	Duke Street
D2	Dungiven Road
D3	Dunnfield Terrace
A1	Eastway
B1	Eglinton Place
A2	Elmwood Road
A2	Elmwood Street
B3	Ewing Street
B1	Fahan Street
B1	Fahan Street
B3	Ferguson Street
C2	Ferry Quay
D3	Fountain Hill

C1	Foyle Embankment
B3	Foyle Road
C2	Foyle Street
B1	Francis Street
B1	Frederick Street
B1	Great James Street
B1	Harvey Street
C2	Hawkin Street
D3	Hayesbank Park
B1	High Street
B3	Ivy Terrace
C3	John Street
D1	King Street
D3	Knockdara Park
A3	Lecky Road
D1	Limavady Road
A2	Limewood Street
C2	Linenhall Street
B1	Lisfannon Park
B1	Little Diamond
B1	Little James Street
B2	London Street
A2	Lone Moor Road
B2	Long Tower Street
B3	Lower Bennett Street
B1	Lower Road
D2	Lower Violet Street
B2	Magazine Street
D3	Malvern Terrace
D3	Margaret Street
C2	Market Street
A1	Marlborough Road
A1	Marlborough Street
B3	Maureen Avenue
B3	Miller Street
A2	Nualamount Drive
A1	Oakfield Crescent
A1	Oakfield Road
C2	Orchard Street
B2	Palace Street
D1	Pine Street

D2	Primrose Street	A3	Southend Park	C3	Wapping Lane
C2	Pump Street	D3	Spencer Road	B1	Waterloo Street
B2	Rossville Street	A2	Stanleys Walk	D2	Waterside Link
B1	Sackville Street	B2	The Diamond	A1	Westland Avenue
A3	St Columbas Walk	C1	Union Hall Place	A1	Westland Street
C2	Shipquay Street	D2	Union Street	A1	Westland Terrace
D2	Simpson's Brae	B3	Upper Bennett Street	B1	William Street

Sligo

Sligo is found on atlas page **52 C6**

C2	Abbey Street	C1	Markievicz Road
B2	Adelaide Street	C2	O'Connell Street
B1	Ballast Quay	C3	Old Market Street
C1	Barrack Street	D3	Pearse Road
C1	Bridge Street	B1	Prin Mill Road
C3	Burton Street	B1	Quay Street
C2	Castle Street	D2	Riverside
C3	Chapel Hill	C3	St Brigets Place
D2	Chapel Street	C1	Stephen Street
C2	Charles Street	C2	Teeling Street
A2	Church Hill	B2	Temple Street
B3	Circular Road	B2	The Lungy
B2	College Road	D1	The Mall
C1	Connaughton Road	C2	Thomas Street
C3	Connolly Street	B1	Union Place
D2	Cranmore Mass Lane	B1	Union Street
A1	Finiskiln Road	A2	Upper John Street
C3	Gallows Hill	B1	Wine Street
D2	Gaol Road	B2	Wolftone Street
C2	Grattan Street		
C2	Harmony Hill		
C2	High Street		
C1	Holborn Hill		
C1	Holborn Street		
B1	Hughes Bridge		
A2	Jinks Avenue		
B2	John Street		
C2	Kennedy Parade		
A2	Knappagh Road		
B2	Lord Edward Street		
D2	Lower Abbey Street		
B1	Lower Quay Street		
B1	Lynn's Place		
C3	Mail Coach Road		
C2	Market Street		

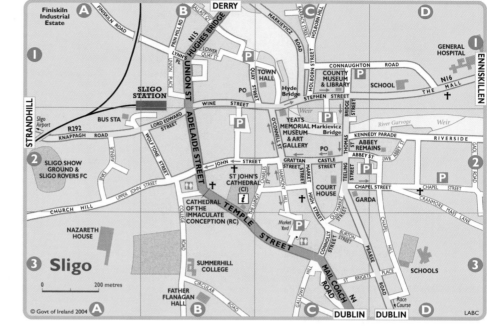

Waterford

Waterford is found on atlas page **14 E6**

D1	Abbey Road	B3	Manor Street
D3	Adelphi Quay	A1	Mary Street
B1	Anne Street	B3	Mayors Walk
D1	Ard Mhuire	B1	Meagher's Quay
B2	Barker Street	C3	Michael Street
B3	Barrack Street	A2	Military Road
C2	Barron Strand Street	A2	Morgan Street
C3	Beau Street	A3	Morrissons Avenue
A3	Bernard Place	A3	Morrissons Road
A1	Bilberry Road	A3	Mount Sion Avenue
C1	Bishopsgrove	B3	New Street
B1	Bridge Street	B3	Newgate Street
C2	Broad Street	B2	Newports Square
D3	Canada Street	B3	Newports Terrace
A3	Cannon Street	B2	O'Connell Street
B3	Castle Street	A2	Ozanam Street
A2	Cathal Brugha Street	C3	Parnell Street
C3	Catherine Street	B2	Patrick Street
B3	Convent Hill	C2	Peter Street
C2	Custom House Quay	A2	Philip Street
B1	Dock Road	A1	Rockfield Park
A3	Doyle's Street	D1	Rockshire Court
A3	Emmett Place	D1	Rockshire Road
D1	Fountain Street	D3	Rose Lane
B2	Francis Street	D3	Scotch Quay
A1	Gracedieu Road	B3	Short Course
A1	Grattan Quay	A3	Slievekeale Road
C2	Great Georges Street	C3	Spring Garden Alley
B2	Green Street	B3	Stephen Street
A3	Griffith Place	B1	Suir Street
B3	Hennessy's Road	A2	Summer Hill
C2	High Street	A1	Summerhill Terrace
C3	John Street	B2	The Glen
B3	Johns Lane	C3	The Mall
C3	Johnstown	B2	Thomas Hill
C3	Lady Lane	B2	Thomas Street
A3	Leamy Street	A2	Upper Yellow Road
D3	Lombard Street	C3	Waterside
A2	Lower Yellow Road	D3	William Street
A3	Luke Wadding Street		
B3	Manor Hill		

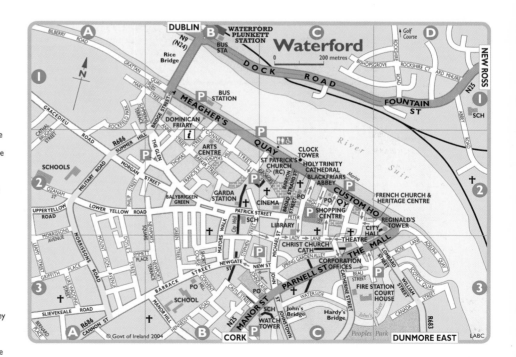

Motorways

The motorway maps on these pages consist of signposting panels, the layout of junctions, road numbers and exit destinations. To reflect the distances shown on the motorway signs, distances are given in miles in Northern Ireland and in kilometres in the Republic of Ireland.

Northern Ireland

M1	Belfast - Dungannon	79-80
M2, M22	Belfast - Randalstown	80
M2	Ballymena Bypass	80

Republic of Ireland

M1	Dublin - Dundalk	77
M4	Leixlip and Maynooth Bypass	78
M7	Naas and Newbridge Bypass	79
M7	Portlaoise Bypass	79
M11	Bray and Shankill Bypass	78
M50	Dublin Ring Road	78

Key to motorway maps

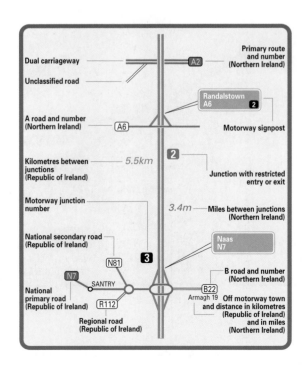

Restricted Motorway Junctions

Northern Ireland

M1 BELFAST – DUNGANNON

Junction		
3 (pg 62)	Westbound	No access. Exit only
	Eastbound	No exit. Access only

M2, M22 BELFAST – RANDALSTOWN

Junction		
2 (pg 63)	Westbound	No restriction.
	Southbound	No exit to M5.
7 (pg 62)	Westbound	No access. Exit only
	Southbound	No access. Exit only

Republic of Ireland

M1 DUBLIN – DUNDALK

Junction		
with R152 (pg 47)	Northbound	No access. Exit only
	Southbound	No exit. Access only
at Donore (pg 47)	Northbound	No restriction.
	Southbound	No access. Exit only
with R132 (pg 47)	Northbound	No exit. Access only
	Southbound	No access. Exit only
with R170 (pg 47)	Northbound	No access. Exit only
	Southbound	No exit. Access only

M7 NAAS & NEWBRIDGE BYPASS

Junction		
9 (pg 30)	Westbound	No access. Exit only to M9 (southbound)
	Eastbound	No exit. Access only from M9 (northbound)

M1 Dublin - Balbriggan

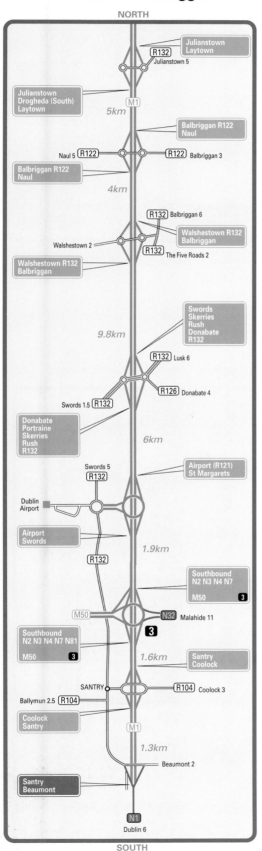

M1 Balbriggan - Dundalk

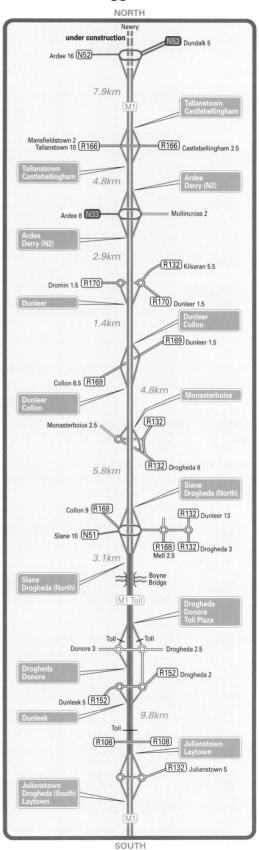

M4 Leixlip & Maynooth Bypass

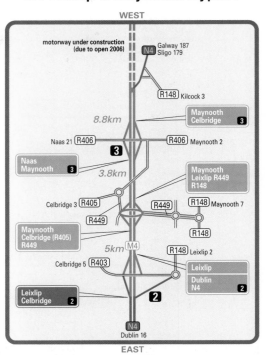

M11 Bray & Shankill Bypass

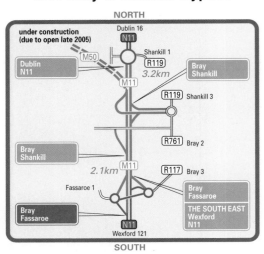

M50 Dublin Ring Road

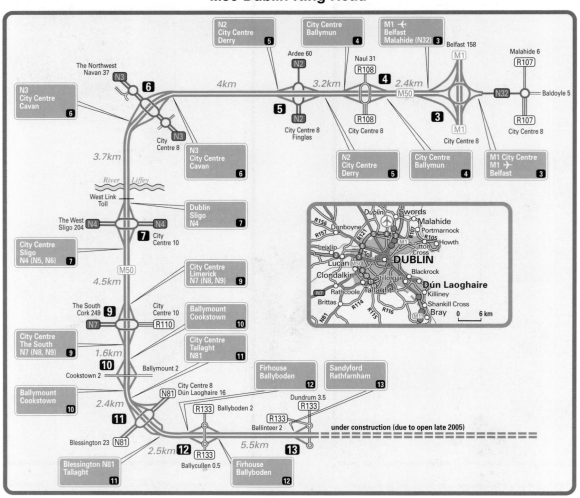

M7 Portlaoise Bypass

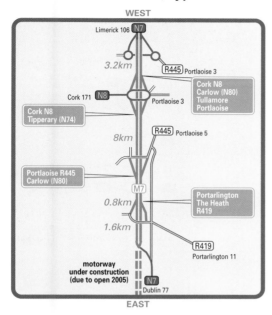

WEST

Limerick 106 · N7

3.2km

R445 · Portlaoise 3

Cork 171 · N8

Cork N8
Carlow (N80)
Tullamore
Portlaoise

Portlaoise 3

Cork N8
Tipperary (N74)

R445 · Portlaoise 5

8km

Portlaoise R445
Carlow (N80)

M7

Portarlington
The Heath
R419

0.8km

1.6km

R419

Portarlington 11

**motorway
under construction
(due to open 2005)**

N7 · Dublin 77

EAST

M7 Naas & Newbridge Bypass

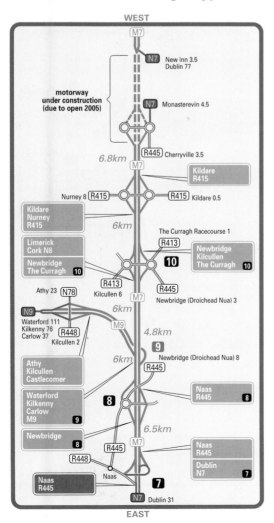

WEST

M7

N7 · New Inn 3.5
Dublin 77

**motorway
under construction
(due to open 2005)**

N7 · Monasterevin 4.5

R445 · Cherryville 3.5

6.8km

M7

Kildare
R415

Nurney 8 · R415

R415 · Kildare 0.5

Kildare
Nurney
R415

6km

The Curragh Racecourse 1

Limerick
Cork N8

R413

Newbridge
Kilcullen
The Curragh · 10

Newbridge
The Curragh · 10

10

Athy 23 · N78

R413

R445

Kilcullen 6

N9

M7

Newbridge (Droichead Nua) 3

Waterford 111
Kilkenny 76
Carlow 37

R448

6km

Kilcullen 2

M9

4.8km

Athy
Kilcullen
Castlecomer

9

6km

Newbridge (Droichead Nua) 8

R445

Waterford
Kilkenny
Carlow
M9 · 9

8

Naas
R445 · 8

Newbridge · 8

6.5km

R445 · M7

Naas
R445

R448

Naas

Dublin
N7 · 7

7

Naas
R445

N7 · Dublin 31

EAST

M1 Belfast - Craigavon

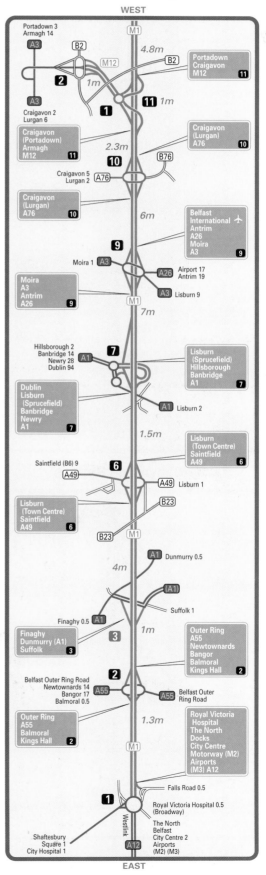

WEST

M1

Portadown 3
Armagh 14

A3

B2

4.8m

M12

B2

Portadown
Craigavon
M12 · 11

2

A3

1m

11 · 1m

Craigavon 2
Lurgan 6

1

Craigavon
(Portadown)
Armagh
M12 · 11

Craigavon
(Lurgan)
A76 · 10

2.3m

10

B76

Craigavon 5
Lurgan 2 · A76

Craigavon
(Lurgan)
A76 · 10

Belfast
International ✈
Antrim
A26
Moira
A3 · 9

6m

9

Moira 1 · A3

Airport 17
Antrim 19

A26

Moira
A3
Antrim
A26 · 9

A3 · Lisburn 9

M1

7m

Hillsborough 2
Banbridge 14
Newry 28
Dublin 94

A1

7

Lisburn
(Sprucefield)
Hillsborough
Banbridge
A1 · 7

Dublin
Lisburn
(Sprucefield)
Banbridge
Newry
A1 · 7

A1 · Lisburn 2

1.5m

Lisburn
(Town Centre)
Saintfield
A49 · 6

Saintfield (B6) 9

A49

6

A49 · Lisburn 1

Lisburn
(Town Centre)
Saintfield
A49 · 6

B23

B23 · M1

A1 · Dunmurry 0.5

4m

(A1)

Suffolk 1

Finaghy 0.5 · A1

1m

Finaghy
Dunmurry (A1)
Suffolk · 3

3

Outer Ring
A55
Newtownards
Bangor
Balmoral
Kings Hall · 2

2

Belfast Outer Ring Road
Newtownards 14
Bangor 17
Balmoral 0.5

A55

Belfast Outer
Ring Road

Outer Ring
A55
Balmoral
Kings Hall · 2

A55

Royal Victoria
Hospital
The North
Docks
City Centre
Motorway (M2)
Airports
(M3) A12

1.3m

M1

Falls Road 0.5

1

Royal Victoria Hospital 0.5
(Broadway)

Westlink

The North
Belfast
City Centre 2
Airports
(M2) (M3)

Shaftesbury
Square 1
City Hospital 1

A12

EAST

M1 Craigavon - Dungannon
M2 Ballymena Bypass
M2, M22 Belfast - Randalstown

M1 Craigavon - Dungannon

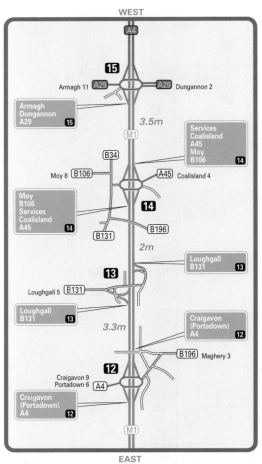

M2 Ballymena Bypass

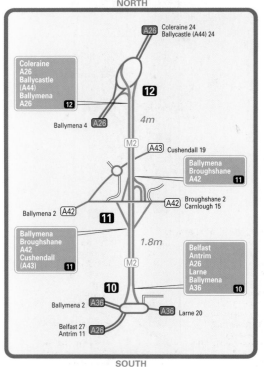

M2, M22 Belfast - Randalstown

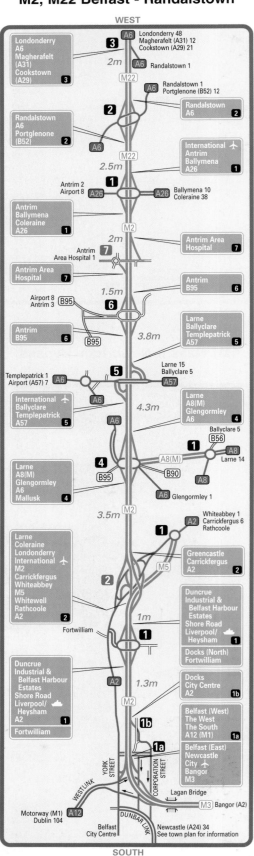

Counties and administrative areas

The index lists places appearing in the main-map section of the atlas in alphabetical order. The reference before each name gives the atlas page number and grid reference of the square in which the place appears. The map shows counties and other internal administration areas in each country, together with a list of the abbreviated county name forms used in the index.

50 places of interest are indexed in red, airports in blue.

Northern Ireland

Antrim	Antrim
Armagh	Armagh
Down	Down
Fermanagh	Ferman
Londonderry	Lderry
Tyrone	Tyrone

Republic of Ireland

Carlow	Carlow	**Leitrim**	Leitrm
Cavan	Cavan	**Limerick**	Limrck
Clare	Clare	**Longford**	Longfd
Cork	Cork	**Louth**	Louth
Donegal	Donegl	**Mayo**	Mayo
Dublin	Dublin	**Meath**	Meath
Dublin City (1)	Dublin	**Monaghan**	Monhan
Dún Laoghaire-		**Offaly**	Offaly
Rathdown (2)	Dublin	**Roscommon**	Roscom
Fingal (3)	Dublin	**Sligo**	Sligo
South Dublin (4)	Dublin	**Tipperary North**	Tippry
Galway	Galway	**Tipperary South**	Tippry
Kerry	Kerry	**Waterford**	Watfd
Kildare	Kildre	**Westmeath**	Wmeath
Kilkenny	Kilken	**Wexford**	Wexfd
Laois	Laois	**Wicklow**	Wicklw

	0	10	20	30	40	50 miles
0	20	40	60	80 km		

A

34 G5 **Abbey** Galway
26 H3 **Abbey** Galway
36 F1 **Abbeyderg Cross Roads** Longfd
16 F10 **Abbeydorney**/*Mainistir Ó dTorna* Kerry
17 L9 **Abbeyfeale**/*Mainistir na Féile* Limrck
45 K8 **Abbeylara**/*Mainistir Leathrátha* Longfd
29 K8 **Abbeyleix**/*Mainistir Laoise* Laois
36 G2 **Abbeyshrule**/*Mainistir Shruthla* Longfd
19 L4 **Abington** Limrck
40 E4 **Achill Sound**/*Gob an Choire* Mayo
51 N8 **Achonry**/*Achadh Conaire* Sligo
51 K8 **Aclare**/*Áth an Chláir* Sligo
56 C5 **Acton** Armagh
15 K3 **Adamstown** Wexfd
18 F5 **Adara**/*Áth Dara* Limrck
34 C7 **Addergoole** Galway
42 D6 **Addergoole** Mayo
3 L4 **Adrigole**/*Eadargóil* Cork
28 H7 **Aghaboe** Laois
44 F7 **Aghaboy** Longfd
11 L9 **Aghabullogue** Cork
44 C1 **Aghacashel**/*Achadh an Chaisil* Leitrm
6 E7 **Aghada** Cork
42 G5 **Aghadiffin** Mayo
48 C3 **Aghadoon** Mayo
67 M8 **Aghadowey** Lderry
4 B8 **Aghadown** Cork
62 E10 **Aghagallon** Antrim
41 L7 **Aghagower** Mayo
62 E10 **Aghalee** Antrim
44 C5 **Aghamore** Leitrm
42 F6 **Aghamore** Mayo
40 E7 **Aghany** Mayo
31 K7 **Aghavannagh** Wicklw
44 F3 **Aghavas** Leitrm
38 E4 **Agher Cross Roads** Meath
12 E8 **Aghern** Cork
48 D6 **Aghleam** Mayo
44 H6 **Aghnacliff**/*Achadh na Cloiche* Longfd
8 F10 **Aghnagar Bridge** Kerry
5 L2 **Aghnamarroge Cross Roads** Cork
55 J10 **Aghnamullen** Monhan
67 M8 **Agivey Bridge** Lderry
8 G5 **Aglish** Kerry
27 M5 **Aglish** Tippry
13 K8 **Aglish** Watfd
11 N7 **Ahadallane Cross Roads** Cork
16 F6 **Ahafona** Kerry
3 M7 **Ahakista** Cork
35 M6 **Ahascragh**/*Áth Eascrach* Galway
5 L1 **Aherla** Cork
12 E3 **Ahnaseed Bridge** Tippry
62 D2 **Ahoghill** Antrim
62 F7 **Aldergrove** Antrim
60 H2 **Alla Cross Roads** Lderry
38 D9 **Allen** Kildre
38 D8 **Allenwood**/*Fiodh Alúine* Kildre
2 F5 **Allihies**/*Na hAilichí* Cork
55 N4 **Allistragh** Armagh
35 K6 **Alloon Lower** Galway
22 F3 **Altamont Gardens** Carlow
59 N3 **Altnapaste** Donegl
48 E4 **An Geata Mór** Mayo
8 H4 **Anascaul**/*Abhainn an Scáil* Kerry
19 N10 **Anglesborough** Limrck
19 P3 **Anglesey Bridge** Tippry
54 F8 **Anlore** Monhan
26 G9 **Annacarriga** Clare
19 Q5 **Annacarty** Tippry
56 E5 **Annaclone** Down
57 L4 **Annacloy** Down
19 J3 **Annacotty** Limrck
31 L9 **Annacurragh** Wicklw
8 H4 **Annagap** Kerry
64 D9 **Annagary**/*Anagaire* Donegl
47 K5 **Annagassan** Louth
19 K3 **Annagh** Limrck
43 K8 **Annagh** Roscom
24 F9 **Annagh Cross Roads** Clare
34 B6 **Annaghdown**/*Eanach Dhúin* Galway
26 D8 **Annaghneal** Clare
18 F1 **Annagore Bridge** Clare
56 G2 **Annahilt** Down
57 J10 **Annalong** Down
31 M5 **Annamoe**/*Áth na mBó* Wicklw
55 L9 **Annayalla** Monhan
11 J3 **Anne's Bridge** Cork
14 B9 **Annestown** Watfd
20 C4 **Annfield** Tippry
57 J6 **Annsborough** Down
62 F5 **Antrim** Antrim
12 F5 **Araglin** Cork
12 E6 **Araglin Bridge** Cork
24 D2 **Aran Islands** Galway
45 P10 **Archerstown** Wmeath

46 E5 **Ardagh** Meath
17 P7 **Ardagh**/*Ardach* Limrck
44 G10 **Ardagh**/*Ardach* Longfd
43 M5 **Ardagh Cross Roads** Roscom
37 J8 **Ardan** Offaly
38 C4 **Ardanew** Meath
58 F4 **Ardara**/*Ard an Ratha* Donegl
22 F3 **Ardattin** Carlow
59 K5 **Ardbane** Donegl
62 B7 **Ardboe** Tyrone
39 K1 **Ardcath** Meath
16 D10 **Ardconnell** Kerry
27 L7 **Ardcrony** Tippry
3 K2 **Ardea Bridge** Kerry
46 H5 **Ardee**/*Baile Átha Fhirdhia* Louth
16 D10 **Ardfert**/*Ard Fhearta* Kerry
5 J7 **Ardfield** Cork
13 J3 **Ardfinnan**/*Ard Fhíonáin* Tippry
6 E3 **Ardglass** Cork
57 N6 **Ardglass** Down
2 H3 **Ardgroom**/*Dhá Dhrom* Cork
2 E2 **Ardkearagh** Kerry
57 P2 **Ardkeen** Down
34 B1 **Ardkill** Mayo
29 K6 **Ardlea** Laois
44 H1 **Ardlougher** Cavan
7 L4 **Ardmore**/*Aird Mhór* Watfd
37 K6 **Ardmorney** Wmeath
18 H2 **Ardnacrusha** Clare
34 F5 **Ardnasodan** Galway
19 J10 **Ardpatrick** Limrck
6 E7 **Ardra** Cork
3 Q5 **Ardrah** Cork
4 C4 **Ardrah** Cork
26 C2 **Ardrahan**/*Ard Raithin* Galway
55 P2 **Ardress** Armagh
30 C5 **Ardscull Cross Roads** Kildre
60 D5 **Ardstraw** Tyrone
61 Q7 **Ardtrea** Tyrone
4 H6 **Argideen Bridge** Cork
23 N2 **Arklow**/*An tInbhear Mór* Wicklw
29 Q8 **Arless** Laois
55 N4 **Armagh** Armagh
68 B6 **Armoy** Antrim
53 P6 **Arney** Ferman
17 P9 **Arranagh** Limrck
14 G6 **Arthurstown** Wexfd
67 K6 **Articlave** Lderry
60 E2 **Artigarvan** Tyrone
44 H4 **Arvagh**/*Armhach* Cavan
39 K3 **Ashbourne**/*Cill Dhéagláin* Meath
17 P10 **Ashford** Limrck
31 P5 **Ashford**/*Áth na Fuinseoige* Wicklw
20 E7 **Ashill** Tippry
23 J5 **Askamore** Wexfd
31 K8 **Askanagap** Wicklw
18 C4 **Askeaton**/*Eas Geitine* Limrck
16 G5 **Astee** Kerry
38 C1 **Athboy**/*Baile Átha Buí* Meath
17 L7 **Athea**/*Áth an tSléibhe* Limrck
34 G8 **Athenry**/*Baile Átha an Rí* Galway
30 E2 **Athgarvan** Kildre
18 H8 **Athlacca** Limrck
35 N2 **Athleague**/*Áth Liag* Roscom
36 C5 **Athlone**/*Baile Átha Luain* Wmeath
36 C5 **Athlone Castle** Wmeath
20 F4 **Athnid** Tippry
30 B6 **Athy**/*Baile Átha Í* Kildre
29 K9 **Attanagh** Laois
56 G10 **Attical** Down
35 N9 **Atticoffey** Galway
35 L6 **Attiregan** Galway
50 G8 **Attymass**/*Áit Tí an Mheasaigh* Mayo
34 H7 **Attymon**/*Áth Tiomáin* Galway
36 E3 **Auburn** Wmeath
34 D6 **Aucloggeen** Galway
9 J2 **Aughacasla** Kerry
54 G3 **Augher** Tyrone
15 L5 **Aughfad** Wexfd
9 L4 **Aughils** Kerry
62 B1 **Aughnacleagh** Antrim
55 J3 **Aughnacloy** Tyrone
20 B10 **Aughnagawer Cross Roads** Galway
44 D1 **Aughnasheelan**/*Acadh na Síleann* Leitrm
25 N5 **Aughrim** Clare
35 M8 **Aughrim**/*Eachroim* Galway
31 L9 **Aughrim**/*Eachroim* Wicklw
31 N9 **Avoca**/*Abhóca* Wicklw

B

38 D5 **Baconstown** Meath
22 C4 **Bagenalstown**/*Muine Bheag* Carlow

24 D4 **Baile an Teampall** Clare
56 H2 **Baileysmill** Down
46 B4 **Bailieborough**/*Coill an Choilligín* Cavan
39 N1 **Balbriggan**/*Baile Brigín* Dublin
51 P1 **Balinfull** Sligo
42 B7 **Balla** Mayo
26 C4 **Ballaba** Galway
5 Q3 **Ballady** Cork
34 F1 **Ballagh** Limrck
17 P9 **Ballagh** Limrck
20 C7 **Ballagh** Tippry
35 Q3 **Ballagh** Roscom
43 Q9 **Ballagh** Roscom
15 J3 **Ballagh** Wexfd
43 J5 **Ballaghaderreen**/*Bealach an Doirín* Roscom
17 L9 **Ballaghbehy** Limrck
20 F8 **Ballaghboy** Tippry
23 K9 **Ballaghkeen** Wexfd
28 F6 **Ballaghmore** Laois
52 D3 **Ballaghnatrillick** Sligo
37 J9 **Ballard** Offaly
22 H3 **Ballard Cross Roads** Wicklw
26 C4 **Ballardiggan** Galway
15 Q7 **Ballare** Wexfd
21 K3 **Balleen** Kilken
29 Q8 **Ballickmoyler** Laois
22 B10 **Balliloque** Kilken
26 H10 **Ballina** Tippry
37 K3 **Ballina** Wmeath
50 F7 **Ballina**/*Béal an Átha* Mayo
5 P2 **Ballinaboy** Galway
32 D4 **Ballinaboy** Galway
37 P5 **Ballinabrackey** Meath
22 B2 **Ballinabranagh** Carlow
31 M8 **Ballinaclash** Wicklw
5 N4 **Ballinadee** Cork
37 L9 **Ballinagar** Offaly
19 L1 **Ballinageragh** Leitrm
29 L8 **Ballinahinch** Tippry
29 L8 **Ballinakill**/*Baile na Coille* Laois
37 K1 **Ballinalack** Wmeath
31 P5 **Ballinalea** Wicklw
44 G7 **Ballinalee**/*Béal Átha na Lao* Longfd
53 Q3 **Ballinamallard** Ferman
21 L5 **Ballinamara Cross Roads** Kilken
43 N5 **Ballinameen** Roscom
35 M4 **Ballinamore Bridge** Galway
5 K5 **Ballinascarty** Cork
35 P7 **Ballinasloe**/*Béal Átha na Sluaighe* Galway
25 H7 **Ballinaspick** Watfd
5 Q4 **Ballinclashet** Cork
15 L3 **Ballinclay** Wexfd
16 F9 **Ballincloher Cross Roads** Kerry
11 P10 **Ballincollig**/*Baile an Chollaigh* Cork
27 M3 **Ballincor** Tippry
14 E5 **Ballincrea** Kilken
6 D3 **Ballincurrig** Cork
22 F7 **Ballindaggan** Wexfd
12 C5 **Ballindangan** Cork
25 N1 **Ballinderreen**/*Baile an Dorín* Galway
27 L5 **Ballinderry** Tippry
42 D10 **Ballindine**/*Baile an Daighin* Mayo
52 E10 **Ballindoon** Sligo
60 D3 **Ballindrait**/*Baile an Droichid* Donegl
8 D4 **Ballineanig** Kerry
4 H4 **Ballineen**/*Béal Átha Fhínín* Cork
43 M2 **Ballinfad**/*Béal an Átha Fada* Sligo
18 D6 **Ballingarrane** Limrck
27 N5 **Ballingarry** Tippry
21 J7 **Ballingarry**/*Baile an Gharraí* Tippry
18 E7 **Ballingary**/*Baile an Gharraí* Limrck
4 E1 **Ballingeary**/*Béal Átha an Ghaorthaidh* Cork
31 K9 **Ballinglen** Wicklw
4 G5 **Ballingurteen** Cork
5 P2 **Ballinhassig** Cork
34 E9 **Ballinillaun** Galway
22 C5 **Ballinkillin** Carlow
18 F8 **Ballinleeny** Limrck
8 E3 **Ballinloghig** Kerry
45 Q8 **Ballinlough** Meath
42 H8 **Ballinlough**/*Baile an Locha* Roscom
6 C8 **Ballinluska** Cork
44 E1 **Ballinmore**/*Béal Átha Móir* Leitrm
44 F5 **Ballinmuck** Longfd
5 K6 **Ballinoroher** Cork
56 H10 **Ballinran** Down
8 D3 **Ballinrannig** Kerry
27 M9 **Ballinree** Tippry
6 B7 **Ballinreeshig** Cork
33 P1 **Ballinrobe**/*Baile an Róba* Mayo
25 P7 **Ballinruan** Clare
2 C1 **Ballinskelligs**/*Baile an Sceilge* Kerry
5 N5 **Ballinspittle**/*Béal Átha an Spidéil* Cork
41 N8 **Ballintober** Mayo

43 L9 **Ballintober** Roscom
52 E8 **Ballintogher**/*Baile an Tóchair* Sligo
67 Q4 **Ballintoy** Antrim
59 K9 **Ballintra**/*Baile an tSratha* Donegl
29 P6 **Ballintubbert** Laois
20 G7 **Ballinunty** Tippry
20 F7 **Ballinure** Tippry
13 Q1 **Ballinurra** Tippry
22 C9 **Ballinvarry** Kilken
20 C2 **Ballinveny** Tippry
5 J2 **Ballinvoher** Cork
5 N5 **Ballinvronig** Cork
30 D5 **Ballitore**/*Béal Átha an Tuair* Kildre
38 B3 **Ballivor**/*Baile Íomhair* Meath
22 E3 **Ballon**/*Balana* Carlow
57 L1 **Balloo** Down
52 E3 **Balloor** Leitrm
46 H1 **Ballsmill** Armagh
54 N4 **Balltculter** Down
58 H10 **Ballure** Donegl
18 E6 **Ballvea** Limrck
12 D4 **Ballyaghaderg Bridge** Cork
18 F9 **Ballyagran** Limrck
18 D7 **Ballyallinan** Limrck
46 H5 **Ballybailie Cross Roads** Louth
35 L5 **Ballybaun** Galway
55 K9 **Ballybay**/*Béal Átha Beithe* Monhan
46 E2 **Ballybay Cross Roads** Monhan
27 P9 **Ballybeg** Tippry
13 K3 **Ballybeg** Tippry
39 L8 **Ballyboden** Dublin
59 P4 **Ballybofey**/*Bealach Feich* Donegl
37 Q5 **Ballyboggan** Meath
39 M3 **Ballyboghil**/*Baile Bachuille* Dublin
67 N6 **Ballybogy** Antrim
36 E5 **Ballybornia** Wmeath
8 F4 **Ballybowler** Kerry
28 F2 **Ballyboy** Offaly
3 M9 **Ballybrack** Cork
2 E1 **Ballybrack** Kerry
38 F6 **Ballybrack** Kildre
7 J2 **Ballybrack** Watfd
20 E3 **Ballybristy** Tippry
29 N3 **Ballybrittas** Laois
16 E10 **Ballybroman** Kerry
19 K5 **Ballybrood** Limrck
28 G8 **Ballybrophy**/*Baile Uí Bhróithe* Laois
18 F2 **Ballybroughan** Clare
37 P6 **Ballybryan** Offaly
16 F6 **Ballybunnion**/*Baile an Bhuinnéanaigh* Kerry
30 D8 **Ballyburn** Kildre
19 M1 **Ballycahane** Tippry
20 D5 **Ballycahill** Tippry
21 L6 **Ballycallan** Kilken
23 L6 **Ballycanew**/*Baile Uí Chonnmhaí* Wexfd
18 H2 **Ballycar** Clare
22 H7 **Ballycarney** Wexfd
63 L4 **Ballycarry** Antrim
14 D7 **Ballycashin** Watfd
68 C4 **Ballycastle** Antrim
50 D3 **Ballycastle**/*Baile an Chaisil* Mayo
62 H4 **Ballyclare** Antrim
44 B10 **Ballyclare** Roscom
13 L1 **Ballyclerahan** Tippry
11 M4 **Ballyclogh**/*Baile Cloch* Cork
15 N6 **Ballycogly** Wexfd
29 J8 **Ballycolla** Laois
3 P6 **Ballycommane** Cork
27 K8 **Ballycommon** Tippry
21 N2 **Ballycomy** Kilken
32 C5 **Ballyconneely**/*Baile Conaola* Galway
53 Q10 **Ballyconnell**/*Béal Átha Conaill* Cavan
17 P1 **Ballycorick Bridge** Clare
6 G7 **Ballycotton**/*Baile Choitín* Cork
27 L2 **Ballycrossaun** Galway
48 H8 **Ballycroy**/*Baile Chruaich* Mayo
13 M8 **Ballycullane** Watfd
14 H6 **Ballycullane**/*Baile Uí Choileáin* Wexfd
31 N5 **Ballycullen** Wicklw
36 G7 **Ballycumber**/*Béal Átha Chomair* Offaly
7 L2 **Ballycurrane** Watfd
12 A7 **Ballydague** Cork
10 G6 **Ballydaly** Cork
35 Q7 **Ballydangan** Roscom
26 F7 **Ballydavid** Cork
26 G1 **Ballydavid** Galway
8 D3 **Ballydavid**/*Baile na nGall* Kerry
29 M4 **Ballydavis** Laois
3 P7 **Ballydehob**/*Béal an Dá Chab* Cork
12 C5 **Ballydeloughy** Cork
10 F4 **Ballydesmond**/*Baile Deasumhan* Cork
2 F6 **Ballydonegan** Cork
26 A6 **Ballydoogan** Galway
14 C7 **Ballydoyle** Cork
14 C7 **Ballyduff** Watfd
23 J6 **Ballyduff** Wexfd

16 F8 **Ballyduff**/*An Baile Dubh* Kerry
12 G7 **Ballyduff**/*An Baile Dubh* Watfd
31 N4 **Ballyduff Cross Roads** Wicklw
12 G5 **Ballyeafy** Watfd
62 H4 **Ballyeaston** Antrim
28 C4 **Ballyeighan** Offaly
35 M8 **Ballyeighter** Galway
8 E4 **Ballyeightragh** Kerry
23 M3 **Ballyfad** Wexfd
42 D7 **Ballyfarnagh** Mayo
43 P1 **Ballyfarnan**/*Baile Átha Fearnáin* Roscom
14 E3 **Ballyfasy** Kilken
6 B8 **Ballyfeard** Cork
8 D4 **Ballyferriter**/*Baile an Fheirtéaraigh* Kerry
23 L6 **Ballyfin** Wexfd
29 J4 **Ballyfin**/*An Baile Fionn* Laois
35 N4 **Ballyforan**/*Béal Átha Feorainne* Roscom
37 P7 **Ballyfore** Offaly
21 N4 **Ballyfoyle** Kilken
28 D5 **Ballygaddy Cross Roads** Offaly
63 K1 **Ballygalley** Antrim
35 M3 **Ballygar**/*Béal Átha Ghártha* Galway
13 R7 **Ballygarran** Watfd
14 B7 **Ballygarran** Watfd
23 N7 **Ballygarrett** Wexfd
41 Q9 **Ballygarries** Mayo
5 Q2 **Ballygarvan** Cork
54 H2 **Ballygawley** Tyrone
52 D8 **Ballygawley**/*Baile Uí Dhálaigh* Sligo
62 F2 **Ballygelly** Antrim
12 E4 **Ballygiblin** Cork
50 D4 **Ballyglass** Mayo
41 Q8 **Ballyglass** Mayo
42 H5 **Ballyglass** Mayo
14 C6 **Ballygorey** Kilken
66 C1 **Ballygorman** Donegl
23 L8 **Ballygortin** Wexfd
63 L10 **Ballygowan** Down
11 L3 **Ballygrady** Cork
20 C8 **Ballygriffin** Tippry
22 B9 **Ballygub** Kilken
18 H9 **Ballygubba** Limrck
14 G6 **Ballyhack** Wexfd
30 E9 **Ballyhacket Cross Roads** Carlow
18 H10 **Ballyhaght** Limrck
17 M5 **Ballyhahill** Limrck
45 L1 **Ballyhaise**/*Béal Átha hÉis* Cavan
63 Q10 **Ballyhalbert** Down
33 Q5 **Ballyhale** Galway
21 N9 **Ballyhale**/*Baile Héil* Kilken
19 Q1 **Ballyhane Cross Roads** Tippry
5 N1 **Ballyhank** Cork
9 Q5 **Ballyhar** Kerry
42 F8 **Ballyhaunis**/*Béal Átha hAmhnais* Mayo
41 N7 **Ballyhean** Mayo
34 D2 **Ballyhear** Galway
45 L6 **Ballyheelan** Cavan
16 D9 **Ballyheige**/*Baile Uí Thaidhg* Kerry
34 B2 **Ballyhenry** Mayo
25 P9 **Ballyhickey** Clare
22 H10 **Ballyhoge** Wexfd
14 E4 **Ballyhomuck** Kilken
11 J4 **Ballyhoolahan** Cork
12 B7 **Ballyhooly**/*Baile Átha Úlla* Cork
57 N5 **Ballyhornan** Down
54 B10 **Ballyhugh** Cavan
37 N8 **Ballyhugh** Offaly
3 N10 **Ballyieragh** Cork
45 N5 **Ballyjamesduff**/*Baile Shéamais Dhuibh* Cavan
37 M9 **Ballykean** Offaly
21 L6 **Ballykeefe Cross Roads** Kilken
56 G3 **Ballykeel** Down
56 D5 **Ballykeeran** Wmeath
66 G8 **Ballykelly** Lderry
37 Q8 **Ballykilleen** Offaly
6 H4 **Ballykilty** Cork
57 K6 **Ballykinler** Down
14 E7 **Ballykinsella** Watfd
31 J3 **Ballyknockan** Wicklw
6 F7 **Ballylanders** Cork
19 M10 **Ballylanders**/*Baile an Londraigh* Limrck
13 R6 **Ballylaneen** Watfd
5 M3 **Ballylangley** Cork
14 B8 **Ballyleen** Watfd
55 Q4 **Ballyleny** Armagh
63 J9 **Ballylesson** Down
3 Q4 **Ballylicky** Cork
66 B3 **Ballyliffin**/*Baile Lifín* Donegl
21 K7 **Ballyline** Kilken
29 M9 **Ballylintagh** Lderry
16 H6 **Ballylongford**/*Béal Átha Longfoirt* Kerry
19 M8 **Ballylooby** Limrck
12 H3 **Ballylooby** Tippry
23 K10 **Ballylucas** Wexfd
63 L2 **Ballylumford** Antrim
29 P7 **Ballylynan**/*Baile Uí Laigheanáin* Laois

Grid	Name
13 L4	Ballymacarbry/Baile Mhac Cairbre Watfd
14 E9	Ballymacaw Watfd
9 Q2	Ballymacelligott Kerry
45 L6	Ballymachugh Cavan
27 M8	Ballymackey Tippry
13 M7	Ballymacmague Watfd
6 H5	Ballymacoda Cork
26 C3	Ballymacquiff Galway
43 N9	Ballymacurly Roscom
35 K6	Ballymacward Galway
7 J5	Ballymadog Cork
66 B6	Ballymagan Donegl
66 G3	Ballymagaraghy Donegl
60 E2	Ballymagorry Tyrone
36 F2	Ballymahon/Baile Uí Mhathain Longfd
10 G9	Ballymakeery/Baile Mhic Íre Cork
47 K7	Ballymakenny Louth
45 M8	Ballymanus Wmeath
56 H10	Ballymartin Down
5 P3	Ballymartle Cork
62 E2	Ballymena Antrim
43 K9	Ballymoe/Béal Átha Mó Galway
67 N7	Ballymoney Antrim
23 N4	Ballymoney Cross Roads Wexfd
6 D6	Ballymore Cork
65 J6	Ballymore Donegl
36 G4	Ballymore/An Baile Mór Wmeath
30 G2	Ballymore Eustace/An Baile Mór Kildre
14 C8	Ballymorris Watfd
52 C10	Ballymote/Baile an Mhóta Sligo
30 E4	Ballymount Kildre
23 J10	Ballymurn Wexfd
22 D7	Ballymurphy Carlow
17 N9	Ballymurragh Limrck
35 Q1	Ballymurray Roscom
14 H4	Ballynabola Wexfd
34 E10	Ballynabucky Galway
2 D6	Ballynacallagh Cork
17 P2	Ballynacally Clare
4 G4	Ballynacarriga Cork
37 J2	Ballynacarrigy/Baile na Carraige Wmeath
51 P6	Ballynacarrow Sligo
27 L10	Ballynaclogh Tippry
6 F4	Ballynacole Cork
6 E5	Ballynacorra Cork
5 Q3	Ballynacourty Cork
13 N8	Ballynacourty Watfd
45 N7	Ballynacree Meath
37 L1	Ballynafid Wmeath
6 C4	Ballynagaul Cork
13 N9	Ballynagaul Watfd
6 A2	Ballynaglogh West Cork
37 K6	Ballynagore Wmeath
11 K8	Ballynagree Cork
5 P2	Ballynagrumoolia Cork
13 L6	Ballynaguilkee Watfd
57 J3	Ballynahinch Down
2 B1	Ballynahow Kerry
36 E7	Ballynahown Wmeath
33 K9	Ballynahown/Baile na hAbhann Galway
50 E6	Ballynahowna Mayo
10 E4	Ballynahulla Kerry
36 D4	Ballynakill Wmeath
3 J6	Ballynakilla Cork
37 M9	Ballynakill Offaly
60 G3	Ballynamallaght Tyrone
5 P3	Ballynamaul Cork
11 P6	Ballynamona Cork
15 J5	Ballynamona Wexfd
47 N2	Ballynamoy Louth
12 B7	Ballynamuddagh Cork
13 L5	Ballynamult Watfd
8 D4	Ballynana Kerry
38 G5	Ballynare Cross Roads Meath
45 L6	Ballynarry Cavan
16 E8	Ballynaskreena Kerry
42 C8	Ballynastangford Mayo
60 H2	Ballyneaner Tyrone
19 J5	Ballyneety Limrck
13 Q2	Ballyneil Tippry
21 J8	Ballynennan Tippry
12 F9	Ballynoe/An Baile Nua Cork
18 D8	Ballynoe Bridge Limrck
63 J4	Ballynure Antrim
12 A3	Ballyorgan Limrck
23 L6	Ballyoughter Wexfd
4 C6	Ballyourane Cork
13 P1	Ballypatrick Tippry
13 J9	Ballyphilip Watfd
12 F4	Ballyporeen/Béal Átha Póirín Tippry
8 G2	Ballyquin Kerry
13 R3	Ballyquin Watfd
21 L2	Ballyragget/Béal Átha Ragad Kilken
67 M6	Ballyrashane Lderry
6 G3	Ballyre Cork
55 J2	Ballyreagh Tyrone
5 P6	Ballyroan/Baile Átha an Róine Laois
43 N6	Ballyroddy Roscom
8 E2	Ballyroe Kerry
22 H5	Ballyroebuck Wexfd
62 A5	Ballyronan Lderry
56 F6	Ballyroney Down
3 K7	Ballyroon Cork
22 C3	Ballyryan Carlow
52 C8	Ballysadare/Baile Easa Dara Sligo
52 G1	Ballyshannon/Béal Átha Seanaidh Donegl
16 E10	Ballysheen Kerry
14 E8	Ballyshoneen Watfd
27 J3	Ballyshrule Galway
11 N6	Ballysimon Cross Roads Cork
20 H6	Ballysloe Tippry
20 F2	Ballysorrell Tippry
18 D3	Ballysteen Limrck
40 D6	Ballytoohy Mayo
25 K3	Ballyvaghan/Baile Uí Bheacháin Clare
23 M9	Ballyvaldon Wexfd
19 N6	Ballyvalode Limrck
11 P8	Ballyvaloon Cork
22 E3	Ballyveal Carlow
13 J3	Ballyveera Tippry
4 G7	Ballyvireen Bridge Cork
12 A4	Ballyvisteen Cork
3 K9	Ballyvoge Cork
35 M5	Ballyvoneen Galway
25 N10	Ballyvonnavaun Clare
6 B9	Ballyvorane Cork
10 F9	Ballyvourney/Baile Bhuirne Cork
68 D4	Ballyvoy Antrim
13 P7	Ballyvoyle Cross Roads Watfd
63 Q9	Ballywalter Down
56 G6	Ballyward Down
12 A5	Ballywater Cork
67 K6	Ballywildrick Lderry
5 N4	Ballywilliam Cork
22 D10	Ballywilliam Wexfd
67 N7	Balnamore Antrim
39 J1	Balrath Meath
37 Q1	Balrath Cross Roads Wmeath
39 N1	Balrothery Dublin
39 M1	Balscaddan Dublin
4 B9	Baltimore/Dún na Séad Cork
30 F7	Baltinglass/Bealach Conglais Wicklw
16 E9	Baltovin Kerry
47 L8	Baltray/Baile Trá Louth
51 L9	Banada Sligo
27 P1	Banagher/Beannchar Offaly
56 D4	Banbridge Down
5 L3	Bandon/Droichead na Bandan Cork
16 G9	Banemore Kerry
63 N6	Bangor Down
49 J6	Bangor/Baingear Mayo
16 D10	Banna Kerry
11 L4	Bannagh Cross Roads Cork
62 B10	Bannfoot Armagh
25 L10	Bansha Clare
20 B10	Bansha/An Bháinseach Tippry
11 K5	Banteer/Bántír Cork
3 P5	Bantry/Beanntraí Cork
3 P5	Bantry Gardens Cork
66 G9	Baranailt Lderry
25 N8	Barefield Clare
4 C9	Barloge Cork
19 M6	Barna Limrck
27 P7	Barna Offaly
33 Q9	Barna/Bearna Galway
42 E4	Barnacahoge Mayo
43 K6	Barnacawley Roscom
34 G4	Barnaderg Galway
3 P6	Barnagheehy Cork
4 D4	Barnagowlane Cork
20 F3	Barnalisheen Tippry
42 E4	Barnalyra Mayo
10 C10	Barnastooka Kerry
48 G4	Barnatra Mayo
59 M6	Barnesmore Donegl
42 D8	Barnycarroll Mayo
3 N3	Barony Bridge Cork
11 L1	Barrack Cross Roads Cork
10 D6	Barraduff Kerry
26 G3	Barratoor Galway
4 D4	Barrboy Cork
21 N9	Barrettstown Kilken
17 P4	Barrigone Limrck
19 K4	Barringtonsbridge Limrck
9 L1	Barrow Kerry
36 F1	Barry Longfd
12 D9	Bartlemy Cork
15 M8	Bastardstown Wexfd
17 K10	Bateman's Bridge Kerry
38 H4	Batterstown Meath
62 G3	Battery Bridge Antrim
37 L5	Baughna Wmeath
4 C5	Baulbrack Cork
21 P9	Baunskeha Kilken
25 J8	Bauntlieve Clare
11 K3	Bawn Cross Roads Cork
44 F10	Bawn Cross Roads Longfd
10 H4	Bawnaneel Cork
4 C5	Bawnboy Cork
53 P10	Bawnboy/An Bábhún Buí Cavan
13 L3	Bawnfune Watfd
4 D9	Bawnlahan Cork
34 F2	Beagh Galway
16 F5	Beal Kerry
25 L3	Bealaclugga Clare
33 J7	Bealadangan/Béal an Daingin Galway
16 G2	Bealaha Clare
9 L8	Bealalaw Bridge Kerry
36 E5	Bealin Wmeath
5 K2	Bealnablath Cork
11 L9	Bealnamorive Cork
9 P6	Beaufort Kerry
38 F2	Bective Meath
12 B9	Behernagh Cork
50 G7	Behy Bridge Mayo
42 E8	Bekan Mayo
41 P7	Belcarra Mayo
34 D4	Belclare Galway
53 L6	Belcoo Ferman
49 L3	Belderg/Béal Deirg Mayo
63 J8	Belfast Antrim
63 K7	Belfast City Antrim
62 E7	Belfast International Antrim
5 Q4	Belgooly Cork
49 L6	Bellacorrick/Béal Átha Chomhraic Mayo
52 C7	Belladrihid Sligo
40 G2	Bellagarvaun Mayo
62 B3	Bellaghy Lderry
35 N7	Bellagill Bridge Galway
42 F3	Bellahy Sligo
49 J4	Bellanaboy Bridge Mayo
43 L6	Bellanagare/Béal Átha na gCarr Roscom
53 P6	Bellanaleck Ferman
36 B5	Bellanamullia Roscom
45 K4	Bellananagh/Béal Átha na nEach Cavan
45 M1	Bellancargy Cavan
35 Q6	Bellaneeny Roscom
59 L2	Bellanmore Donegl
54 H6	Bellanode Monhan
41 Q5	Bellavary/Béal Átha Bhearaigh Mayo
55 Q8	Belleek Armagh
52 H2	Belleek Ferman
50 F6	Belleek Mayo
52 H2	Belleek Pottery Ferman
47 K10	Bellewstown Meath
36 D9	Bellmount Offaly
48 F4	Belmullet/Béal an Mhuirthead Mayo
63 L4	Beltoy Antrim
41 M3	Beltra Mayo
51 N4	Beltra/Béal Trá Sligo
54 C10	Belturbet/Béal Tairbirt Cavan
6 C5	Belvelly Cork
55 M3	Benburb Tyrone
67 N8	Bendooragh Antrim
30 D9	Bennekerry Carlow
21 P7	Bennettsbridge/Droichead Binéid Kilken
67 J5	Benone Lderry
60 H9	Beragh Tyrone
11 M8	Bernard Cross Roads Cork
11 N9	Berrings Cork
56 B8	Bessbrook Armagh
47 M9	Bettystown/Baile an Bhiataigh Meath
59 N6	Big Bridge Tyrone
62 G3	Big Collin Antrim
21 Q2	Bilboa Carlow
19 L1	Birdhill Tippry
28 C3	Birr/Biorra Offaly
28 C4	Birr Castle Demesne Offaly
57 N5	Bishops Court Down
14 D5	Bishopshall Kilken
12 F6	Black Watfd
39 J4	Black Bull Meath
36 H10	Black Lion Meath
20 E10	Blackcastle Tippry
15 L3	Blackhall Wexfd
53 L6	Blacklion Cavan
6 B5	Blackrock Cork
39 N8	Blackrock Dublin
47 K3	Blackrock/Na Creagacha Dubha Louth
48 D7	Blacksod/An Fód Dubh Mayo
9 L7	Blackstones Bridge Kerry
23 L10	Blackwater/An Abhainn Dubh Wexfd
3 K1	Blackwater Bridge Kerry
38 C5	Blackwater Bridge Kildre
55 M3	Blackwatertown Armagh
38 D8	Blackwood/Coil Dubh Kildre
67 M5	Blagh Lderry
39 K6	Blanchardstown Dublin
17 L7	Blane Bridge Watfd
11 Q9	Blarney/An Bhlarna Cork
11 Q9	Blarney Castle Cork
56 C3	Bleary Down
9 N2	Blennerville Kerry
30 H2	Blessington/Baile Coimín Wicklw
36 H10	Blue Ball Offaly
10 H3	Blueford Cork
6 B8	Boardee Cork
57 J2	Boardmills Down
43 J4	Bockagh Roscom
26 E8	Bodyke Clare
41 N3	Bofeenaun Mayo
39 M1	Bog of The Ring Dublin
21 J5	Boggan Kilken
46 C6	Boggan Cross Roads Meath
28 E9	Boggaun Tippry
4 F1	Bohane's Cross Roads Cork
9 L8	Boheeshil Kerry
19 K4	Boher Limrck
28 E5	Boheraphuca Offaly
13 K7	Boheravaghera Cross Roads Watfd
10 H4	Boherboy Cork
11 P3	Boherboy Cross Roads Cork
19 J4	Bohereen Limrck
38 F7	Boherhole Cross Roads Kildre
20 D7	Boherlahan Tippry
46 E10	Bohermeen/An Bóthar Mín Meath
12 G2	Bohernarnane Tippry
45 K9	Boherquill Wmeath
19 L6	Boherroe Limrck
42 C4	Bohola/Both Chomhla Mayo
67 J7	Bolea Lderry
67 L9	Boleran Lderry
29 P7	Boley Laois
22 H3	Boley Wicklw
30 C4	Boley Cross Roads Kildre
30 G3	Boleybeg Cross Roads Kildre
23 K7	Boleyvogue Wexfd
40 E5	Bolinglanna Mayo
17 J8	Bolton's Cross Roads Kerry
7 J3	Boola Watfd
12 G2	Boolakennedy Tippry
22 C6	Borris/An Bhuiríos Carlow
28 F7	Borris in Ossory/Buiríos Mór Osraí Laois
27 M6	Borrisokane/Buiríos Uí Chéin Tippry
20 C3	Borrisoleigh/Buiríos Ó Luigheach Tippry
25 N5	Boston Clare
19 K8	Bottomstown Limrck
45 K10	Bottomy Wmeath
20 D4	Bouladuff Tippry
67 M10	Bovedy Lderry
66 H10	Bovevagh Lderry
43 N3	Boyle/Mainistir na Búille Roscom
34 H1	Boyounagh Galway
37 N9	Brackagh Offaly
12 E3	Brackbaun Bridge Limrck
3 J1	Brackloon Kerry
43 L7	Brackloon Roscom
43 M6	Brackloon Cross Roads Roscom
37 P2	Bracklyn Wmeath
36 B1	Bracknagh Roscom
37 Q10	Bracknagh Offaly
36 E10	Brackny Offaly
50 F8	Brackwanshagh Mayo
3 N6	Brahalish Cork
8 G2	Brandon Kerry
54 H7	Brandrum Monhan
30 F3	Brannockstown Kildre
39 P10	Bray/Bré Wicklw
60 E1	Bready Tyrone
5 J4	Breaghna Cork
16 E4	Breaghva Clare
41 P6	Breaghwy Mayo
22 G10	Bree Wexfd
6 H2	Breeda Cork
42 E8	Brickeens Mayo
12 D8	Bridebridge Cork
35 Q5	Brideswell Roscom
66 B8	Bridge End Donegl
23 J2	Bridgeland Wicklw
59 K8	Bridgetown Donegl
19 J1	Bridgetown/Baile an Droichid Clare
15 M7	Bridgetown/Baile an Droichid Wexfd
61 Q8	Brigh Tyrone
64 E6	Brinlack/Bun na Leaca Donegl
13 P6	Briska Watfd
39 J9	Brittas Dublin
12 E9	Britway Cork
38 B5	Broadford Kildre
18 C10	Broadford Limrck
26 E10	Broadford/Áth Leathan Clare
15 Q7	Broadway Wexfd
67 K10	Brockagh Lderry
18 D9	Broken Bridge Limrck
54 C5	Brookeborough Ferman
19 P8	Brookville Bridge Tippry
46 E1	Broomfield Monhan
25 N5	Brosna Offaly
10 E1	Brosna Kerry
11 Q3	Brough Cross Roads Cork
28 E1	Broughal Offaly
62 F1	Broughshane Antrim
66 F5	Brown Shoulder Donegl
7 J2	Brown's Cross Roads Watfd
45 J8	Browne's Cross Roads Longfd
46 G10	Brownstown Meath
14 E9	Brownstown Watfd
30 D3	Brownstown Cross Roads Kildre
20 E4	Brownstown Cross Roads Tippry
20 G3	Bruckana Kilken
58 F7	Bruckles Donegl
19 J7	Bruff/An Brú Limrck
43 E6	Bruff Cross Roads Mayo
18 H8	Bruree/Brú Rí Limrck
56 H7	Bryansford Down
14 B7	Buck's Cross Roads Watfd
62 G1	Buckna Antrim
52 G3	Buckode Leitrm
35 J9	Bulgaden Limrck
35 J9	Bullaun Galway
40 D3	Bunacurry/Bun an Churraigh Mayo
3 N2	Bunane Kerry
3 K2	Bunaw Kerry
64 E8	Bunbeg/An Bun Beag Donegl
37 K1	Bunbrosna Wmeath
22 G5	Bunclody/Bun Clóidí Wexfd
65 Q6	Buncrana/Bun Cranncha Donegl
52 F2	Bundoran/Bun Dobhráin Donegl
9 K7	Bunglasha Kerry
58 F6	Bungosteen Bridge Donegl
44 H7	Bunlahy Longfd
14 A9	Bunmahon/Bun Machan Watfd
33 Q3	Bunnafollistran Mayo
48 G5	Bunnahowen/Bun na hAbhna Mayo
32 G5	Bunnahown/Bun na hAbhann Galway
51 P8	Bunnanaddan Sligo
41 M5	Bunnyconnellan Mayo
18 F2	Bunratty Clare
18 F2	Bunratty Castle and Folk Park Clare
21 M7	Burnchurch Kilken
12 F3	Burncourt Tippry
66 B8	Burnfoot/Bun na hAbhann Donegl
11 P6	Burnfort Cork
11 N2	Burren Clare
56 D9	Burren Down
25 L2	Burren/Boirinn Clare
17 M2	Burrenfadda Clare
66 B8	Burt Donegl
64 C9	Burtonport/Ailt an Chórrain Donegl
30 C6	Burtown Cross Roads Kildre
45 N4	Bushmills Antrim
45 L1	Butlers Bridge/Droichead an Bhuiléaraigh Cavan
5 L7	Butlerstown Cork
11 N3	Buttevant/Cill na Mallach Cork
11 N7	Bweeng Cork

C

Grid	Name
55 K1	Cabragh Tyrone
28 F3	Cadamstown Offaly
38 C6	Cadamstown Kildre
62 D4	Caddy Antrim
67 M9	Caheny Bridge Lderry
3 K7	Caher Cork
26 E6	Caher Clare
13 J2	Caher/An Chathair Tippry
13 J2	Caher Castle Tippry
17 L10	Caher Hill Limrck
9 K4	Caheracruttera Kerry
34 D9	Caheradrine Galway
4 C6	Caheragh Cork
35 L9	Caherakillen Galway
2 E1	Caherbarnagh Kerry
19 K5	Caherconlish/Cathair Chinn Lis Limrck
2 F3	Caherdaniel/Cathair Dónall Kerry
17 P1	Caherea Clare
34 E7	Caherlea Galway
34 C3	Caherlistrane Galway
2 F6	Cahermore Kerry
25 P3	Cahermore Galway
4 C3	Cahermuckee Cork
17 K1	Cahermurphy Clare
24 G9	Caherogan Clare
34 F5	Caherphuca Galway
25 J7	Cahersherkin Clare
8 F9	Cahersiveen/Cathair Saidhbhín Kerry
22 G8	Caim Wexfd
43 N5	Caldragh Cross Roads Roscom
55 L4	Caledon Tyrone
21 L8	Callan/Callain Kilken
42 C3	Callow Mayo
43 L4	Callow Roscom
35 L5	Caltra Galway
35 M7	Caltraghlea Galway
30 E4	Calverstown Kildre
56 B8	Camlough Armagh
23 K6	Camolin/Cam Eolaing Wexfd
9 K3	Camp Kerry
14 G5	Campile/Ceann Poill Wexfd

28 G6 **Camross**/Camros Laois
33 K6 **Camus** Galway
45 Q3 **Canningstown** Cavan
68 B5 **Cape Castle** Antrim
4 C2 **Cappaboy Beg** Cork
12 C7 **Cappagh** Cork
18 D5 **Cappagh** Limrck
61 L9 **Cappagh** Tyrone
19 P5 **Cappagh White/** An Cheapach Tippry
25 M3 **Cappaghmore** Galway
28 F2 **Cappagowlan** Offaly
28 F9 **Cappalinnan** Laois
19 M4 **Cappamore/An Cheapach Mhór** Limrck
35 L8 **Cappataggle** Galway
4 H2 **Cappeen** Cork
13 K7 **Cappoquin/Ceapach Choinn** Watfd
9 K6 **Caragh Bridge** Kerry
43 M8 **Caran** Roscom
38 B7 **Carbury** Kildre
10 D4 **Carker** Kerry
61 N9 **Carland** Tyrone
46 D8 **Carlanstown/ Droichead Chearbhalláin** Meath
47 M1 **Carlingford/Cairlinn** Louth
30 C9 **Carlow/Ceatharlach** Carlow
61 M1 **Carn** Lderry
48 E4 **Carn** Mayo
36 H4 **Carn** Wmeath
32 F7 **Carna** Galway
62 H1 **Carnalbanagh Sheddings** Antrim
61 J2 **Carnanreagh** Lderry
46 B8 **Carnaross/Carn na Ros** Meath
63 K1 **Carncastle** Antrim
66 D3 **Carndonagh/Carn Domhnach** Donegl
23 J4 **Carnew/Carn a Bhua** Wicklw
52 C5 **Carney** Sligo
27 L6 **Carney** Tippry
68 M9 **Carnlough** Antrim
63 J6 **Carnmoney** Antrim
34 D8 **Carnmore Cross Roads** Galway
34 E6 **Carnoneen** Galway
55 J3 **Carnteel** Tyrone
42 G3 **Carracastle** Mayo
38 E9 **Carragh** Kildre
43 J3 **Carraghs** Roscom
41 K6 **Carraholly** Mayo
25 L5 **Carran** Clare
21 P6 **Carran** Kilken
33 J9 **Carraroe/An Cheathrú Rua** Galway
15 K6 **Carrick** Wexfd
58 C7 **Carrick/An Charraig** Donegl
68 B4 **Carrick-a-Rede Rope Bridge NT** Antrim
43 Q4 **Carrick-on-Shannon/Cora Droma Rúisc** Leitrm
13 R2 **Carrick-on-Suir/Carraig na Siúire** Tippry
45 L4 **Carrickaboy** Cavan
65 L5 **Carrickart/Carraig Airt** Donegl
46 E4 **Carrickashedoge** Monhan
36 G1 **Carrickboy/An Charraig Bhui** Longfd
63 L5 **Carrickfergus** Antrim
46 E3 **Carrickmacross/Carraig Mhachaire Rois** Monhan
39 N9 **Carrickmines** Dublin
61 K8 **Carrickmore or Termon Rock** Tyrone
54 H4 **Carrickroe** Monhan
27 P4 **Carrig** Tippry
30 H2 **Carrig** Wicklw
9 J2 **Carrigaday** Kerry
11 L10 **Carrigadrohid** Cork
11 K8 **Carrigagulla** Cork
16 E4 **Carrigaholt/Carrig an Chabhaltaigh** Clare
27 M4 **Carrigahorig** Tippry
6 B7 **Carrigaline/Carraig Uí Leighin** Cork
44 G3 **Carrigallen/Carraig Álainn** Leitrm
45 K5 **Carrigan** Cavan
10 H8 **Carriganimmy** Cork
12 F3 **Carriganroe** Tippry
66 B10 **Carrigans/An Carraigín** Donegl
27 K9 **Carrigatogher** Tippry
4 E6 **Carrigbaun Cross Roads** Cork
4 E6 **Carrigeeny** Cork
31 N3 **Carriggower** Wicklw
17 N7 **Carrigkerry** Limrck
11 R8 **Carrignavar** Cork
6 D5 **Carrigtohill/Carrig Thuathail** Cork
14 B7 **Carroll's Cross Roads** Watfd
20 B7 **Carrow** Tippry
63 P8 **Carrowdore** Down
24 G6 **Carrowduff** Cork
43 M9 **Carrowduff** Roscom
51 M6 **Carroweden** Sligo
26 G2 **Carrowkeel** Galway
33 Q1 **Carrowkeel** Mayo

65 N6 **Carrowkeel/An Cheathrú Chaol** Donegl
34 G1 **Carrowkeelanahglass** Galway
41 K9 **Carrowkennedy** Mayo
66 F3 **Carrowmenagh** Donegl
34 D10 **Carrowmore** Galway
50 E4 **Carrowmore** Mayo
42 C9 **Carrowmore** Mayo
34 C1 **Carrowmore** Mayo
51 M7 **Carrowmore** Sligo
52 C7 **Carrowmore Megalithic Cemetery** Sligo
33 Q5 **Carrowmoreknock** Galway
41 P8 **Carrownacon** Mayo
50 H3 **Carrowpadeen** Sligo
35 P6 **Carrowreagh** Roscom
36 C2 **Carrowrory** Longfd
48 H2 **Carrowteige/Ceathrú Thaidhg** Mayo
53 Q6 **Carry Bridge** Ferman
63 K9 **Carryduff** Down
26 E1 **Cartron** Galway
22 D6 **Cashel** Carlow
29 L6 **Cashel** Laois
40 E3 **Cashel** Mayo
32 G5 **Cashel/An Caiseal** Galway
20 D8 **Cashel/Caiseal** Tippry
65 M4 **Cashel Glebe** Donegl
52 C4 **Cashelgarran** Sligo
34 E8 **Cashla** Galway
32 D1 **Cashleen** Galway
14 H4 **Cassagh** Wexfd
53 Q5 **Castle Coole NT** Ferman
2 F2 **Castle Cove** Kerry
43 M1 **Castlebaldwin/Béal Átha na gCarraigíní** Sligo
41 N5 **Castlebar/Caislean an Bharraigh** Mayo
47 K4 **Castlebellingham/Baile an Ghearlánaigh** Louth
12 B7 **Castleblagh** Cork
35 K5 **Castleblakeney** Galway
55 M10 **Castleblaney/Baile na Lorgan** Monhan
15 P3 **Castlebridge/ Droichead an Chaisleáin** Wexfd
67 P5 **Castlecat** Antrim
61 N10 **Castlecaulfield** Tyrone
21 N2 **Castlecomer/Caisleán an Chomair** Kilken
19 K2 **Castleconnell/Caisleán Uí Chonnaill** Limrck
50 G6 **Castleconor** Sligo
35 N1 **Castlecoote** Roscom
11 M3 **Castlecor** Cork
28 G2 **Castlecuffe Cross Roads** Laois
62 A4 **Castledawson** Lderry
60 C6 **Castlederg** Tyrone
30 D7 **Castledermot/Diseart Diarmada** Kildre
22 G7 **Castledockerell** Wexfd
60 C3 **Castlefinn/Caisleán na Finne** Donegl
4 H7 **Castlefreke** Cork
52 D2 **Castlegal** Sligo
9 J2 **Castlegregory/Caisleán Ghriaire** Kerry
50 D8 **Castlehill** Mayo
40 G2 **Castlehill** Mayo
10 C3 **Castleisland/Oileán Ciarraí** Kerry
37 P6 **Castlejordan** Meath
39 K6 **Castleknock** Dublin
20 E2 **Castleleiny** Tippry
23 K9 **Castlellis** Wexfd
12 D8 **Castlelyons/Caisleán Ó Liatháin** Cork
9 N4 **Castlemaine/Caisleán na Mainge** Kerry
6 G5 **Castlemartyr/Baile na Martra** Cork
43 M8 **Castleplunket** Roscom
45 M9 **Castlepollard/Baile na gCros** Wmeath
34 C6 **Castlequarter** Galway
45 N6 **Castlerahan** Cavan
43 K7 **Castlerea/An Caisleán Riabhach** Roscom
67 K5 **Castlerock** Lderry
55 K7 **Castleshane** Monhan
25 L5 **Castletown** Clare
4 H3 **Castletown** Cork
18 E8 **Castletown** Limrck
46 E7 **Castletown** Meath
45 L8 **Castletown** Wmeath
23 N4 **Castletown** Wexfd
28 H6 **Castletown/Baile an Chaisleáin** Laois
37 J5 **Castletown Geoghegan** Wmeath
2 H5 **Castletown Bearhaven/Baile Chaisleáin Bhéarra** Cork
38 H7 **Castletown House** Kildre
12 A6 **Castletownroche/Baile Chaisleáin an Róistigh** Cork
4 E8 **Castletownshend/Baile an Chaisleáin** Cork
21 Q4 **Castlewarren** Kilken
56 H6 **Castlewellan** Down
16 E8 **Causeway/An Tóchar** Kerry

45 L2 **Cavan/An Cabhán** Cavan
55 J8 **Cavanagarvan** Monhan
59 K10 **Cavangarden** Donegl
12 F3 **Caves** Tippry
4 D5 **Ceancullig** Cork
11 M4 **Cecilstown** Cork
49 M2 **Ceide Fields** Mayo
38 H7 **Celbridge/Cill Droichid** Kildre
46 H3 **Chanonrock** Louth
22 F10 **Chapel Village** Wexfd
57 N6 **Chapeltown** Down
8 D9 **Chapeltown** Kerry
55 N2 **Charlemont** Armagh
42 F3 **Charlestown/Baile Chathail** Mayo
18 G10 **Charleville/An Ráth** Cork
14 F6 **Cheekpoint** Watfd
30 B2 **Cherryville** Kildre
62 C3 **Chesney's Corner** Antrim
6 D7 **Church Bay** Cork
4 C8 **Church Cross** Cork
9 M1 **Church Hill** Kerry
65 K9 **Church Hill/Mín an Lábáin** Donegl
65 Q10 **Church Town** Donegl
35 Q2 **Churchboro Cross** Roscom
41 M10 **Churchfield** Cork
43 L5 **Churchstreet** Roscom
6 F7 **Churchtown** Cork
14 G9 **Churchtown** Watfd
15 Q7 **Churchtown** Wexfd
11 N2 **Churchtown/Baile an Teampail** Cork
66 E8 **City of Derry** Lderry
54 D3 **Clabby** Ferman
32 B2 **Claddaghduff** Galway
62 B2 **Clady** Antrim
60 C4 **Clady** Tyrone
55 Q6 **Cladymilltown** Armagh
40 F3 **Claggan** Mayo
10 F3 **Clamper Bridge** Cork
38 F8 **Clane/Claonadh** Kildre
36 H7 **Clara/Clóirtheach** Offaly
29 J2 **Clarahill** Laois
56 B5 **Clare** Armagh
25 M10 **Clarecastle/Droichead an Chláir** Clare
18 C1 **Clareen Bridge** Clare
28 D4 **Clareen** Offaly
34 D7 **Claregalway/Baile Chláir** Galway
42 C9 **Claremorris/Clár Chlainne Mhuiris** Mayo
18 G4 **Clarina** Limrck
34 E9 **Clarinbridge/Droichead an Chláirín** Galway
37 K2 **Clark's Cross Roads** Wmeath
27 N8 **Clash** Tippry
17 M8 **Clash North** Limrck
17 M8 **Clash South** Limrck
19 M7 **Clashdrumsmith** Tippry
7 K3 **Clashmore/Clais Mhór** Watfd
14 B5 **Clashroe** Watfd
60 H1 **Claudy** Lderry
32 C2 **Cleggan/An Cloigeann** Galway
18 D2 **Clenagh** Clare
13 M6 **Cleristown** Wexfd
43 K6 **Clerragh** Roscom
32 D3 **Clifden/An Clochán** Galway
45 N3 **Clifferna** Cavan
52 D3 **Cliffony/Cliafuine** Sligo
24 F6 **Cliffs of Moher** Clare
37 P4 **Clocrave** Wmeath
61 K9 **Clogfin** Tyrone
14 C5 **Clogga** Kilken
23 P3 **Clogga** Wicklw
29 N9 **Clogh/An Chloch** Kilken
68 B10 **Clogh** Antrim
28 H8 **Clogh** Laois
23 L5 **Clogh** Wexfd
68 B9 **Clogh Mills** Antrim
18 D6 **Clogh West** Limrck
37 N2 **Cloghan** Wmeath
36 D10 **Cloghan/An Clochán** Offaly
59 J4 **Cloghan/An Clochan** Donegl
3 J10 **Cloghane** Cork
8 G2 **Cloghane/An Clochán** Kerry
34 C1 **Cloghans Hill** Mayo
21 P3 **Clogharinka** Kilken
38 B6 **Clogharinka** Kildre
17 K1 **Cloghaun** Clare
34 D6 **Cloghaun** Galway
26 E8 **Cloghaun Bridge** Clare
51 P2 **Cloghboley** Sligo
17 J10 **Cloghboola** Kerry
33 L2 **Cloghbrack** Galway
38 B2 **Cloghbrack Bridge** Meath
60 E2 **Clogher** Tyrone
13 L4 **Clogheen** Watfd
12 H4 **Clogheen/An Chloichín** Tippry
48 D6 **Clogher** Mayo
41 L6 **Clogher** Mayo
41 P8 **Clogher** Mayo
44 B5 **Clogher** Roscom
54 F7 **Clogher** Tyrone
18 H1 **Cloghera** Clare

47 M7 **Clogherhead/Ceann Chlochair** Louth
40 E5 **Cloghmore** Mayo
21 P4 **Cloghpook** Kilken
39 M5 **Cloghran** Dublin
11 P10 **Cloghroe** Cork
10 F2 **Cloghvoula** Cork
57 P2 **Cloghy** Down
22 G6 **Clohamon/Cloch Ámainn** Wexfd
14 E8 **Clohernagh** Watfd
23 K6 **Cologe** Wexfd
28 D8 **Clonakenny** Tippry
5 J6 **Clonakilty/Cloich na Coillte** Cork
39 K1 **Clonalvy** Meath
2 J5 **Clonard** Cork
38 B4 **Clonard** Meath
15 N4 **Clonard** Wexfd
36 C7 **Clonascra** Offaly
28 H2 **Clonaslee/Cluain na Slí** Laois
37 P9 **Clonavoe** Offaly
34 H2 **Clonbern** Galway
37 Q9 **Clonbulloge/Cluain Bolg** Offaly
33 M2 **Clonbur/An Fhairche** Galway
37 P9 **Cloncreen** Offaly
36 F3 **Cloncullen** Wmeath
28 F6 **Cloncully** Laois
38 E5 **Clancurry** Kildre
39 K7 **Clondalkin** Dublin
10 H9 **Clondrohid** Cork
12 E7 **Clondulane** Cork
13 Q4 **Clonea** Watfd
39 J5 **Clonee** Meath
37 L7 **Cloneen** Offaly
20 H9 **Cloneen** Tippry
22 G4 **Clonegall/Cluain na nGall** Carlow
59 P9 **Clonelly** Ferman
54 F8 **Clones/Cluain Eois** Monhan
23 M7 **Clonevin Cross Roads** Wexfd
36 B9 **Clonfert/Cluain Fearta** Galway
36 B10 **Clonfert Cross Roads** Galway
15 J5 **Clongeen** Wexfd
28 H6 **Cloninurragh** Laois
10 D8 **Clonkeen** Kerry
29 K5 **Clonkeen** Laois
35 J6 **Clonkeenkerrill** Galway
27 N9 **Clonlea** Tippry
37 Q1 **Clonleame Cross Roads** Wmeath
37 N2 **Clonlost** Wmeath
36 C7 **Clonmacnoise/Cluain Mhic Nóis** Offaly
21 K4 **Clonmantagh** Kilken
66 B3 **Clonmany/Cluain Maine** Donegl
20 G2 **Clonmeen** Laois
13 M2 **Clonmel/Cluain Meala** Tippry
45 Q10 **Clonmellon** Wmeath
40 H9 **Clonmore** Carlow
47 L6 **Clonmore** Louth
28 E9 **Clonmore** Tippry
6 F3 **Clonmult** Cork
36 D9 **Clonony** Offaly
20 C6 **Clonoulty** Tippry
22 F10 **Clonroche/Cluain an Róistigh** Wexfd
23 L3 **Clonroe Cross Roads** Wexfd
39 K6 **Clonsilla** Dublin
39 N6 **Clontarf** Dublin
55 L8 **Clontibret** Monhan
21 L3 **Clontubbrid** Kilken
38 B3 **Clonycavan** Meath
29 L1 **Clonygowan/Cluain na nGamhan** Offaly
29 L2 **Clonyquin** Offaly
34 C7 **Cloonacauneen** Galway
51 L7 **Cloonacool** Sligo
45 J6 **Cloonagh** Longfd
34 C6 **Cloonboo** Galway
36 B1 **Clooncah** Roscom
44 D8 **Cloondara** Longfd
44 E4 **Cloone/An Chluain** Leitrm
44 D6 **Clooneagh** Leitrm
45 J6 **Cloonagh** Longfd
58 F3 **Clooney** Donegl
43 K5 **Cloonfad Cross Roads** Roscom
42 G9 **Cloonfad** Roscom
35 Q8 **Cloonfad** Roscom
42 D6 **Cloonfallagh** Mayo
25 L9 **Cloonfinish** Mayo
42 E3 **Cloonfinish** Mayo
43 J7 **Cloonfower** Roscom
50 H6 **Cloonkeelaun** Sligo
42 H10 **Cloonkeen** Galway
41 N6 **Cloonkeen** Roscom
43 J8 **Cloonkeen** Roscom
51 P7 **Cloonkeen** Sligo
19 J2 **Cloonlara/Cluain Lára** Clare
42 D7 **Cloonlee** Mayo
19 N5 **Cloonlusk** Limrck
42 G3 **Cloonmore Cross Roads** Mayo
43 P8 **Clonmurray** Roscom
34 H1 **Cloonnacat** Galway
8 G2 **Cloonsharragh** Kerry

43 K6 **Cloonsheever** Roscom
42 H3 **Cloontia** Mayo
26 F7 **Cloonusker** Clare
35 K8 **Cloonymorris** Galway
43 P8 **Cloonyogan** Roscom
43 N7 **Cloonyquin** Roscom
46 B10 **Cloran Cross Roads** Wmeath
57 K5 **Clough** Down
5 L1 **Cloughduv** Cork
27 N7 **Cloughjordan/Cloch Shiurdáin** Tippry
18 D8 **Clouncagh** Limrck
45 L1 **Cloverhill** Cavan
6 F6 **Cloyne/Cluain** Cork
4 G5 **Clubhouse Cross Roads** Cork
10 L10 **Clydagh Bridge** Kerry
11 M10 **Coachford/Áth an Choiste** Cork
61 Q7 **Coagh** Tyrone
20 H6 **Coalbrook** Tippry
61 P9 **Coalisland** Tyrone
21 P2 **Coan** Kilken
6 C6 **Cobh/An Cóbh** Cork
30 E5 **Colbinstown** Kildre
67 L6 **Coleraine** Lderry
15 N4 **Colestown** Wexfd
13 M7 **Colligan Bridge** Watfd
45 N10 **Collinstown/Baile na gCailleach** Wmeath
46 H7 **Collon/Collann** Louth
52 C8 **Collooney/Cúil Mhuine** Sligo
3 J3 **Collorus** Kerry
20 F10 **Colman** Tippry
34 H6 **Colmanstown** Galway
47 L9 **Colp** Meath
63 M9 **Comber** Down
19 Q1 **Commaun More** Tippry
59 M3 **Commeen** Donegl
58 F5 **Common Bridge** Donegl
5 K2 **Commons** Cork
21 J6 **Commons** Tippry
33 N2 **Cong/Conga** Mayo
63 N7 **Conlig** Down
12 F8 **Conna** Cork
25 K9 **Connolly/Fíoch Rua** Clare
4 F7 **Connonagh** Cork
62 F3 **Connor** Antrim
67 P7 **Conogher Cross Roads** Antrim
60 B2 **Convoy/Conmhaigh** Donegl
61 P7 **Cookstown** Tyrone
12 H6 **Cool** Watfd
52 E9 **Coola Cross Roads** Sligo
37 N9 **Coolagary** Offaly
51 P5 **Coolaney/Cúil Aine** Sligo
13 K7 **Coolanheen** Watfd
23 J3 **Coolattin** Wicklw
20 G8 **Coolbaun Cross Roads** Tippry
27 K6 **Coolbaun** Tippry
21 P2 **Coolbaun** Kilken
65 M9 **Coolboy** Donegl
12 D3 **Coolboy** Limrck
23 J3 **Coolboy** Wicklw
28 D5 **Coolderry** Offaly
45 L9 **Coole** Wmeath
12 E7 **Coole Abbey** Cork
12 B8 **Coolea** Cork
10 F9 **Coolea/Cúil Aodha** Cork
21 P5 **Coolgrange** Kilken
23 M3 **Coolgreany/Cúil Ghréine** Wexfd
6 B3 **Coolgreen** Cork
12 B7 **Coolinny** Cork
4 E4 **Coolkellure** Cork
53 J8 **Coollegreane** Leitrm
17 M3 **Coolmeen** Clare
59 J9 **Coolmore** Donegl
42 G8 **Coolnafarna** Mayo
45 K9 **Coolnagun** Wmeath
39 M6 **Coolock** Dublin
28 G6 **Coolrain** Laois
23 M8 **Coolroe** Wexfd
27 N2 **Coolross** Tippry
6 B7 **Coolsallagh** Cork
44 B10 **Coolshaghtena** Roscom
43 P10 **Coolteige Cross** Roscom
6 G8 **Coomduff** Kerry
3 P3 **Coomhola Bridge** Cork
4 D4 **Coomleagh** Cork
18 G3 **Coonagh** Limrck
54 E5 **Cooneen** Ferman
43 L3 **Coonloogh** Sligo
17 J2 **Cooraclare/Cuar an Chláir** Clare
21 Q4 **Coorleagh** Kilken
3 P7 **Coosane** Cork
43 P3 **Cootehall** Roscom
45 Q1 **Coothill/Muinchille** Cavan
11 N4 **Copsetown Cross Roads** Cork
12 F2 **Corbally** Clare
50 H5 **Corbally** Sligo
30 E2 **Corbally Cross Roads** Kildre
44 G9 **Corboy** Longfd
48 E3 **Corclogh** Mayo
46 G3 **Corcreeghagh** Louth
49 M8 **Corcullin** Mayo
10 D3 **Cordal** Kerry
41 L8 **Cordarragh** Mayo
38 D8 **Corduff** Kildre
5 Q1 **Cork** Cork

6 A5 **Cork**/*Corcaigh* Cork
68 B8 **Corkey** Antrim
36 D1 **Corlea** Longfd
26 F5 **Corlea Bridge** Clare
50 H9 **Corlee** Mayo
53 N10 **Corlough** Cavan
36 B6 **Cornafulla** Roscom
33 L3 **Cornamona**/*Corr na Móna* Galway
41 Q9 **Cornanagh** Mayo
37 K8 **Corndarragh** Offaly
36 E8 **Corr Hill** Offaly
26 F6 **Corrakyle** Clare
55 P6 **Corran Cross Roads** Armagh
34 C6 **Corrandulla** Galway
40 E5 **Corraun** Mayo
62 F1 **Correen** Antrim
37 P4 **Correllstown** Wmeath
22 C5 **Corries Cross** Carlow
34 E5 **Corrofin** Galway
25 L7 **Corrofin**/*Cora Finne* Clare
53 J9 **Corry** Leitrm
46 D9 **Cortown** Meath
21 L5 **Corstown Cross Roads** Kilken
49 N5 **Corvoley** Mayo
33 K8 **Costelloe**/*Casla* Galway
8 H4 **Coumduff** Kerry
12 F6 **Countygate** Watfd
15 J3 **Courthoyle** Wexfd
5 M6 **Courtmacsherry**/*Cúirt Mhic Shéafraidh* Cork
18 C6 **Courtmatrix** Limrck
23 M5 **Courtown**/*Baile na Cúirte* Wexfd
4 D3 **Cousane** Cork
23 K4 **Craan** Wexfd
23 K5 **Craanford** Wexfd
31 L8 **Crafield** Wicklw
24 H3 **Craggagh** Clare
26 D8 **Cragroe** Clare
60 H3 **Craig** Tyrone
67 M10 **Craigavole** Lderry
56 C2 **Craigavon** Armagh
62 C1 **Craigs** Antrim
62 C1 **Craigs Cross** Antrim
61 J4 **Cranagh** Tyrone
23 J8 **Crane** Wexfd
65 M6 **Cranford** Donegl
17 M2 **Cranny** Clare
61 P5 **Cranny** Lderry
18 F2 **Cratloe** Clare
34 G9 **Craughwell**/*Creachmhaoil* Galway
63 M6 **Crawfordsburn** Down
37 M2 **Crazy Corner** Wmeath
4 C8 **Creagh** Cork
55 M8 **Creaghanroe** Monhan
11 M8 **Crean's Cross Roads** Cork
18 G5 **Crecora** Limrck
17 J1 **Creegh** Clare
35 M1 **Creegs** Galway
65 K6 **Creeslough**/*An Craoslach* Donegl
50 D4 **Creevagh** Mayo
18 C5 **Creeves** Limrck
25 J3 **Cregg** Clare
4 G8 **Cregg** Cork
55 P10 **Creggan** Armagh
36 D8 **Creggan** Offaly
61 K7 **Creggan** Tyrone
40 G9 **Cregganbaun** Mayo
29 N9 **Crettyard** Laois
66 H7 **Crindle** Lderry
28 C4 **Crinkill** Offaly
58 G6 **Croagh** Donegl
18 E6 **Croagh** Limrck
50 G6 **Crockets Town** Mayo
45 P4 **Croghan** Roscom
37 M7 **Croghan** Offaly
64 E8 **Crolly** Donegl
9 L5 **Cromane** Kerry
53 M10 **Cromlin** Leitrm
29 J6 **Cromoge Cross Roads** Laois
16 F8 **Crompaun Bridge** Kerry
37 M1 **Crookedwood** Wmeath
3 L9 **Crookhaven**/*An Cruachán* Cork
5 K1 **Crookstown** Cork
30 E5 **Crookstown** Kildre
18 G6 **Croom**/*Cromadh* Limrck
16 D4 **Cross** Clare
7 K2 **Cross** Watfd
33 P2 **Cross**/*An Chrois* Mayo
5 N2 **Cross Barry** Cork
45 M4 **Cross Keys** Cavan
45 P9 **Cross Keys** Meath
5 L4 **Cross Mahon** Cork
59 Q4 **Cross Roads** Donegl
15 N3 **Crossabeg** Wexfd
45 Q9 **Crossakeel**/*Crosa Caoil* Meath
42 C9 **Crossboyne** Mayo
35 N9 **Crossconnell** Galway
45 K3 **Crossdoney**/*Cros Domhnaigh* Cavan
44 G10 **Crossea** Longfd
45 M5 **Crosserlough** Cavan
57 L3 **Crossgar** Down
67 L7 **Crossgare** Lderry
6 C7 **Crosshaven**/*Bun an Tábhairne* Cork
29 Q3 **Crosskeys** Kildre
55 P10 **Crossmaglen** Armagh

50 D7 **Crossmolina**/*Crois Mhaoiliona* Mayo
43 P2 **Crossna** Roscom
25 N2 **Crossooha** Galway
20 H3 **Crosspatrick** Kilken
23 K3 **Crosspatrick** Wicklw
6 G4 **Crowbally** Cork
62 F7 **Crumlin** Antrim
2 H4 **Crumpane** Cork
25 N7 **Crusheen**/*Croisín* Clare
29 M8 **Crutt** Kilken
28 H8 **Cuffsborough Cross Roads** Laois
50 E9 **Cuilkillew** Mayo
56 F1 **Culcavy** Down
66 E3 **Culdaff**/*Cúil Dabhcha* Donegl
43 K2 **Culfadda** Sligo
66 E2 **Culkeeny** Donegl
21 K2 **Cullahill**/*An Chúlchoill* Laois
19 M10 **Cullane** Limrck
46 F1 **Cullaville** Armagh
18 E1 **Culleen** Clare
51 J5 **Culleens** Sligo
10 G5 **Cullen** Cork
19 N7 **Cullen** Tippry
12 B4 **Cullenagh** Cork
15 K7 **Cullenstown** Wexfd
42 C2 **Cullin** Mayo
4 B6 **Cullomane Cross Roads** Cork
62 D1 **Cullybackey** Antrim
55 P9 **Cullyhanna** Armagh
66 D8 **Culmore** Lderry
38 G4 **Culmullin Cross Roads** Meath
61 Q2 **Culnady** Lderry
12 F7 **Currabeha** Cork
15 P3 **Curracloe** Wexfd
5 J2 **Curraclogh** Cork
7 L4 **Curragh** Watfd
30 D2 **Curragh Camp** Kildre
42 H10 **Curragh West** Galway
39 J2 **Curragha** Meath
4 F5 **Curraghalicky** Cork
35 Q4 **Curraghboy** Roscom
23 K2 **Curraghlawn** Wicklw
21 Q10 **Curraghmore** Kilken
27 J10 **Curraghmore** Tippry
44 B8 **Curraghroe** Roscom
12 G8 **Curraglass** Cork
28 D8 **Curragunneen** Tippry
61 Q3 **Curran** Lderry
9 Q3 **Currans** Kerry
19 Q2 **Curreeny** Tippry
10 B4 **Currow** Kerry
42 F2 **Curry** Sligo
68 E7 **Cushendall** Antrim
68 F6 **Cushendun** Antrim
29 N1 **Cushina** Offaly

D

37 M8 **Daingean**/*An Daingean* Offaly
39 P8 **Dalkey**/*Deilginis* Dublin
13 N6 **Dalligan Bridge** Watfd
37 L5 **Dalystown** Wmeath
39 L2 **Damastown** Dublin
67 M7 **Damhead** Lderry
6 G3 **Dangan** Cork
20 C9 **Dangandargan** Tippry
22 H9 **Darby's Gap** Wexfd
55 N7 **Darkley** Armagh
54 H10 **Dartry** Monhan
22 G9 **Davidstown** Wexfd
49 M7 **Deel Bridge** Mayo
31 P2 **Delgany**/*Deilgne* Wicklw
40 G10 **Delphi** Mayo
37 Q1 **Delvin**/*Dealbhna* Wmeath
10 H5 **Dernagree** Cork
53 M10 **Derradda** Leitrm
25 L10 **Derragh** Clare
36 D1 **Derraghan Cross Roads** Longfd
24 F7 **Derreen** Clare
8 F10 **Derreen** Kerry
40 E4 **Derreen** Mayo
41 M2 **Derreen** Mayo
3 M4 **Derreenacarrin** Cork
4 B7 **Derreenard** Cork
2 G2 **Derreenauliff** Kerry
3 K5 **Derreeny** Cork
36 H8 **Derries** Offaly
38 B8 **Derries** Offaly
36 B7 **Derrineel** Roscom
43 Q1 **Derrinisky** Roscom
38 C7 **Derrinturn** Kildre
66 C9 **Derry City Walls** Lderry
56 B1 **Derryadd** Armagh
64 E7 **Derrybeg**/*Doirí Beaga* Donegl
57 L2 **Derryboy** Down
26 E4 **Derrybrien** Galway
4 E6 **Derryclogh** Cork
28 H4 **Derrycon** Laois
36 G9 **Derrycooly** Offaly
28 F1 **Derryclohy** Offaly
20 G3 **Derryfadda** Tippry
10 F10 **Derryfineen** Cork
19 M2 **Derrygareen** Tippry
29 L3 **Derrygile** Laois
37 K7 **Derrygolan** Wmeath
53 M3 **Derrygonnelly** Ferman
36 D1 **Derrygowna** Longfd

13 K2 **Derrygrath** Tippry
37 L8 **Derrygrogan** Offaly
67 P6 **Derrykeighan** Antrim
36 B7 **Derrylahan** Roscom
53 Q8 **Derrylin** Ferman
56 B1 **Derrymacash** Armagh
9 L2 **Derrymore** Kerry
4 E3 **Derrynacaheragh** Cork
32 H6 **Derryrush**/*Doire Iorrais* Galway
32 H3 **Derryvoreada** Galway
43 J9 **Derrywode** Galway
67 P6 **Dervock** Antrim
6 D2 **Desert** Cork
61 Q4 **Desertmartin** Lderry
53 P4 **Devenish** Ferman
8 E4 **Dingle**/*An Daingean* Kerry
62 H5 **Doagh** Antrim
65 N4 **Doagh Beg** Donegl
27 L10 **Dolla** Tippry
56 D2 **Dollingstown** Down
39 N6 **Dollymount** Dublin
39 N4 **Donabate**/*Domhnach Bat* Dublin
47 L9 **Donacarney** Meath
38 E7 **Donadea** Kildre
54 C8 **Donagh** Ferman
63 P7 **Donaghadee** Down
56 D3 **Donaghcloney** Down
28 G8 **Donaghmore** Laois
39 K3 **Donaghmore** Meath
61 N9 **Donaghmore** Tyrone
46 E9 **Donaghpatrick** Meath
22 E10 **Donard** Wexfd
30 G5 **Donard**/*Dún Ard* Wicklw
20 B8 **Donaskeagh** Tippry
59 K7 **Donegal**/*Dún na nGall* Donegl
64 D8 **Donegal** Donegl
59 K7 **Donegal Castle** Donegl
11 P3 **Doneraile**/*Dún ar Aill* Cork
19 Q6 **Donohill** Tippry
38 C3 **Donore** Meath
47 J9 **Donore** Meath
11 M8 **Donoughmore** Cork
40 C3 **Dooagh**/*Dumha Acha* Mayo
49 N6 **Doobehy** Mayo
45 N1 **Doocarrick** Cavan
51 N9 **Doocastle** Mayo
59 J1 **Doocharry**/*An Dúchoraidh* Donegl
40 D4 **Dooega**/*Dumha Éige* Mayo
44 G2 **Doogary** Cavan
40 G5 **Dooghbeg** Mayo
48 E9 **Doogort**/*Dumha Goirt* Mayo
55 L9 **Doohamlat** Monhan
54 G9 **Doohat** Monhan
48 F7 **Doohooma** Mayo
49 M7 **Dooleeg** Mayo
24 G5 **Doolin**/*Dúlainn* Clare
35 M6 **Doon** Galway
12 G5 **Doon** Tippry
19 N4 **Doon**/*Dún* Limrck
36 E7 **Doon Cross Roads** Offaly
48 G8 **Doona** Mayo
16 F4 **Doonaha** Clare
16 H1 **Doonbeg** Clare
8 G5 **Doonmanagh** Kerry
32 F5 **Doonreaghan** Galway
14 C6 **Doornane** Kilken
48 F7 **Dooyork** Mayo
3 K9 **Dough** Cork
34 C8 **Doughiska** Galway
6 B6 **Douglas**/*Dúglas* Cork
60 E5 **Douglas Bridge** Tyrone
20 D4 **Dovea** Tippry
14 B4 **Dowling** Kilken
67 J5 **Downhill** Lderry
65 K5 **Downies**/*Na Dúnaibh* Donegl
12 D6 **Downing** Cork
57 L5 **Downpatrick** Down
53 J8 **Dowra**/*An Damhshraith* Cavan
36 C5 **Doyle's Bridge** Roscom
20 H8 **Drangan**/*Drongán* Tippry
61 N4 **Draperstown** Lderry
61 K2 **Dreen** Lderry
16 C8 **Dreenagh** Kerry
9 M1 **Drehidasillagh** Kerry
4 E6 **Driminidy** Cork
28 H5 **Drimmo** Laois
4 D5 **Drimoleague**/*Drom Dhá Liag* Cork
4 F6 **Drinagh** Cork
32 C4 **Drinagh** Galway
44 C8 **Drinagh** Roscom
15 P5 **Drinagh** Wexfd
50 H4 **Drinaghan** Sligo
44 H6 **Dring** Longfd
11 M10 **Dripsey** Cork
3 N7 **Drishane Bridge** Cork
47 K9 **Drogheda**/*Droichead Átha* Louth
8 G2 **Drom** Kerry
20 D3 **Drom** Tippry
11 J5 **Dromagh** Cork
52 F7 **Dromahair**/*Droim Dhá Thiar* Leitrm
9 K8 **Dromalonhurt Bridge** Kerry
56 G4 **Dromara** Down
8 G10 **Dromaragh** Kerry

11 Q8 **Dromboy South** Cork
18 D10 **Dromcolliher**/*Drom Collachair* Limrck
16 E10 **Dromcunnig** Kerry
11 Q8 **Dromgarriff** Cork
19 J8 **Dromin** Limrck
47 J6 **Dromin** Louth
11 M1 **Dromina**/*Drom Aidhne* Cork
27 K7 **Dromineer** Tippry
47 K4 **Dromiskin** Louth
11 N6 **Drommahane** Cork
3 L7 **Dromnea** Cork
4 C5 **Dromore** Cork
56 F3 **Dromore** Down
60 E10 **Dromore** Tyrone
13 K8 **Dromore** Watfd
51 K4 **Dromore West** Sligo
11 J9 **Dromree Cross Roads** Cork
17 M10 **Dromtrasna** Limrck
54 G10 **Drum** Monhan
36 B6 **Drum** Roscom
66 D10 **Drumahoe** Lderry
55 N10 **Drumakill** Monhan
26 D6 **Drumandoora** Clare
57 J4 **Drumanass** Down
25 K9 **Drumanure** Clare
51 N4 **Drumard** Sligo
57 J5 **Drumaroad** Down
27 J1 **Drumatober** Galway
20 C5 **Drumbane** Tippry
19 M1 **Drumbaun** Tippry
63 J9 **Drumbo** Down
63 J10 **Drumbo** Down
47 K5 **Drumcar** Louth
26 D8 **Drumcharley** Clare
25 M8 **Drumcliff** Clare
52 C5 **Drumcliff**/*Droim Chliabh* Sligo
46 F6 **Drumcondra**/*Droim Conrach* Meath
45 P10 **Drumcree** Wmeath
22 D5 **Drumfea** Carlow
52 D9 **Drumfin** Sligo
66 B5 **Drumfree** Donegl
34 C6 **Drumgriftin** Galway
59 L6 **Druminnin** Donegl
26 G3 **Drumkeary** Galway
59 Q2 **Drumkeen** Donegl
52 H9 **Drumkeeran**/*Droim Caorthainn* Leitrm
44 F2 **Drumlea** Leitrm
44 F6 **Drumlish**/*Droim Lis* Longfd
36 C7 **Drumlosh** Roscom
52 E9 **Drummacool** Sligo
24 G10 **Drummin** Clare
41 J9 **Drummin** Mayo
43 Q6 **Drummullin** Roscom
44 E3 **Drumna** Leitrm
60 H8 **Drumnakilly** Tyrone
44 D6 **Drumod**/*Drómad* Leitrm
60 C1 **Drumoghill** Donegl
45 P10 **Drumone** Meath
60 D8 **Drumquin** Tyrone
36 F4 **Drumraney** Wmeath
38 G3 **Drumree** Meath
13 J7 **Drumroe** Watfd
44 B1 **Drumshanbo**/*Droim Seanbhó* Leitrm
33 N2 **Drumsheel** Mayo
44 B4 **Drumsna**/*Droim ar Snámh* Leitrm
67 J9 **Drumsurn** Lderry
45 N1 **Drung** Cavan
17 K8 **Duagh**/*Dubháth* Kerry
20 E8 **Dually** Tippry
39 M7 **Dublin** Dublin
39 M5 **Dublin** Dublin
38 B6 **Duffy's Cross Roads** Kildre
36 B6 **Duggarry** Roscom
47 J10 **Duleek**/*Damhliag* Meath
39 N8 **Dún Laoghaire** Dublin
62 G6 **Dunadry** Antrim
65 Q3 **Dunaff** Donegl
35 M1 **Dunamon** Roscom
47 L5 **Dunany** Louth
21 P6 **Dunbell** Kilken
39 J3 **Dunboyne** Meath
38 D9 **Dunbyrne** Kildre
14 G7 **Duncannon**/*Dún Canann* Wexfd
15 L7 **Duncormick** Wexfd
47 K2 **Dundalk**/*Dún Dealgan* Louth
5 N4 **Dunderrow** Cork
38 E1 **Dunderry** Meath
55 J4 **Dundian** Monhan
63 L8 **Dundonald** Down
35 M7 **Dundoogan** Galway
62 G7 **Dundrod** Antrim
57 K6 **Dundrum** Down
39 M8 **Dundrum** Dublin
20 B7 **Dundrum**/*Dún Droma* Tippry
65 J5 **Dunfanaghy**/*Dún Fionnachaidh* Donegl
38 D6 **Dunfierth Cross Roads** Kildre
55 L1 **Dungannon** Tyrone
14 F4 **Dunganstown** Wexfd
21 Q7 **Dungarvan** Kilken
13 N6 **Dungarvan**/*Dún Garbhán* Watfd
61 L1 **Dungiven** Lderry
64 D10 **Dunglow**/*An Clochán Liath* Donegl

6 F4 **Dungourney** Cork
14 C8 **Dunhill** Watfd
26 H3 **Duniry** Galway
28 C8 **Dunkerrin** Offaly
58 G7 **Dunkineely**/*Dún Clonnaola* Donegl
14 D5 **Dunkitt** Kilken
30 F4 **Dunlavin**/*Dún Luáin* Wicklw
47 K6 **Dunleer**/*Dún Léire* Louth
64 G9 **Dunlewy**/*Dún Lúiche* Donegl
67 Q9 **Dunloy** Antrim
67 N4 **Dunluce Castle** Antrim
1 L8 **Dunmanus** Cork
4 F4 **Dunmanway**/*Dún Mánmhaí* Cork
12 H9 **Dunmoon** Watfd
34 G1 **Dunmore**/*Dún Mór* Galway
14 F8 **Dunmore East**/*Dún Mór* Watfd
62 H9 **Dunmurry** Antrim
21 M9 **Dunnamaggan** Kilken
60 F2 **Dunnamanagh** Tyrone
16 L6 **Dunnamore** Tyrone
21 M5 **Dunningstown** Kilken
8 C4 **Dunquin**/*Dún Chaoin* Kerry
38 G2 **Dunsany Cross Roads** Meath
38 H3 **Dunshaughlin**/*Dún Seachlainn* Meath
29 K9 **Durrow**/*Darú* Laois
3 N6 **Durrus**/*Dúras* Cork
35 P4 **Dysart** Roscom
37 K4 **Dysart** Wmeath

E

38 H10 **Eadestown** Kildre
20 H6 **Earlshill** Tippry
51 J3 **Easky**/*Iascaigh* Sligo
53 J6 **East Barrs** Leitrm
64 F3 **East Town**/*Baile Thoir* Donegl
63 L5 **Eden** Antrim
37 Q7 **Edenderry**/*Eadan Doire* Offaly
60 B10 **Ederney** Ferman
44 H7 **Edgeworthstown**/*Meathas Troim* Longfd
66 E8 **Eglinton** Lderry
55 L2 **Eglish** Tyrone
45 P6 **Eighter** Cavan
43 P6 **Elphin**/*Ail Finn* Roscom
19 K8 **Elton** Limrck
26 D7 **Emlagh Cross Roads** Galway
8 F10 **Emlaghmore** Kerry
19 M8 **Emly**/*Imleach* Tippry
40 Q10 **Emmoo** Roscom
29 M3 **Emo**/*Ioma* Laois
55 J5 **Emyvale**/*Scairb na gCaorach* Monhan
25 M9 **Ennis**/*Inis* Clare
22 H9 **Enniscorthy**/*Inis Córthaidh* Wexfd
5 J4 **Enniskean**/*Inis Céin* Cork
31 N1 **Enniskerry**/*Áth na Sceire* Wicklw
53 P5 **Enniskillen** Ferman
24 H7 **Ennistimon**/*Inis Díomáin* Clare
24 C2 **Eochaill** Clare
44 C9 **Erra** Roscom
41 K10 **Erriff Bridge** Mayo
28 F9 **Errill** Laois
66 E10 **Ervey Cross Roads** Lderry
54 F6 **Eshnadarragh** Ferman
34 G8 **Esker** Galway
44 F7 **Esker South** Longfd
49 M7 **Eskeragh Bridge** Mayo
9 L10 **Eskine** Kerry
54 F2 **Eskragh** Tyrone
44 D4 **Eslinbridge** Leitrm
2 G4 **Eyeries**/*Na hAorai* Cork
27 M1 **Eyrecourt**/*Dún an Uchta* Galway

F

9 P5 **Faha** Kerry
13 Q6 **Faha Glen** Watfd
10 C2 **Fahaduff** Kerry
9 J1 **Fahamore** Kerry
65 Q7 **Fahan** Donegl
8 C5 **Fahan** Kerry
19 M10 **Fahanasoodry** Limrck
35 L8 **Fahy** Galway
27 L2 **Fahy** Galway
25 N8 **Fair Green** Clare
36 F5 **Fairfield** Roscom
43 K6 **Fairymount** Roscom
64 G6 **Falcarragh**/*An Fál Carrach* Donegl
26 G1 **Fanore More** Clare
12 A4 **Farahy** Cork
36 D6 **Fardrum** Wmeath
9 P2 **Farmer's Bridge** Kerry
36 F6 **Farnagh** Wmeath

44 E5 **Farnaght** Leitrm
4 E3 **Farnanes** Cork
5 L1 **Farnanes** Cork
14 E4 **Farnoge** Kilken
5 L1 **Farran** Cork
29 J8 **Farran Cross Roads** Laois
9 Q4 **Farranfore**/*An Fearann Fuar* Kerry
46 B7 **Fartagh Cross Roads** Cavan
44 H1 **Fartrin Cross Roads** Cavan
26 E7 **Feakle**/*An Fhiacail* Clare
24 B2 **Fearann an Choirce** Clare
18 H6 **Fedamore**/*Feadamair* Limrck
16 D4 **Feeard** Clare
25 J3 **Feenagh** Clare
18 D9 **Feenagh** Limrck
43 L1 **Feenaghmore** Sligo
61 K1 **Feeny** Lderry
44 E2 **Fenagh** Leitrm
9 L1 **Fenit**/*An Fhianait* Kerry
22 D4 **Fennagh** Carlow
14 C8 **Fennor** Watfd
37 N1 **Fennor** Wmeath
18 C9 **Feohanagh** Limrck
8 D3 **Feohanagh**/*An Fheothanach* Kerry
3 L1 **Feoramore** Kerry
36 E9 **Ferbane**/*An Féar Bán* Offaly
12 D7 **Fermoy**/*Mainistir Fhear Maí* Cork
23 J7 **Ferns**/*Fearna* Wexfd
18 F4 **Ferry Bridge** Limrck
23 P2 **Ferrybank** Wicklw
20 G10 **Fethard**/*Fiodh Ard* Tippry
14 H8 **Fethard**/*Fiodh Ard* Wexfd
13 Q5 **Fews** Watfd
19 M2 **Fiddane** Tippry
14 B4 **Fiddown**/*Fiodh Dúin* Kilken
9 Q4 **Fieries** Kerry
42 H6 **Figh Bridge** Roscom
13 Q2 **Figlash** Tippry
25 L2 **Finavarra** Clare
45 L7 **Finnea**/*Fiodh an Átha* Wmeath
56 G4 **Finnis** Down
33 L2 **Finny** Mayo
54 D1 **Fintona** Tyrone
59 K2 **Fintown**/*Baile na Finne* Donegl
16 H8 **Finuge**/*Fionnúig* Kerry
67 P9 **Finvoy** Antrim
2 E6 **Firkeel** Cork
24 G5 **Fisherstreet** Clare
62 H4 **Five Corners** Antrim
28 D2 **Fivealley** Offaly
52 E6 **Fivemilebourne** Leitrm
5 Q2 **Fivemilebridge** Cork
54 D4 **Fivemiletown** Tyrone
26 E6 **Flagmount** Clare
21 Q5 **Flagmount** Kilken
32 H6 **Flannery Bridge** Galway
9 J4 **Flemingstown** Kerry
53 N7 **Florence Court NT** Ferman
8 G8 **Foilmore Bridge** Kerry
3 P8 **Foilnamuck** Cork
19 J9 **Foley's Cross Roads** Limrck
30 C4 **Fontstown** Kildre
46 C10 **Fordstown** Meath
45 N9 **Fore** Wmeath
56 B10 **Forkill** Armagh
25 J3 **Formoyle** Clare
25 J9 **Formoyle** Clare
36 C1 **Formoyle** Longfd
40 F8 **Formoyle** Mayo
11 N8 **Fornaght** Cork
18 G9 **Fort Middle** Limrck
36 D2 **Forthill** Longfd
6 C5 **Fota Wildlife Park** Cork
15 K5 **Foulkesmill** Wexfd
20 F8 **Foulkstown** Tippry
25 M9 **Fountain Cross** Clare
43 P9 **Four Mile House** Roscom
35 P3 **Four Roads** Roscom
44 D2 **Foxfield** Leitrm
42 B3 **Foxford**/*Béal Easa* Mayo
17 P4 **Foynes**/*Faing* Limrck
11 K2 **Freemount**/*Cillín an Chrónáin* Cork
43 L5 **Frenchpark**/*Dún Gar* Roscom
21 L4 **Freshford**/*Achadhúr* Kilken
30 F5 **Freynestown** Wicklw
18 H5 **Friarstown** Limrck
58 H6 **Frosses**/*Na Frosa* Donegl
35 N1 **Fuerty** Roscom
25 M3 **Funshin More** Galway
3 N4 **Furkeal** Cork
13 P5 **Furraleigh** Watfd
17 M1 **Furroor** Clare
12 E4 **Furrow** Cork
9 M4 **Fybagh** Kerry

G

17 J6 **Gabbett's Bridge** Kerry
37 L4 **Gainstown** Wmeath
15 L3 **Galbally** Wexfd
19 M9 **Galbally**/*An Gallbhaile* Limrck
20 E6 **Galbertstown** Tippry
16 H7 **Galey Cross Roads** Kerry
62 D2 **Galgorm** Antrim
44 B10 **Gallagh** Roscom
20 H2 **Gallmoy** Kilken
28 C2 **Galros Cross Roads** Offaly
38 F3 **Galtrim** Meath
34 D8 **Galway** Galway
34 C8 **Galway**/*Gaillimh* Galway
19 N3 **Gannavane** Limrck
54 D10 **Gannon's Cross** Cavan
38 F4 **Garadice** Meath
35 N7 **Garbally Demesne** Galway
13 J2 **Garnavilla** Tippry
37 N6 **Garr** Offaly
42 F10 **Garrafrauns** Galway
50 D5 **Garranard** Mayo
11 P1 **Garrane Cross Roads** Cork
5 J2 **Garranereagh** Cork
42 H9 **Garranlahan** Roscom
16 G3 **Garraun** Clare
9 P3 **Garraun** Kerry
27 J2 **Garraun** Galway
30 F8 **Garrettstown** Carlow
52 H3 **Garrison** Ferman
39 K2 **Garristown**/*Baile Cháire* Dublin
12 F9 **Garrycaheragh** Cork
50 E7 **Garrycloonagh** Mayo
15 L3 **Garrycullen** Wexfd
67 P8 **Garryduff** Antrim
18 G9 **Garryfine** Limrck
22 D5 **Garryhill** Carlow
27 J8 **Garrykennedy** Tippry
6 H5 **Garrymore** Cork
27 N9 **Garrynafana** Tippry
6 G9 **Garryvoe** Cork
67 L9 **Garvagh** Lderry
44 D3 **Garvagh** Leitrm
54 G2 **Garvaghy** Tyrone
19 L9 **Garyspillane** Limrck
21 K3 **Gattabaun** Kilken
34 M4 **Gaybrook** Wmeath
37 M9 **Geashill**/*Géisill* Offaly
52 F10 **Geevagh**/*An Chaobhach* Sligo
46 E8 **Georges Cross Roads** Meath
14 A8 **Georgestown** Watfd
3 M6 **Gerahies** Cork
67 N4 **Giant's Causeway NT** Antrim
46 E9 **Gibstown** Meath
56 C4 **Gilford** Down
46 G5 **Glack Cross Roads** Louth
3 N8 **Glan** Cork
4 G2 **Glan Cross Roads** Cork
3 L7 **Glanalin** Cork
9 K7 **Glanbehy Bridge** Kerry
4 C5 **Glandart** Cork
4 F7 **Glandore**/*Cuan Dor* Cork
53 L8 **Glangevlin** Cavan
3 M6 **Glanlough** Cork
6 B5 **Glanmire**/*Gleann Maghair* Cork
16 G9 **Glanoe** Kerry
3 K7 **Glanroon** Cork
11 M6 **Glantane** Cork
12 C6 **Glanworth**/*Gleannúir* Cork
68 B10 **Glarryford** Antrim
28 G9 **Glasha Cross Roads** Laois
8 D3 **Glashabeg** Kerry
11 R7 **Glashaboy East** Cork
11 Q7 **Glashaboy North** Cork
17 J10 **Glashananoon** Kerry
17 L6 **Glashapullagh** Limrck
46 C3 **Glasleck** Cavan
55 K5 **Glaslough**/*Glasloch* Monhan
36 D4 **Glassan**/*Glasán* Wmeath
57 P1 **Glastry** Down
66 H6 **Glebe** Lderry
65 L6 **Glen** Donegl
61 P2 **Glen** Lderry
6 G2 **Glenacroghery** Cork
12 E3 **Glenade** Leitrm
27 N8 **Glenahilty** Tippry
49 K4 **Glenamoy**/*Gleann na Muaidhe* Mayo
68 E8 **Glenariff or Waterfoot** Antrim
68 G10 **Glenarm** Antrim
62 F8 **Glenavy** Antrim
9 K6 **Glenbeigh**/*Gleann Beithe* Kerry
52 H6 **Glenboy** Leitrm
23 J9 **Glenbrien** Wexfd
19 L9 **Glenbrohane** Limrck
9 L8 **Glencar** Kerry
52 E5 **Glencar**/*Gleann an Chairthe* Leitrm
58 B6 **Glencolumbkille**/*Gleann Cholm Cille* Donegl
33 Q3 **Glencorrib** Mayo

39 L10 **Glencree** Wicklw
39 M9 **Glencullen** Dublin
31 N3 **Glendarragh** Wicklw
16 C9 **Glenderry** Kerry
6 E3 **Glendine Bridge** Cork
65 J10 **Glendowan**/*Gleann Domhain* Donegl
26 D7 **Glendree** Clare
12 E4 **Glenduff** Cork
68 E6 **Glendun Viaduct** Antrim
50 N4 **Glenealy** Wicklw
50 D4 **Glenedagh** Mayo
66 E4 **Gleneely**/*Gleann Daoile* Donegl
53 K6 **Glenfarne** Leitrm
10 D7 **Glenflesk** Kerry
3 N3 **Glengarriff**/*An Gleann Garbh* Cork
12 G8 **Glengoura** Cork
66 G9 **Glenhead** Lderry
61 K5 **Glenhull** Tyrone
40 F9 **Glenkeen Bridge** Mayo
60 B1 **Glenmaquin** Donegl
17 L1 **Glenmore** Clare
14 F4 **Glenmore**/*An Gleann Mhór* Kilken
13 K1 **Glennagat** Tippry
10 G2 **Glennaknockane** Cork
35 J1 **Glennamaddy**/*Gleann na Madadh* Galway
10 G3 **Glennamucklagh East** Cork
13 R4 **Glennaphuca Cross Roads** Watfd
34 D8 **Glenoe** Antrim
63 K3 **Glenoe** Antrim
20 B6 **Glenough Lower** Tippry
20 B6 **Glenough Upper** Tippry
12 B3 **Glenroe** Limrck
6 F2 **Glentane** Cork
58 H4 **Glenties**/*Na Gleannta* Donegl
66 D4 **Glentogher** Donegl
33 K5 **Glentrasna**/*Gleann Trasna* Galway
67 Q10 **Glenvale** Antrim
59 P6 **Glenveagh** Donegl
65 K9 **Glenveagh Castle** Donegl
12 B9 **Glenville**/*Gleann an Phréacháin* Cork
17 L5 **Glin**/*An Gleann* Limrck
43 L10 **Glinsk** Galway
32 F6 **Glinsk**/*Glinsce* Galway
6 C5 **Glounthaune** Cork
63 L3 **Glynn** Antrim
22 C9 **Glynn** Carlow
15 M3 **Glynn** Wexfd
10 E5 **Gneevgullia** Kerry
20 C9 **Golden**/*An Gabhailín* Tippry
39 N9 **Golden Ball** Dublin
3 L9 **Goleen**/*An Góilín* Cork
20 C7 **Goold's Cross** Tippry
22 B6 **Goresbridge**/*An Droichead Nua* Kilken
23 M5 **Gorey**/*Guaire* Wexfd
13 J3 **Gormanston** Tippry
47 M10 **Gormanstown**/*Baile Mhic Gormáin* Meath
26 C4 **Gort**/*An Gort* Galway
24 B3 **Gort na gCapall** Clare
61 L7 **Gortaclady** Tyrone
3 J1 **Gortagowan** Kerry
64 G6 **Gortahork**/*Gort an Choirce* Donegl
20 C3 **Gortalough** Tippry
27 N2 **Gortarevan** Offaly
7 J4 **Gortaroo** Cork
53 M6 **Gortatole** Ferman
61 M7 **Gorteagh** Tyrone
35 J6 **Gorteen** Galway
29 N9 **Gorteen** Kilken
18 E9 **Gorteen** Limrck
43 K2 **Gorteen** Sligo
13 M9 **Gorteen** Watfd
28 H1 **Gorteen Bridge** Offaly
14 E6 **Gorteens** Kilken
27 J5 **Gorteeny** Galway
2 G4 **Gortgarriff** Cork
52 F7 **Gortgarrigan** Leitrm
10 C3 **Gortglass** Kerry
66 F10 **Gortilea Cross Roads** Lderry
60 G5 **Gortin** Tyrone
44 E5 **Gortletteragh** Leitrm
4 D2 **Gortloughra Bridge** Cork
33 J6 **Gortmore** Galway
50 D3 **Gortmore** Mayo
35 L1 **Gortnadeeve** Galway
21 K5 **Gortnagap Cross Roads** Kilken
17 N3 **Gortnahaha** Clare
66 H10 **Gortnahey** Lderry
20 H5 **Gortnahoo** Tippry
4 F2 **Gortnahoughtee** Cork
49 N6 **Gortnahurra** Mayo
9 Q1 **Gortnaleaha** Kerry
26 C7 **Gortnamearacaun** Clare
43 M7 **Gortnasillagh** Roscom
9 L7 **Gortrelig** Kerry
25 N3 **Gortskeagh** Galway
3 L6 **Gouladoo** Cork
32 E1 **Gour Bridge** Cork
32 E1 **Gowlaun** Galway
22 D8 **Gowlin** Cork
21 Q6 **Gowran**/*Gabhrán* Kilken
62 D2 **Gracehill** Antrim

19 J10 **Graigue Cross Roads** Limrck
13 P5 **Graiguearush** Watfd
22 C8 **Graiguenamanagh**/*Gráig na Manach* Kilken
31 J4 **Granabeg** Wicklw
45 J7 **Granard**/*Gránard* Longfd
30 E8 **Graney** Kildre
37 Q6 **Grange** Kildre
21 M6 **Grange** Kilken
14 B5 **Grange** Kilken
47 M2 **Grange** Louth
7 L3 **Grange** Watfd
15 M7 **Grange** Watfd
52 C4 **Grange**/*An Ghráinseach* Sligo
30 B2 **Grange Beg** Kildre
28 G8 **Grange Beg** Laois
18 C7 **Grange Bridge** Limrck
30 E6 **Grange Con** Wicklw
38 H2 **Grange Cross Roads** Meath
47 K6 **Grangebellew** Louth
22 E2 **Grangeford** Carlow
46 H7 **Grangegeeth** Meath
52 D10 **Graniamore** Sligo
26 C2 **Grannagh** Galway
55 L1 **Granville** Tyrone
28 G8 **Green Cross Roads** Laois
31 L7 **Greenan** Wicklw
54 H8 **Greenans Cross Roads** Monhan
39 L1 **Greenanstown** Meath
61 J6 **Greencastle** Tyrone
66 G4 **Greencastle**/*An Caisleán Nua* Donegl
63 K5 **Greenisland** Antrim
47 N1 **Greenore**/*An Grianfort* Louth
11 P8 **Grenagh** Cork
63 P9 **Greyabbey** Down
17 L1 **Greygrove** Clare
66 F8 **Greysteel** Lderry
55 L2 **Greystone** Tyrone
31 P2 **Greystones**/*Na Clocha Liatha* Wicklw
19 L10 **Griston** Limrck
36 F7 **Grogan** Offaly
63 N6 **Groomsport** Down
53 K7 **Gubaveeny** Cavan
14 B6 **Guilcagh Cross Roads** Watfd
61 Q3 **Gulladuff** Lderry
10 E5 **Gullaun** Kerry
52 F5 **Gurteen** Leitrm
14 H5 **Gusserane** Wexfd
64 E4 **Gweedore**/*Gaoth Dobhair* Donegl
48 G6 **Gweesala** Mayo
6 E7 **Gyleen** Cork

H

46 H1 **Hackballs Cross** Louth
30 H8 **Hacketstown**/*Baile Haicéid* Carlow
5 P2 **Halfway** Cork
14 F7 **Halfway House** Watfd
46 E10 **Halltown Cross Roads** Meath
55 P5 **Hamiltonsbawn** Armagh
62 H8 **Hannahstown** Antrim
14 C3 **Harristown** Kilken
34 B4 **Headford**/*Áth Cinn* Galway
10 D7 **Headfort** Kerry
15 M6 **Heavenstown Cross Roads** Wexfd
16 D8 **Heirhill** Kerry
63 M6 **Helen's Bay** Down
19 K6 **Herbertstown**/*Baile Hiobaird* Limrck
36 D9 **Highstreet** Offaly
6 D2 **Hightown** Cork
43 Q5 **Hill Street** Roscom
38 B4 **Hill of Down** Meath
62 H10 **Hillhall** Down
56 F2 **Hillsborough** Down
56 F8 **Hilltown** Down
15 K5 **Hilltown** Wexfd
15 N6 **Hilltown** Wexfd
18 C4 **Hogan's Bridge** Limrck
19 Q4 **Hollyford** Tippry
23 L4 **Hollyfort** Wexfd
42 B10 **Hollymount** Mayo
26 D3 **Hollymount** Galway
30 G3 **Hollywood**/*Cillín Chaoimhín* Wicklw
19 J7 **Holycross** Limrck
20 D6 **Holycross**/*Mainistir na Croiche* Tippry
53 L6 **Holywell** Ferman
57 P6 **Holywood** Down
14 G9 **Hook Lighthouse** Wexfd
46 D7 **Horath Cross Roads** Meath
15 P6 **Horetown** Wexfd
20 F6 **Horse & Jockey**/*An Marcach* Tippry
36 H6 **Horseleap**/*Baile Átha an Urchair* Offaly
19 L7 **Hospital**/*An tOspidéal* Limrck

39 P6 **Howth**/*Binn Éadair* Dublin
21 N10 **Hugginstown** Kilken
18 H3 **Hunt Museum** Limrck
18 E2 **Hurlers Cross** Clare

I

9 K5 **Illaunstookagh** Kerry
25 K8 **Inagh**/*Eidhneach* Clare
6 E7 **Inch** Cork
6 H3 **Inch** Cork
65 Q8 **Inch** Donegl
19 Q3 **Inch** Tippry
23 M3 **Inch** Wexfd
9 K4 **Inch**/*Inse* Kerry
29 N5 **Inch Cross Roads** Laois
17 M9 **Inchabaun** Limrck
38 C4 **Inchamore Bridge** Meath
21 L3 **Inchbeg** Kilken
10 D10 **Inchee Bridge** Kerry
4 F3 **Inchicahan Cross Roads** Cork
4 F1 **Inchigeelagh**/*Inse Geimhleach* Cork
12 B6 **Inchinapallas** Cork
12 G3 **Inchnamuck** Tippry
5 M3 **Inishannon**/*Inis Eonáin* Cork
50 G5 **Inishcrone**/*Inis Crabhann* Sligo
62 A2 **Inishrush** Lderry
46 G2 **Iniskeen**/*Inis Caoin* Monhan
21 Q9 **Inistioge**/*Inis Tíog* Kilken
38 D5 **Innfield**/*An Bóthar Buí* Meath
58 H7 **Inver**/*Inbhear* Donegl
33 L9 **Inveran**/*Indreabhán* Galway
30 C2 **Irish National Stud** Kildre
42 E10 **Irishtown** Mayo
53 P2 **Irvinestown** Ferman
58 H5 **Ivy Bridge** Donegl

J

31 P8 **Jack White's Cross Roads** Wicklw
29 N3 **Jamestown** Laois
44 B4 **Jamestown** Leitrm
21 M3 **Jenkinstown** Kilken
47 L2 **Jenkinstown** Louth
56 C7 **Jerrettspass** Armagh
14 G5 **John F. Kennedy Ancestral Home** Wexfd
42 D4 **Johnsfort** Mayo
44 D6 **Johnstonsbridge** Longfd
6 B6 **Johnstown** Cork
46 F10 **Johnstown** Meath
38 G9 **Johnstown** Kildre
15 L6 **Johnstown** Wexfd
23 M2 **Johnstown** Wicklw
31 P9 **Johnstown** Wicklw
20 H3 **Johnstown**/*Baile Sheáin* Kilken
38 D6 **Johnstown Bridge** Kildre
15 N5 **Johnstown Castle** Wexfd
21 P4 **Johnswell** Kilken
56 C10 **Jonesborough** Armagh
47 L9 **Julianstown** Meath

K

11 K4 **Kanturk**/*Ceann Toirc* Cork
9 P7 **Kate Kearney's Cottage** Kerry
56 F5 **Katesbridge** Down
43 Q1 **Keadew**/*Céideadh* Roscom
55 M7 **Keady** Armagh
9 L10 **Kealariddig** Kerry
2 H5 **Kealincha Bridge** Cork
8 B3 **Kealkill** Cork
4 E2 **Kealvaugh** Cork
33 P7 **Keeagh**/*An Chaothach* Galway
40 C3 **Keel**/*An Caol* Mayo
8 G9 **Keelnagore** Kerry
35 K1 **Keeloges** Galway
49 M8 **Keenagh** Mayo
36 E1 **Keenagh**/*Caonach* Longfd
13 K8 **Keereen** Watfd
22 D2 **Kellistown Cross Roads** Carlow
62 E3 **Kells** Antrim
8 H7 **Kells** Kerry
21 M8 **Kells**/*Ceanannas* Kilken
46 C8 **Kells**/*Ceanannas* Meath
21 Q2 **Kelly's Bridge** Kilken
30 G7 **Kelshabeg** Wicklw
9 Q10 **Kenmare**/*Neidín* Kerry
28 C3 **Kennedy's Cross Roads** Offaly
46 H10 **Kentstown** Meath
15 N1 **Kerloge** Wexfd

Kerry - Laragh 87

9 Q4 Kerry Kerry
9 N2 Kerry the Kingdom Kerry
17 P6 Kerryikyle Limrck
59 Q10 Kesh Ferman
44 C2 Keshcarrigan/Ceis Charraigín Leitrm
7 M3 Kiely's Cross Roads Watfd
16 C5 Kilbaha/Cill Bheathach Clare
22 D2 Kilballyhue Carlow
26 F10 Kilbane Clare
4 G1 Kilbarry Cork
14 D7 Kilbarry Watfd
26 C4 Kilbeacanty Galway
14 B8 Kilbeg Watfd
37 J6 Kilbeggan/Cill Bheagáin Wmeath
35 M1 Kilbegnet Roscom
12 E3 Kilbeheny Limrck
34 E2 Kilbenan Cross Roads Galway
29 Q5 Kilberry Kildre
46 F9 Kilberry Meath
13 P3 Kilbrack Watfd
18 E5 Kilbreedy Limrck
18 H9 Kilbreedy Limrck
20 C8 Kilbreedy Tippry
33 J6 Kilbrickan/Cill Bhreacáin Galway
20 E3 Kilbrickane Tippry
29 J7 Kilbricken Laois
42 D4 Kilbride Mayo
38 D1 Kilbride Meath
31 J1 Kilbride Wicklw
31 P7 Kilbride Wicklw
39 K4 Kilbride Cross Roads Meath
12 C8 Kilbrien Cork
13 M6 Kilbrien Watfd
11 L3 Kilbrin Cork
5 M5 Kilbrittain/Cill Briotáin Cork
34 D9 Kilcaimin Galway
29 M1 Kilcappagh Offaly
58 D7 Kilcar/Cill Charthaigh Donegl
14 E7 Kilcaragh Cross Roads Watfd
31 J8 Kilcarney Wicklw
31 J8 Kilcarney Cross Roads Wicklw
17 J3 Kilcarroll Clare
13 P1 Kilcash Tippry
35 Q7 Kilcashel Roscom
29 K1 Kilcavan Laois
26 E2 Kilchreest/Cill Chríost Galway
26 E7 Kilclaran Clare
57 N4 Kilclief Down
16 D5 Kilcloher Clare
37 L7 Kilclonfert Offaly
38 F6 Kilcock/Cill Choca Kildre
4 B8 Kilcoe Cork
45 K6 Kilcogy Cavan
14 E7 Kilcohan Watfd
34 E10 Kilcolgan/Cill Cholgáin Galway
5 K4 Kilcolman Cork
17 P6 Kilcolman Limrck
7 M3 Kilcolman Watfd
27 P6 Kilcomin Offaly
19 Q2 Kilcommon Tippry
12 H2 Kilcommon Tippry
34 G9 Kilconierin Galway
34 D2 Kilconly Galway
35 L7 Kilconnell/Cill Chonaill Galway
11 Q3 Kilconnor Cork
56 G7 Kilcoo Down
53 J4 Kilcoo Cross Roads Ferman
31 P3 Kilcoole/Cill Chomhghuill Wicklw
12 E9 Kilcor Cork
25 N5 Kilcorkan Clare
28 E2 Kilcormac/Cill Chormaic Offaly
11 J6 Kilcorney Cork
23 J9 Kilcotty Wexfd
6 H6 Kilcredan Cork
43 K10 Kilcroan Cross Roads Galway
3 L7 Kilcrohane Cork
12 G9 Kilcronat Cork
30 E3 Kilcullen/Cill Chuillinn Kildre
8 H2 Kilcummin Kerry
10 B5 Kilcummin Kerry
47 J2 Kilcurly Louth
47 J1 Kilcurry Louth
10 C2 Kilcusnaun Kerry
38 C2 Kildalkey Meath
29 Q3 Kildangan Kildre
30 C2 Kildare/Cill Dara Kildre
22 F5 Kildavin/Cill Damháin Carlow
14 B7 Kildermody Watfd
18 F4 Kildimo New Limrck
18 F4 Kildimo Old Limrck
12 B4 Kildorrery/Cill Dairbhre Cork
61 N7 Kildress Tyrone
66 B10 Kildrum Donegl
8 D4 Kildurrihy Kerry
20 B9 Kilfeakle Tippry
16 F3 Kilfearagh Clare
25 J6 Kilfenora/Cill Fhionnúrach Clare
19 K10 Kilfinnane/Cill Fhíonáin Limrck
18 F6 Kilfinny Limrck
16 F10 Kilflyn Kerry
10 C10 Kilgarvan/Cill Gharbháin Kerry
50 H4 Kilglass Sligo
35 M5 Kilglass Galway
35 Q2 Kilglass Roscom
9 N6 Kilgobnet Kerry
13 M7 Kilgobnet Watfd
30 E4 Kilgowan Kildre
18 E5 Kilgrogan Limrck
30 C7 Kilkea Kildre
21 N10 Kilkeasy Kilken
16 F2 Kilkee/Cill Chaoi Clare
47 Q1 Kilkeel Down
42 E5 Kilkelly/Cill Cheallaigh Mayo
21 N5 Kilkenny/Cill Chainnigh Kilken
21 N5 Kilkenny Castle Kilken
36 E4 Kilkenny West Wmeath
5 N5 Kilkerran Cork
35 J2 Kilkerrin Galway
32 G7 Kilkieran/Cill Chiaráin Galway
21 N4 Kilkieran Cross Roads Kilken
4 B8 Kilkilleen Cork
17 K10 Kilkinlea Lower Limrck
26 C10 Kilkishen/Cill Chisin Clare
45 P2 Kill Cavan
32 C3 Kill Galway
14 B8 Kill Watfd
38 G9 Kill/An Chill Kildre
36 F5 Killachonna Wmeath
12 C4 Killaclug Cork
18 F9 Killacolla Limrck
53 P3 Killadeas Ferman
35 M5 Killaderry Galway
40 F9 Killadoon Mayo
17 P3 Killadysert/Cill an Dísirt Clare
26 C5 Killafeen Galway
15 M7 Killag Wexfd
17 N8 Killaghteen Limrck
13 J7 Killahaly Watfd
21 K5 Killahy Cross Roads Kilken
50 F5 Killala/Cill Ala Mayo
45 Q9 Killallon Meath
26 H10 Killaloe/Cill Dalua Clare
60 H1 Killaloo Lderry
21 K9 Killamery Kilken
36 H4 Killane Wmeath
26 D6 Killanena Clare
22 F8 Killann/Cill Anna Wexfd
16 H1 Killard Clare
52 G7 Killarga Leitrm
10 B6 Killarney/Cill Airne Kerry
36 H4 Killaroo Wmeath
45 J2 Killashandra/Cill na Seanrátha Cavan
44 D9 Killashee Longfd
42 D3 Killasser Mayo
33 L1 Killateeaun Mayo
28 D3 Killaun Offaly
41 N8 Killavally Mayo
12 F8 Killavarilly Cork
11 R9 Killavarrig Cork
51 P9 Killavil Sligo
34 H2 Killavoher Galway
11 Q5 Killavullen/Cill an Mhuilinn Cork
52 H5 Killea Leitrm
20 D2 Killea Tippry
14 F8 Killea Watfd
62 F6 Killead Antrim
6 H4 Killeagh/Cill Ia Cork
24 C3 Killeany/Cill Éinne Clare
22 D6 Killedmond Carlow
12 C4 Killee Bridge Cork
17 P9 Killeedy Limrck
26 C6 Killeen Galway
40 F8 Killeen Mayo
27 P4 Killeen Tippry
61 Q9 Killeen Tyrone
25 N1 Killeenaran Galway
20 C9 Killeenasteena Tippry
25 P2 Killeenavarra Galway
34 F10 Killeeneenmore Galway
4 C6 Killeenleagh Cork
11 R9 Killeens Cross Cork
54 G8 Killeevan Monhan
35 P5 Killeglan Roscom
37 K10 Killeigh/Cill Aichidh Offaly
60 B6 Killen Tyrone
23 M6 Killenagh Wexfd
29 N3 Killenard Laois
27 P3 Killenaule Tippry
20 G7 Killenaule/Cill Náile Tippry
43 M4 Killerdoo Roscom
30 E9 Killerrig Cross Roads Carlow
37 M7 Killeshil Offaly
30 B9 Killeshin Laois
60 B6 Killeter Tyrone
34 H10 Killilan Bridge Galway
17 J4 Killimer Clare
27 K2 Killimor/Cill Íomair Galway
25 L6 Killinaboy/Cill Inine Baoith Clare
11 L10 Killinardrish Cork
14 C4 Killinaspick Kilken
57 M1 Killinchy Down
23 M9 Killincooly Wexfd
9 J2 Killiney Kerry
39 P8 Killiney/Cill Iníon Léinín Dublin
15 P6 Killinick Wexfd
23 M3 Killinierin Wexfd
45 Q5 Killinkere Cavan
25 N3 Killinny Galway
38 B9 Killinthomas Kildre
31 P4 Killiskey Wicklw
10 H10 Killnamartery/Cill na Martra Cork
44 G8 Killoe Longfd
50 E3 Killogeary Mayo
36 E6 Killogeenaghan Wmeath
8 E10 Killoluaig Kerry
25 P3 Killomoran Galway
37 N8 Killoneen Offaly
35 M9 Killoran Galway
9 M5 Killorglin/Cill Orglan Kerry
35 J5 Killoscobe Galway
57 M6 Killough Down
33 P1 Killour Mayo
56 E10 Killowen Down
39 L4 Killsallaghan Dublin
37 P3 Killucan/Cill Liúcainne Wmeath
43 Q4 Killukin Roscom
37 J10 Killurin Offaly
15 M3 Killurin Wexfd
2 C1 Killurly Kerry
20 G10 Killusty Tippry
62 D3 Killybegs Antrim
58 F7 Killybegs/Na Cealla Beaga Donegl
60 G8 Killyclogher Tyrone
44 H2 Killygar Leitrm
60 B4 Killygordon/Cúil na gCuirridín Donegl
67 L9 Killykergan Lderry
55 L5 Killylea Armagh
57 M3 Killyleagh Down
55 K6 Killyneill Monhan
28 D3 Killyon Offaly
6 F6 Kilmacahill Cork
31 N2 Kilmacanoge Wicklw
11 N3 Kilmaclenine Cross Roads Cork
14 D5 Kilmacow/Cill Mhic Bhúith Kilken
65 L8 Kilmacrenan/Cill Mhic Réanáin Donegl
13 Q5 Kilmacthomas/Coill Mhic Thomáisín Watfd
43 N1 Kilmactranny Sligo
21 M10 Kilmaganny/Cill Mogeanna Kilken
34 B2 Kilmaine Mayo
46 D6 Kilmainham Wood Meath
25 L10 Kilmaley/Cill Mháile Clare
39 N10 Kilmalin Wicklw
19 J9 Kilmallock/Cill Mocheallóg Limrck
21 K6 Kilmanagh Kilken
17 K10 Kilmaniheen Kerry
35 Q3 Kilmass Roscom
30 C5 Kilmead Kildre
14 C6 Kilmeadan Watfd
38 D9 Kilmeage Kildre
18 D9 Kilmeedy/Cill Míde Limrck
38 F2 Kilmessan/Cill Mheasáin Meath
2 D6 Kilmichael Cork
4 G1 Kilmichael Cork
17 L2 Kilmihil/Cill Mhicíl Clare
11 Q8 Kilmona Cork
3 Q10 Kilmoon Cork
55 P3 Kilmore Armagh
19 J1 Kilmore Clare
57 K3 Kilmore Down
16 E7 Kilmore Kerry
42 B3 Kilmore Mayo
44 B5 Kilmore Roscom
15 M7 Kilmore Wexfd
38 F4 Kilmore Cross Roads Meath
15 M8 Kilmore Quay Wexfd
44 D9 Kilmore Upper Longfd
17 K8 Kilmorna Kerry
30 B7 Kilmorony Laois
42 G5 Kilmovee Mayo
23 M8 Kilmuckridge/Cill Mhucraise Wexfd
14 B9 Kilmurrin Watfd
18 F1 Kilmurry/Cill Mhuire Clare
24 F10 Kilmurry Clare
5 J1 Kilmurry Cork
18 E9 Kilmurry Limrck
30 F7 Kilmurry Wicklw
17 L3 Kilmurry McMahon Clare
24 B2 Kilmurvy/Cill Mhuirbhigh Clare
22 G6 Kilmyshall Wexfd
13 J8 Kilnacarriga Watfd
18 G1 Kilnacreagh Clare
44 C3 Kilnagross Leitrm
35 M8 Kilnahown Galway
45 L5 Kilnaleck/Cill na Leice Cavan
23 L8 Kilnamanagh Wexfd
25 L8 Kilnamona/Cill na Móna Clare
5 M3 Kilpatrick Cork
18 H5 Kilpeacon Cross Roads Limrck
31 P3 Kilpedder Wicklw
8 E3 Kilquane Kerry
22 H2 Kilquiggin Wicklw
67 Q7 Kilraghts Antrim
15 Q6 Kilrane Wexfd
67 N10 Kilrea Lderry
58 G4 Kilrean Donegl
35 K9 Kilreekill Galway
34 C8 Kilroghter Galway
24 C3 Kilronan/Cill Rónáin Clare
43 Q10 Kilroosky Roscom
19 N8 Kilross Tippry
16 H3 Kilrush/Cill Rois Clare
43 K10 Kilsallagh Galway
40 H7 Kilsallagh Mayo
47 K5 Kilsaran Louth
38 C6 Kilshanchoe Kildre
9 J1 Kilshannig Kerry
24 H6 Kilshanny Clare
13 N2 Kilsheelan Tippry
5 L5 Kilshinahan Cork
46 B9 Kilskeer Meath
53 Q3 Kilskeery Tyrone
42 C6 Kiltamagh/Caillte Mach Mayo
41 M8 Kiltarsaghaun Mayo
26 C3 Kiltartan Galway
22 F7 Kiltealy/Cill Téile Wexfd
38 H9 Kilteel Kildre
19 L6 Kilteely/Cill Tíle Limrck
43 Q10 Kilteevan Cross Roads Roscom
30 G8 Kiltegan Wicklw
23 J6 Kilthomas Cross Roads Wexfd
25 P1 Kiltiernan Galway
39 N9 Kiltiernan Dublin
37 K7 Kiltober Wmeath
36 B4 Kiltoom Roscom
45 L10 Kiltoom Wmeath
35 N9 Kiltormer Galway
34 H8 Kiltullagh/Cill Tulach Galway
53 J4 Kiltyclogher/Coillte Clochair Leitrm
21 J9 Kilvemnon Tippry
42 E10 Kilvine Mayo
12 H8 Kilwatermoy Watfd
63 K2 Kilwaughter Antrim
38 H7 Kilwoghan Kildre
12 D6 Kilworth/Cill Uird Cork
12 D5 Kilworth Camp Cork
36 H6 Kimalady Offaly
17 L5 Kinard Limrck
53 P7 Kinawley Ferman
64 C9 Kincaslough/Cionn Caslach Donegl
50 D5 Kincon Mayo
45 Q9 King's Cross Roads Meath
18 H3 King John's Castle Limrck
59 L1 Kingarrow Donegl
46 D4 Kingscourt/Dún an Rí Cavan
61 Q7 Kingsmill Tyrone
52 F2 Kinlough/Cionn Locha Leitrm
40 E9 Kinnadoohy Mayo
37 P4 Kinnegad/Cionn Átha Gad Wmeath
28 E3 Kinnitty/Cion Eitigh Offaly
5 P4 Kinsale/Cionn tSáile Cork
7 K4 Kinsalebeg Watfd
39 N5 Kinsaley Dublin
33 K7 Kinvarra Galway
25 N2 Kinvarra/Cinn Mharra Galway
4 G5 Kippagh Bridge Cork
63 Q10 Kircubbin Down
67 P7 Kirkhills Antrim
57 P2 Kirkistown Down
10 G4 Kishkeam Cork
41 K7 Knappagh Mayo
8 E9 Knights Town Kerry
17 K4 Knock Clare
28 F7 Knock Tippry
42 D7 Knock/An Cnoc Mayo
42 F4 Knock International Mayo
25 L8 Knockacaurhin Clare
10 B5 Knockacullig Kerry
50 E7 Knockadangan Bridge Mayo
18 C7 Knockaderry Limrck
19 K7 Knockainy/Cnoc Áine Limrck
13 P3 Knockalafalla Watfd
43 M8 Knockalaghta Roscom
17 L2 Knockalough Clare
31 J8 Knockananna Wicklw
42 F8 Knockanarra Mayo
30 H6 Knockanarrigan Wicklw
4 H2 Knockane Cork
12 B3 Knockanevin Cork
50 E7 Knockanillaun Mayo
13 J9 Knockanore Watfd
17 K7 Knockanure Kerry
28 G7 Knockaroe Laois
54 G6 Knockatallan Monhan
12 E6 Knockatrasnane Cork
24 H8 Knockatullaghaun Clare
35 M10 Knockaun Galway
12 H6 Knockaunarast Watfd
17 J9 Knockaunbrack Kerry
9 L5 Knockaunnaglashy Kerry
9 K6 Knockaunroe Kerry
8 E4 Knockavrogeen Kerry
17 M8 Knockawahig Limrck
13 M5 Knockboy Watfd
16 F10 Knockbrack Kerry
26 E9 Knockbrack Clare
60 B1 Knockbrack Donegl
46 B3 Knockbride Cavan
46 H3 Knockbridge Louth
20 F9 Knockbrit Tippry
5 L5 Knockbrown Cork
5 N1 Knockburden Cork
16 G9 Knockburrane Cross Roads Kerry
61 Q3 Knockcloghrim Lderry
35 Q2 Knockcroghery/Cnoc an Chrochaire Roscom
18 H8 Knockdarnan Limrck
37 L2 Knockdrin Wmeath
11 N6 Knockdrislagh Cork
10 B2 Knockeen Cross Roads Kerry
10 G4 Knockeenadallane Cork
10 D1 Knockeencreen Kerry
24 G5 Knockfin Cross Roads Clare
13 K2 Knocklofty Tippry
19 L8 Knocklong Limrck
25 P7 Knockmael West Clare
21 K2 Knockmannon Cross Roads Kilken
50 F9 Knockmore Mayo
12 F8 Knockmourne Cork
41 L4 Knockmoyle Bridge Mayo
17 N5 Knocknaboly Limrck
10 E4 Knocknaboul Cross Kerry
68 E6 Knocknacarry Antrim
30 D8 Knocknacree Cross Roads Kildre
5 M4 Knocknacurra Cork
17 K10 Knocknagashel/Cnoc na gCaiseal Kerry
26 G8 Knocknagower Clare
10 F5 Knocknagree Cork
9 N1 Knocknahaha Kerry
24 G10 Knocknahila Clare
5 M1 Knocknahilan Cork
48 G3 Knocknalina Mayo
48 G4 Knocknalower Mayo
6 G5 Knocknaskagh Cork
24 H7 Knockpatrick Clare
6 C4 Knockraha Cork
9 J9 Knockroe Kerry
13 M7 Knockroe Watfd
5 J5 Knocks Cork
29 J4 Knocks Laois
5 J5 Knockskagh Cork
11 J2 Knockskavane Cork
21 N9 Knocktopher/Cnoc an Tóchair Kilken
15 L6 Knocktown Cross Roads Wexfd
43 P2 Knockvicar Roscom
5 M4 Knoppoge Bridge Cork
11 Q6 Knuttery Cork
29 N6 Kyle Laois
26 G3 Kylebrack Galway
19 N4 Kylegarve Limrck
35 Q9 Kylemore Galway
32 E2 Kylemore Abbey Galway

L

26 C2 Laban Galway
17 M4 Labasheeda/Leaba Shíoda Clare
60 C9 Lack Ferman
10 E10 Lackabaun Cork
29 Q2 Lackagh Kildre
27 J9 Lackamore Tippry
21 Q4 Lackan Carlow
43 Q8 Lackan Roscom
45 K10 Lackan Wmeath
31 J2 Lackan Wicklw
35 P3 Lackan Cross Roscom
5 J2 Lackareagh Cork
10 D1 Lackbrooder Kerry
12 B8 Lackendarragh North Cork
14 H3 Lacken Wexfd
28 F6 Lackey Laois
15 Q7 Lady's Island Wexfd
6 G5 Ladysbridge/Droichead na Scuab Cork
67 Q4 Lagavara Antrim
20 C10 Lagganstown Tippry
55 M1 Laghey Corner Tyrone
59 K8 Laghy/An Lathaigh Donegl
11 M6 Laharan Cross Roads Cork
50 D9 Lahardaun/Leathardán Mayo
17 L4 Lakyle Clare
21 L10 Lamoge Kilken
44 C10 Lanesborough/Béal Átha Liag Roscom
26 D5 Lannaght Clare
38 E3 Laracor Meath
46 D1 Laragh Monhan
38 F6 Laragh Kildre

31 L5 **Laragh**/*Láithreach* Wicklw
11 L10 **Larchill Cross Roads** Cork
49 K6 **Largan** Mayo
51 J7 **Largan** Sligo
43 Q6 **Largan** Roscom
58 E7 **Largy** Donegl
52 E3 **Largydonnell** Leitrm
63 L2 **Larne** Antrim
54 H8 **Latnamard** Monhan
25 N10 **Latoon Bridge** Clare
19 N7 **Lattin** Tippry
46 B1 **Latton** Monhan
3 K3 **Lauragh**/*Láithreach* Kerry
56 B4 **Laurelvale** Armagh
35 P9 **Laurencetown**/*An Baile Mór* Galway
51 N7 **Lavagh** Sligo
56 C4 **Lawrencetown** Down
47 M9 **Laytown**/*An Inse* Meath
64 B9 **Leabgarrow**/*An Leadhb Gharbh* Donegl
6 D4 **Leamlara** Cork
4 F7 **Leap**/*An Léim* Cork
36 B3 **Lecarrow** Roscom
66 F4 **Leckemy** Donegl
32 H1 **Leenaun**/*An Lionán* Galway
36 G1 **Legan or Lenamore** Longfd
44 G5 **Leggah** Longfd
63 J7 **Legoniel** Antrim
24 G7 **Lehinch**/*An Leacht* Clare
22 B3 **Leighlinbridge**/*Leithghlinn an Droichid* Carlow
38 B5 **Leinster Bridge** Meath
17 K1 **Leitrim** Clare
56 H6 **Leitrim** Down
44 B3 **Leitrim**/*Liatroim* Leitrm
17 K6 **Leitrim East** Kerry
4 D5 **Leitry Bridge** Cork
39 J6 **Leixlip** Kildre
36 F8 **Lemanaghan** Offaly
13 P6 **Lemybrien**/*Léim Uí Bhriain* Watfd
14 F8 **Leperstown** Watfd
16 E10 **Lerrig** Kerry
59 J6 **Letterbarra** Donegl
53 N5 **Letterbreen** Ferman
32 H8 **Lettercallow** Galway
32 E2 **Letterfrack**/*Leitir Fraic* Galway
24 H9 **Letterkelly** Clare
65 M10 **Letterkenny**/*Leitir Ceanainn* Donegl
67 L7 **Letterloan** Lderry
58 H2 **Lettermacaward**/*Leitir Mhic an Bhaird* Donegl
41 K4 **Lettermaghera** Mayo
32 H8 **Lettermore**/*Leitir Móir* Galway
32 C9 **Lettermullan**/*Leitir Mealláin* Galway
41 Q10 **Levally** Mayo
34 G3 **Levally** Galway
14 C6 **Licketstown** Kilken
60 D3 **Lifford**/*Leifear* Donegl
60 F4 **Ligfordrum or Douglas** Tyrone
66 H8 **Limavady** Lderry
18 H3 **Limerick**/*Luimneach* Limrck
19 P7 **Limerick Junction** Tippry
65 Q5 **Linsfort** Donegl
63 M10 **Lisbane** Down
54 B5 **Lisbellaw** Ferman
45 N1 **Lisboduff** Cavan
62 H10 **Lisburn** Antrim
34 D7 **Liscananaun** Galway
24 G7 **Liscannor**/*Lios Ceannúir* Clare
41 K8 **Liscarney** Mayo
11 M2 **Liscarroll**/*Lios Cearúill* Cork
17 N1 **Liscasey** Clare
38 B1 **Lisclogher Cross Roads** Meath
60 G2 **Liscloon** Tyrone
8 G4 **Lisdargan** Kerry
24 H5 **Lisdoonvarna**/*Lios Dúin Bhearna* Clare
21 L2 **Lisdowney** Kilken
45 Q7 **Lisduff** Cavan
11 Q9 **Lisduff** Cork
28 E2 **Lisduff** Offaly
44 E9 **Lisduff Cross Roads** Longfd
27 M8 **Lisgarode** Tippry
6 E3 **Lisgoold** Cork
45 P5 **Lisgrea Cross Roads** Cavan
17 P1 **Lisheen** Clare
35 N10 **Lisheenaguile** Galway
43 L2 **Liskeagh** Sligo
45 K9 **Lismacaffry** Wmeath
11 K3 **Lismire** Cork
12 H7 **Lismore**/*Lios Mór* Watfd
35 P4 **Lismoyle** Roscom
55 N6 **Lisnadill** Armagh
19 K3 **Lisnagry** Limrck
14 C7 **Lisnakill Cross** Watfd
54 H10 **Lisnalong** Monhan
61 P3 **Lisnamuck** Lderry
53 N2 **Lisnarrick** Ferman
54 C7 **Lisnaskea** Ferman
5 P6 **Lispatrick** Cork

8 G4 **Lispole**/*Lios Póil* Kerry
25 K10 **Lisroe** Clare
13 M1 **Lisronagh** Tippry
45 J8 **Lisryan** Longfd
10 H10 **Lissacresig** Cork
43 L8 **Lissalway** Roscom
3 P10 **Lissamona** Cork
35 P10 **Lissanacody** Galway
43 K7 **Lissananny** Roscom
5 L4 **Lissaphooca Cross Roads** Cork
9 J9 **Lissatinnig Bridge** Kerry
4 H7 **Lissavard** Cork
16 G7 **Lisselton Cross Roads** Kerry
9 N1 **Listellick** Kerry
14 E3 **Listerlin** Kilken
57 K3 **Listooder** Down
16 H8 **Listowel**/*Lios Tuathail* Kerry
19 N9 **Lisvarrinane** Tippry
6 C5 **Little Island** Cork
20 F6 **Littleton**/*An Baile Beag* Tippry
16 F9 **Lixnaw**/*Leic Snámha* Kerry
62 G6 **Loanends** Antrim
46 F7 **Lobinstown** Meath
45 J5 **Loch Gowna**/*Loch Gamhna* Cavan
17 M5 **Loghill** Limrck
12 H6 **Logleagh** Watfd
2 H1 **Lomanagh** Kerry
11 M5 **Lombardstown** Cork
66 C9 **Londonderry**/*Derry* Lderry
28 E4 **Longford** Offaly
44 E8 **Longford**/*An Longfort* Longfd
19 J6 **Longford Bridge** Limrck
20 G4 **Longfordpass Bridge** Tippry
38 C4 **Longwood** Meath
27 M4 **Lorrha**/*Lothra* Tippry
22 C5 **Lorum** Carlow
7 N2 **Loskeran** Watfd
35 L7 **Loughaclerybeg** Galway
12 H2 **Loughacutteen** Tippry
37 J4 **Loughanavally** Wmeath
64 E9 **Loughanure** Donegl
33 M9 **Loughaunbeg** Galway
56 D5 **Loughbrickland** Down
45 K5 **Loughduff** Cavan
9 J3 **Lougher** Kerry
55 P3 **Loughgall** Armagh
43 J6 **Loughglinn**/*Loch Glinne* Roscom
68 B7 **Loughguile** Antrim
57 K4 **Loughinisland** Down
61 J7 **Loughmacory** Tyrone
20 E3 **Loughmore** Tippry
46 D1 **Loughmorne** Monhan
26 F1 **Loughrea**/*Baile Locha Riach* Galway
39 P2 **Loughshinny** Dublin
40 G7 **Louisburgh**/*Cluain Cearbán* Mayo
46 H3 **Louth**/*Lú* Louth
62 E9 **Lower Ballinderry** Antrim
3 M8 **Lowertown** Cork
56 G5 **Lowtown** Down
39 J6 **Lucan** Dublin
51 L4 **Lugdoon** Sligo
29 N7 **Luggacurren** Laois
14 D3 **Lukeswell** Kilken
38 C8 **Lullymore** Kildre
42 F4 **Lurga** Mayo
56 C2 **Lurgan** Armagh
36 F6 **Lurgan** Offaly
43 M5 **Lurgan** Roscom
52 G5 **Lurganboy** Leitrm
65 P6 **Lurganboy** Donegl
39 N3 **Lusk**/*Lusca* Dublin
44 D10 **Lyneen Bridge** Longfd
16 H10 **Lyracrumpane** Kerry
11 P7 **Lyradane** Cork
11 L6 **Lyre** Cork
12 G9 **Lyre** Cork
10 D2 **Lyre** Kerry
12 F6 **Lyrenaglogh** Watfd

M

33 K4 **Maam Cross**/*An Teach Dóite* Galway
58 G3 **Maas** Donegl
41 M7 **Mace** Mayo
53 P7 **Mackan** Ferman
67 L7 **Macosquin** Lderry
12 E6 **Macroney** Cork
11 J10 **Macroom**/*Maigh Chromtha* Cork
4 Q2 **Madabawn** Cavan
21 N6 **Maddockstown** Kilken
30 C8 **Maganey** Kildre
62 F10 **Maghaberry** Antrim
57 M7 **Maghera** Down
61 Q2 **Maghera** Lderry
25 P8 **Maghera Cross Roads** Clare
65 N3 **Magheradrumman** Donegl
61 Q4 **Magherafelt** Lderry
56 D2 **Magheralin** Down
66 B10 **Magheramason** Tyrone
63 L3 **Magheramorne** Antrim
54 E8 **Maghraveely** Ferman

62 A10 **Maghery** Armagh
58 F1 **Maghery**/*An Machaire* Donegl
54 B6 **Maguiresbridge** Ferman
18 C8 **Mahoonagh** Limrck
9 Q3 **Maine Bridge** Kerry
38 F7 **Mainham** Kildre
39 N4 **Malahide**/*Mullach Íde* Dublin
66 D2 **Malin**/*Málainn* Donegl
58 A6 **Malin Beg**/*Málainn Bhig* Donegl
58 B6 **Malin More** Donegl
40 G4 **Mallaranny**/*An Mhala Raithní* Mayo
11 P5 **Mallow**/*Mala* Cork
62 H6 **Mallusk** Antrim
4 G4 **Manch Bridge** Cork
36 D7 **Mannion's Cross Roads** Offaly
65 N10 **Manorcunningham**/*Mainear Uí Chuinneagáin* Donegl
52 G6 **Manorhamilton**/*Cluainín* Leitrm
20 F4 **Manselstown** Tippry
47 J4 **Mansfieldstown** Louth
43 N6 **Mantua** Roscom
41 Q6 **Manulla** Mayo
53 M7 **Marble Arch Caves** Ferman
20 G7 **Mardyke** Tippry
55 Q6 **Markethill** Armagh
13 L2 **Marlfield** Tippry
22 H7 **Marshalstown** Wexfd
68 C10 **Martinstown** Antrim
19 K9 **Martinstown** Limrck
46 C10 **Martinstown Cross Roads** Meath
46 D9 **Marty** Meath
8 H10 **Mastergeehy** Kerry
20 C10 **Masterstown** Tippry
11 P9 **Matehy** Cork
4 E7 **Maulatrahane** Cork
4 C3 **Maulavanig** Cork
3 M8 **Maulawaddra** Cork
33 K3 **Maum** Galway
33 K1 **Maumtrasna** Mayo
25 K8 **Mauricesmills** Clare
15 N6 **Mayglass** Wexfd
38 G6 **Maynooth**/*Maigh Nuad* Kildre
42 B8 **Mayo** Mayo
56 E8 **Mayobridge** Down
62 G10 **Mazetown** Antrim
68 C10 **McGregor's Corner** Antrim
67 N10 **McLaughlins Corner** Antrim
18 H6 **Meanus** Limrck
27 M2 **Meelick** Galway
10 H2 **Meelin** Cork
64 F6 **Meenaclady**/*Mín an Chladaigh* Donegl
58 C5 **Meenacross** Donegl
58 G1 **Meenacross** Donegl
58 D6 **Meenaneary** Donegl
64 D9 **Meenbannad** Donegl
64 D1 **Meenbannivane** Kerry
64 F6 **Meenlaragh**/*Mín Larach* Donegl
10 F1 **Meennaraheeny** Cork
31 M8 **Meeting of the Waters** Wicklw
56 C9 **Meigh** Armagh
34 B8 **Menlough** Galway
35 J5 **Menlough**/*Mionlach* Galway
55 L6 **Middletown** Armagh
42 D5 **Midfield** Mayo
6 E5 **Midleton**/*Mainistir an Corann* Cork
22 H8 **Milehouse** Wexfd
30 F3 **Milemill** Kildre
19 Q3 **Milestone** Tippry
55 N5 **Milford** Armagh
18 E10 **Milford**/*Áth an Mhuilinn* Cork
62 E5 **Mill Town** Antrim
63 K2 **Millbrook** Lderry
4 E7 **Milleen Bridge** Cork
65 M7 **Milford**/*Baile na nGallóglach* Donegl
63 P7 **Millisle** Down
12 E5 **Millstreet** Cork
13 L6 **Millstreet** Watfd
10 H6 **Millstreet**/*Sráid an Mhuilinn* Cork
55 Q4 **Milltown** Armagh
45 J1 **Milltown** Cavan
58 H7 **Milltown** Donegl
58 M5 **Milltown** Donegl
39 J7 **Milltown** Dublin
34 E1 **Milltown** Galway
35 K3 **Milltown** Galway
38 D10 **Milltown** Kildre
14 C3 **Milltown** Kilken
67 K6 **Milltown** Lderry
67 M8 **Milltown** Lderry
37 J3 **Milltown** Wmeath
8 E4 **Milltown**/*Baile an Mhuilinn* Kerry
9 N4 **Milltown**/*Baile an Mhuilinn* Kerry
18 G10 **Milltown Cross Roads** Cork
24 G9 **Milltown Malbay**/*Sráid na Cathrach* Clare

37 N5 **Milltownpass**/*Bealach Bhaile an Mhuileann* Wmeath
6 B8 **Minane Bridge** Cork
57 L6 **Minerstown** Down
13 P2 **Minorstown** Tippry
12 D4 **Mitchelstown**/*Baile Mhistéala* Cork
16 H3 **Moanmore** Clare
19 M8 **Moanmore** Tippry
44 G8 **Moat Farrell** Longfd
36 F6 **Moate**/*An Móta* Wmeath
11 M9 **Model Village** Cork
11 P10 **Model Village** Cork
13 L7 **Modelligo** Watfd
27 N7 **Modreeny** Tippry
6 G4 **Mogeely** Cork
21 N4 **Mohil** Kilken
44 D4 **Mohill**/*Maothail* Leitrm
56 D1 **Moira** Down
9 P9 **Moll's Gap** Kerry
23 J8 **Monagear** Wexfd
55 J7 **Monaghan**/*Muineachán* Monhan
55 J7 **Monaghan County Museum** Monhan
12 F8 **Monagoun** Cork
13 J6 **Monalour** Watfd
14 E7 **Monamintra Cross Roads** Watfd
23 L7 **Monamolin** Wexfd
7 M2 **Monamraher** Watfd
19 N6 **Monard** Tippry
23 K4 **Monaseed** Wexfd
18 G6 **Monaster** Limrck
43 K4 **Monasteraden** Sligo
47 J7 **Monasterboice** Louth
29 P2 **Monasterevin**/*Mainistir Eimhin* Kildre
53 N4 **Monea** Ferman
11 P6 **Monea Cross Roads** Cork
16 C5 **Moneen** Clare
34 D4 **Moneen** Galway
29 N9 **Moneenroe** Kilken
29 J1 **Monettia Bog** Laois
64 G8 **Money More** Donegl
4 H1 **Moneycusker** Cork
67 M9 **Moneydig** Lderry
27 P8 **Moneygall**/*Muine Gall* Offaly
53 L7 **Moneygashel** Cavan
62 C4 **Moneyglass** Antrim
61 Q6 **Moneymore** Lderry
61 N3 **Moneyneany** Lderry
63 L9 **Moneyreagh** Down
56 F6 **Moneyslane** Down
37 M2 **Monilea** Wmeath
34 G6 **Monivea**/*Muine Mheá* Galway
63 J5 **Monkstown** Antrim
6 C6 **Monkstown** Cork
19 K1 **Montpelier** Limrck
14 C5 **Mooncoin**/*Móin Choinn* Kilken
30 D6 **Moone**/*Maoin* Kildre
7 K4 **Moord** Watfd
27 L1 **Moorfield Cross Roads** Galway
62 F3 **Moorfields** Antrim
61 R1 **Moran's Cross Roads** Lderry
18 F7 **Morenane** Limrck
10 C9 **Morley's Bridge** Kerry
47 L8 **Mornington** Meath
19 Q6 **Morpeth Bridge** Tippry
19 K10 **Mortlestown** Limrck
5 L2 **Moskeagh** Cork
47 M10 **Mosney Camp** Meath
67 Q5 **Moss-Side** Antrim
63 J6 **Mossley** Antrim
13 Q3 **Mothel** Watfd
45 M6 **Mount Nugent** Cavan
63 P9 **Mount Stewart** Down
55 N3 **Mount Talbot** Roscom
52 C3 **Mount Temple** Sligo
36 F5 **Mount Temple** Wmeath
6 G3 **Mount Uniacke** Cork
47 M2 **Mountain Bay** Louth
43 Q1 **Mountallen** Roscom
35 K4 **Mountbellew Bridge**/*An Creagán* Galway
28 F1 **Mountbolus** Offaly
6 C2 **Mountcatherine** Cork
59 J7 **Mountcharles**/*Moin Séarlas* Donegl
10 F1 **Mountcollins** Cork
60 H7 **Mountfield** Tyrone
23 L7 **Mounthoward Cross Roads** Wexfd
60 F7 **Mountjoy** Tyrone
13 J6 **Mountmelleray** Watfd
29 L3 **Mountmellick**/*Móinteach Milic* Laois
55 Q7 **Mountnorris** Armagh
29 J6 **Mountrath**/*Maighean Rátha* Laois
16 H1 **Mountrivers Bridge** Clare
26 H7 **Mountshannon**/*Baile Uí Bheoláin* Clare
16 E3 **Moveen** Clare
66 G5 **Moville**/*Bun an Phobail* Donegl
25 N3 **Moy** Galway
55 M2 **Moy** Tyrone
32 D2 **Moyard** Galway

16 H3 **Moyasta** Clare
20 E6 **Moycarky** Tippry
33 Q7 **Moycullen**/*Maigh Cuilinn* Galway
44 E10 **Moydow** Longfd
55 M1 **Moygashel** Tyrone
20 F8 **Moyglass** Tippry
22 D2 **Moyle** Carlow
22 G3 **Moylisha** Wicklw
51 M9 **Moylough** Sligo
26 C9 **Moymore** Clare
35 J4 **Moylough** Galway
46 C7 **Moynalty**/*Maigh nEalta* Meath
38 F4 **Moynalvy** Meath
44 G4 **Moyne** Longfd
43 J6 **Moyne** Roscom
20 F4 **Moyne** Tippry
31 J8 **Moyne** Wicklw
4 D5 **Moyny Bridge** Cork
48 F4 **Moyrahan** Mayo
17 N6 **Moyreen** Limrck
32 F6 **Moyrus** Galway
66 H9 **Moys** Lderry
38 C5 **Moyvally** Kildre
36 G3 **Moyvore** Wmeath
36 G5 **Moyvoughly** Wmeath
38 D6 **Mucklon** Kildre
10 B7 **Muckross** Kerry
10 B7 **Muckross House** Kerry
66 D8 **Muff**/*Magh* Donegl
10 C1 **Muinganear** Kerry
1 L6 **Muingaphuca** Kerry
9 Q1 **Muingnaminnane** Kerry
17 J10 **Muingwee** Kerry
8 F10 **Muingydowda** Kerry
39 K5 **Mulhuddart** Dublin
50 E5 **Mullafarry** Mayo
24 F10 **Mullagh** Clare
35 L10 **Mullagh** Galway
40 H8 **Mullagh** Mayo
38 G4 **Mullagh** Meath
46 B6 **Mullagh**/*An Mullach* Cavan
55 Q10 **Mullaghbane** Armagh
52 D2 **Mullaghmore** Sligo
43 K3 **Mullaghroe** Sligo
67 L8 **Mullan** Lderry
67 P9 **Mullan Head** Antrim
51 K8 **Mullany's Cross** Sligo
47 K7 **Mullary Cross Roads** Louth
43 L6 **Mullen** Roscom
11 R6 **Mullenaboree** Cork
21 K10 **Mullennaglogh** Tippry
21 Q10 **Mullennakill** Kilken
22 H2 **Mullinacuff** Wicklw
21 J8 **Mullinahone**/*Muileann na hUamhan* Tippry
14 D4 **Mullinavat**/*Muileann an Bhata* Kilken
41 Q9 **Mullingar Bridge** Mayo
37 L3 **Mullingar**/*An Muileann gCearr* Wmeath
37 L1 **Multyfarnham**/*Muilte Farannáin* Wmeath
18 G4 **Mungret**/*Mungairit* Limrck
17 K7 **Murher** Kerry
6 G2 **Murley's Cross Roads** Cork
15 N5 **Murntown** Wexfd
8 D3 **Murreagh**/*An Mhuiríoch* Kerry
41 J7 **Murrisk** Mayo
19 L3 **Murroe** Limrck
24 H3 **Murroogh** Clare
40 D3 **Mweelin** Kerry
10 B2 **Mweennalaa** Kerry
4 F8 **Myross** Cork
6 C8 **Myrtleville** Cork
22 E4 **Myshall**/*Miseal* Carlow

N

33 P9 **Na Forbacha** Galway
38 F10 **Naas**/*An Nás* Kildre
11 L6 **Nad** Cork
37 P10 **Nahana** Offaly
58 F3 **Naran** Donegl
30 D4 **Narraghmore**/*An Fhorrach Mhór* Kildre
39 L1 **Naul**/*An Aill* Dublin
46 F10 **Navan**/*An Uaimh* Meath
33 P2 **Neale**/*An Éill* Mayo
28 E6 **Nealstown** Laois
2 G3 **Nedanone** Kerry
27 L9 **Nenagh**/*An tAonach* Tippry
20 G6 **New Birmingham** Tippry
66 C10 **New Buildings** Lderry
45 N4 **New Inn** Cavan
35 K8 **New Inn** Galway
29 M4 **New Inn** Laois
14 G3 **New Ross**/*Ros Mhic Thriúin* Wexfd
11 N4 **New Twopothouse Village** Cork
15 J4 **Newbawn** Wexfd
54 G9 **Newbliss**/*Cúil Darach* Monhan
35 L3 **Newbridge** Galway
18 C5 **Newbridge** Limrck
30 E2 **Newbridge**/*An Droichead Nua* Kildre
57 J7 **Newcastle** Down
34 H7 **Newcastle** Galway

13 K4 **Newcastle** Tippry
39 J8 **Newcastle/An Caisleán Nua** Dublin
31 P4 **Newcastle/An Caisleán Nua** Wicklw
17 P8 **Newcastle West/An Caisleán Nua** Limrck
5 K3 **Newcestown** Cork
13 L1 **Newchapel** Tippry
37 K5 **Newell's Bridge** Wmeath
47 J9 **Newgrange Megalithic Passage Tomb** Meath
20 D10 **Newinn/Loch Ceann** Tippry
21 N9 **Newmarket** Kilken
11 J3 **Newmarket/Áth Trasna** Cork
10 D3 **Newmarket Cross Roads** Kerry
18 D1 **Newmarket on Fergus/Cora Chaitlin** Clare
4 H7 **Newmills** Cork
59 P1 **Newmills** Donegl
61 P9 **Newmills** Tyrone
19 L2 **Newport/An Port Nua** Tippry
41 K5 **Newport/Baile Ui Fhiacháin** Mayo
56 C8 **Newry** Down
35 L9 **Newtown** Galway
38 E6 **Newtown** Kildre
21 J5 **Newtown** Kilken
29 N9 **Newtown** Laois
19 K8 **Newtown** Limrck
41 P7 **Newtown** Mayo
46 G6 **Newtown** Meath
27 N2 **Newtown** Offaly
43 M9 **Newtown** Roscom
35 P7 **Newtown** Roscom
27 K8 **Newtown** Tippry
19 P9 **Newtown** Tippry
28 E8 **Newtown** Tippry
7 L3 **Newtown** Watfd
13 M8 **Newtown** Watfd
13 R5 **Newtown** Watfd
15 J7 **Newtown** Wexfd
15 M7 **Newtown** Wexfd
36 C2 **Newtown Cashel** Longfd
50 F8 **Newtown Cloghans** Mayo
65 Q9 **Newtown Cunningham/An Baile Nua Chuinneagain** Donegl
44 E8 **Newtown Forbes/An Lios Breac** Longfd
44 G1 **Newtown Gore** Leitrm
31 P3 **Newtown Mount Kennedy/Baile an Chinnéidigh** Wicklw
68 C9 **Newtown-Crommelin** Antrim
63 J6 **Newtownabbey** Antrim
13 J2 **Newtownadam** Tippry
63 M8 **Newtownards** Down
54 D8 **Newtownbutler** Ferman
55 P8 **Newtownhamilton** Armagh
37 K6 **Newtownlow** Wmeath
25 M2 **Newtownlynch** Galway
17 K7 **Newtownsandes Moyvane/Maigh Mheáin** Kerry
18 F10 **Newtownshandrum/ Baile Nua Sheandroma** Cork
60 F5 **Newtownstewart** Tyrone
14 E5 **Nicholastown** Kilken
21 K10 **Ninemilehouse/Tigh na Naoi Mile** Tippry
46 E6 **Nobber/An Obair** Meath
6 B9 **Nohaval** Cork
28 E7 **Nore Bridge** Tippry
5 K6 **North Ring** Cork
46 C3 **Northlands** Cavan
25 K5 **Noughaval** Clare
25 N9 **Noughaval** Clare
30 C3 **Nurney** Kildre
22 C3 **Nurney/An Urnai** Carlow
39 J4 **Nuttstown Cross Roads** Meath

O

24 G7 **O'Brien's Bridge** Clare
19 K1 **O'Briensbridge/ Droichead Ui Bhriain** Clare
26 D9 **O'Callaghansmills** Clare
16 G8 **Oaghley** Kerry
18 G1 **Oatfield** Clare
35 P9 **Oghill** Galway
26 G8 **Ogonnelloe** Clare
23 J10 **Oilgate/Maolán na nGabhar** Wexfd
67 N4 **Old Bushmills Distillery** Antrim
12 B9 **Old Bride Bridge** Cork
19 M5 **Old Bridge** Limrck
38 G3 **Old Cross Keys** Meath
5 P6 **Old Head** Cork
30 E3 **Old Kilcullen** Kildre

43 K5 **Old Lung Bridge** Roscom
47 J8 **Old Mellifont Abbey** Louth
6 E5 **Old Midleton Distillery** Cork
13 N7 **Old Pike Bridge** Watfd
14 H3 **Old Ross** Wexfd
29 K8 **Old Town** Laois
35 Q8 **Old Town** Roscom
11 P4 **Old Twopothouse Cross Roads** Cork
45 P7 **Oldcastle/An Seanchaisleán** Meath
13 K3 **Oldgrange** Dublin
29 Q8 **Oldleagh** Laois
22 B3 **Oldleighlin** Carlow
39 L3 **Oldtown** Dublin
36 C6 **Oldtown** Roscom
60 G8 **Omagh** Tyrone
56 D10 **Omeath/Ó Méith** Louth
24 B2 **Onaght/Eoghanacht** Clare
19 N6 **Oola/Úlla** Limrck
34 D9 **Oranmore/Orán Mór** Galway
46 E8 **Oristown** Meath
61 N7 **Orritor** Tyrone
36 G9 **Oughter** Offaly
33 N5 **Oughterard/Uachtar Ard** Galway
23 K8 **Oulart/An tAbhallort** Wexfd
13 J1 **Outeragh** Tippry
46 C2 **Ouvry Cross Roads** Monhan
11 N10 **Ovens** Cork
51 J4 **Owenbeg** Sligo
25 P2 **Owenbristy** Galway
41 J9 **Owenmore Bridge** Mayo
51 J5 **Owenykeevan or Tawnamaddoo** Sligo
33 Q4 **Ower** Galway
14 A3 **Owning** Kilken
9 J9 **Owroe Bridge** Kerry

P

22 E10 **Palace** Wexfd
19 M6 **Palatine Street** Limrck
30 D9 **Palatine** Carlow
35 L6 **Pallas** Laois
29 K5 **Pallas** Laois
20 C4 **Pallas Cross** Tippry
19 M5 **Pallas Green New** Limrck
19 M6 **Pallas Green** Limrck
37 L7 **Pallasboy** Wmeath
18 E4 **Pallaskenry/Pailis Chaonrai** Limrck
23 L3 **Pallis** Wexfd
39 K7 **Palmerstown** Dublin
41 Q4 **Park** Mayo
61 J2 **Park** Lderry
15 L7 **Park** Wexfd
22 G4 **Park Bridge** Wicklw
12 B6 **Parkacunna** Cork
5 K3 **Parkbane** Cork
62 G5 **Parkgate** Antrim
25 N2 **Parkmore** Galway
3 J2 **Parknasilla** Kerry
18 H2 **Parteen** Clare
41 P9 **Partry/Partrai** Mayo
35 N2 **Passage** Roscom
14 G6 **Passage East/An Pasáiste** Watfd
6 C6 **Passage West/An Pasáiste** Cork
18 G5 **Patrickswell/Tobar Phádraig** Limrck
22 B5 **Paulstown/Baile Phóil** Kilken
35 L9 **Peak** Galway
62 E4 **Peters Bridge** Antrim
26 D3 **Peterswell/Tobar Pheadair** Galway
59 P9 **Pettigo/Paiteagó** Donegl
6 A4 **Piercetown** Cork
15 N5 **Piercetown** Wexfd
3 Q4 **Pierson's Bridge** Cork
27 N3 **Pike** Tippry
38 F3 **Pike Corner** Meath
28 H7 **Pike of Rush Hall** Laois
14 B4 **Piltown/Baile an Phoill** Kilken
65 N10 **Pluck** Donegl
60 G4 **Plumbridge** Tyrone
25 N2 **Pollagh** Galway
36 F8 **Pollagh** Offaly
35 L9 **Pollatlugga** Galway
48 H3 **Pollatomish/Poll an Tómais** Mayo
35 P8 **Pollboy** Galway
43 J10 **Pollshask** Galway
61 L8 **Pomeroy** Tyrone
41 Q3 **Pontoon** Mayo
41 Q3 **Pontoon Bridge** Mayo
19 P6 **Pope's Bridge** Tippry
47 L6 **Port** Louth
29 L5 **Portlaoise/Port Laoise** Laois
48 H2 **Portacloy** Mayo
56 B3 **Portadown** Armagh
57 N3 **Portaferry** Down

66 E2 **Portaleen** Donegl
29 M2 **Portarlington/Cuil an tSúdaire** Laois
57 Q2 **Portavogie** Down
67 N4 **Portballintrae** Antrim
62 B2 **Portglenone** Antrim
27 L3 **Portland** Tippry
14 B5 **Portlaw/Port Lách** Watfd
8 D10 **Portmagee/An Caladh** Kerry
39 N5 **Portmarnock/Port Mearnóg** Dublin
63 M2 **Portmuck** Antrim
65 J5 **Portnablaghy/Port na Blaiche** Donegl
40 D7 **Portnakilly** Mayo
37 L1 **Portnashangan** Wmeath
58 F3 **Portnoo/Port Nua** Donegl
39 P3 **Portraine/Port Reachrainn** Dublin
27 J8 **Portroe/An Port Rua** Tippry
67 M5 **Portrush** Antrim
65 N5 **Portsalon/Port an tSalainn** Donegl
67 L5 **Portstewart** Lderry
27 L4 **Portumna/Port Omna** Galway
49 J2 **Porturlin** Mayo
27 N9 **Poulakerry** Tippry
5 J1 **Poulanargid** Cork
67 P3 **Poulgorm Bridge** Kerry
13 K1 **Poulnamucky** Tippry
27 J4 **Power's Cross** Galway
12 B8 **Powers Bridge** Cork
31 N1 **Powerscourt Gardens** Wicklw
56 C6 **Poyntz Pass** Armagh
12 B8 **Prap** Cork
60 E7 **Priest's Bridge** Tyrone
14 G5 **Priesthaggard** Wexfd
13 L5 **Priesttown** Tippry
38 E8 **Prosperous/An Chorrchoill** Kildre
27 K7 **Puckaun** Tippry

Q

5 K2 **Quarry Cross Roads** Cork
62 E1 **Quarrytown** Antrim
25 L2 **Quay** Clare
6 C6 **Queenstown Story** Cork
16 G4 **Querrin** Clare
66 E6 **Quigley's Point/Rinn Ui Choigligh** Donegl
24 F10 **Quilty/Coillte** Clare
25 P10 **Quin/Cuinche** Clare
28 D8 **Quinlisk's Cross Roads** Tippry

R

21 N4 **Radestown** Kilken
57 L2 **Raffrey** Down
51 N2 **Raghly** Sligo
45 P8 **Rahaghy** Meath
36 H8 **Rahan/Raithean** Offaly
37 Q3 **Raharney/Ráth Fhearna** Wmeath
30 G9 **Raheen** Carlow
5 M2 **Raheen** Cork
10 D6 **Raheen** Kerry
12 H2 **Raheen** Tippry
36 G5 **Raheen** Wmeath
15 J3 **Raheen** Wexfd
23 M8 **Raheenlusk** Wexfd
3 N7 **Raheenroe** Cork
57 M4 **Raholp** Down
50 D8 **Rake Street** Mayo
14 G6 **Ramsgrange** Wexfd
26 H2 **Ranamackan** Galway
62 D4 **Randalstown** Antrim
28 C2 **Rapemills** Offaly
60 C2 **Raphoe/Ráth Bhoth** Donegl
10 G3 **Rascalstreet** Cork
67 P10 **Rasharkin** Antrim
59 P1 **Rashedoge** Donegl
43 N4 **Ratallen Cross Roads** Roscom
28 D3 **Rath** Offaly
39 K3 **Rath Cross Roads** Meath
38 B10 **Rathangan/Ráth Iomgháin** Kildre
9 Q2 **Rathanny** Kerry
44 H10 **Rathaspick** Wmeath
20 F9 **Rathbrit** Tippry
27 N3 **Rathcabban** Tippry
38 D1 **Rathcarran/Ráth Chairn** Meath
38 F7 **Rathcoffey** Kildre
43 N9 **Rathconor** Roscom
37 J3 **Rathconrath** Wmeath
11 J6 **Rathcool** Cork
39 J8 **Rathcoole/Ráth Cúil** Dublin
38 D4 **Rathcore** Meath
12 D8 **Rathcormack/Ráth Chormaic** Cork

43 M7 **Rathcroghan Cross Roads** Roscom
25 K10 **Rathcrony** Clare
30 H7 **Rathdangan/Ráth Daingin** Wicklw
28 G9 **Rathdowney/Ráth Domhnaigh** Laois
31 M7 **Rathdrum/Ráth Droma** Wicklw
36 H1 **Rathduff** Longfd
17 P9 **Ratheenagh** Limrck
38 D9 **Rathernan** Kildre
47 J6 **Rathescar Cross Roads** Louth
39 J1 **Rathfeigh** Meath
6 C3 **Rathfilode** Cork
56 E7 **Rathfriland** Down
22 F9 **Rathflyane** Watfd
29 L9 **Rathgarry** Laois
13 P3 **Rathgormuck** Watfd
34 B1 **Rathgranagher** Mayo
19 N8 **Rathkea** Tippry
18 D6 **Rathkeale/Ráth Caola** Limrck
46 F8 **Rathkenny** Meath
43 N8 **Rathkeva** Roscom
13 L2 **Rathkevin** Tippry
43 M6 **Rathkineely** Roscom
50 E3 **Rathlackan/Ráth Leacáin** Mayo
50 H3 **Rathlee** Sligo
30 F9 **Rathlyon** Carlow
13 Q5 **Rathmaiden** Watfd
65 N8 **Rathmelton/Ráth Mealtain** Donegl
46 D10 **Rathmore** Meath
10 F6 **Rathmore/An Ráth Mhór** Kerry
38 H10 **Rathmore/An Ráth Mhór** Kildre
14 F9 **Rathmoylan** Watfd
38 D4 **Rathmoylon** Meath
65 P7 **Rathmullan/Ráth Maolain** Donegl
31 P3 **Rathnew/Ráth Naoi** Wicklw
22 E9 **Rathnure** Wexfd
50 E5 **Rathoma** Mayo
6 F3 **Rathorgan** Cork
45 J10 **Rathowen/Ráth Eoghainn** Wmeath
50 F6 **Rathroeen** Mayo
3 P7 **Rathruane** Cork
16 E9 **Rathscannel** Kerry
22 E2 **Rathtoe** Carlow
30 F8 **Rathvilly/Ráth Bhile** Carlow
37 P3 **Rathwire** Wmeath
39 J3 **Ratoath/Ráth Tó** Meath
3 M8 **Ratooragh** Cork
47 K1 **Ravensdale** Louth
56 G1 **Ravernet** Down
65 P7 **Ray** Donegl
4 C7 **Rea Cross Roads** Cork
46 G4 **Reaghstown** Louth
7 M3 **Reanaclogheen** Watfd
25 J10 **Reanagishagh** Clare
10 B1 **Reanagowan Cross Roads** Kerry
10 G10 **Reananerree** Cork
4 G6 **Reanascreena** Cork
19 N3 **Rearcross** Tippry
36 C10 **Reask** Galway
4 F6 **Reavouler Bridge** Cork
32 H4 **Recess/Sraith Salach** Galway
61 L10 **Reclain** Tyrone
66 F6 **Redcastle** Donegl
31 N8 **Redcross/An Chrois Dhearg** Wicklw
23 J10 **Redgate** Wexfd
54 D10 **Redhills/An Cnoc Rua** Cavan
27 M3 **Redwood** Tippry
3 N2 **Releagh Bridge** Kerry
3 J6 **Rerrin** Cork
67 N5 **Revallagh North** Antrim
37 N7 **Rhode/Ród** Offaly
55 P4 **Richill** Armagh
8 E3 **Riesk** Cork
15 Q7 **Ring** Wexfd
6 C7 **Ringaskiddy/Rinn an Scidigh** Cork
67 L8 **Ringsend** Lderry
29 J5 **Ringstown** Laois
13 N9 **Ringville/An Rinn** Watfd
64 D8 **Rinnafarset** Donegl
24 G8 **Rinneen** Clare
4 E8 **Rinneen** Cork
34 D9 **Rinville** Galway
32 D1 **Rinvyle** Galway
23 M5 **Riverchapel** Wexfd
5 Q3 **Riverstick** Cork
6 B5 **Riverstown** Cork
27 P4 **Riverstown** Cork
52 D9 **Riverstown/Baile Idir Dhá Abhainn** Sligo
9 Q3 **Riverville Cross Roads** Kerry
24 G5 **Roadford** Clare
38 D8 **Robertstown/Baile Riobaird** Kildre
38 E1 **Robinstown** Meath
15 L6 **Robinstown** Wexfd
14 C4 **Rochestown** Kilken
14 F5 **Rochestown** Kilken
13 J2 **Rochestown** Tippry

37 M5 **Rochfortbridge/ Droichead Chaisleán Loiste** Wmeath
20 D8 **Rock of Cashel** Tippry
10 G1 **Rockchapel** Cork
54 H10 **Rockcorry/Buíochar** Monhan
31 N7 **Rocketstown** Wicklw
18 G9 **Rockhill** Limrck
12 B5 **Rockmills** Cork
43 Q5 **Rodeen** Roscom
34 E10 **Roevehagh** Galway
27 N1 **Rooaun** Galway
42 H2 **Roosky** Mayo
44 C6 **Roosky/Rúscaigh** Roscom
35 Q7 **Rooty Cross Roads** Roscom
65 L5 **Rosapenna** Donegl
14 G3 **Rosbercon** Wexfd
22 E2 **Roscat** Carlow
35 P1 **Roscommon/Ros Comáin** Roscom
28 D7 **Roscrea/Ros Cré** Tippry
20 E9 **Rosegreen** Tippry
36 G5 **Rosemount** Wmeath
29 J3 **Rosenallis** Laois
33 J7 **Rosmuck/Ros Muc** Galway
20 C5 **Rosmult** Tippry
65 M5 **Rosnakill** Donegl
45 M7 **Ross** Meath
9 J6 **Ross Behy** Kerry
4 G7 **Ross Carbery/Ros Ó gCairbre** Cork
48 H3 **Ross Port/Ros Dumhach** Mayo
41 P4 **Ross West** Mayo
19 Q9 **Rossadrehid** Tippry
10 B4 **Rossanean** Kerry
33 K8 **Rossaveel/Ros an Mhil** Galway
58 E3 **Rossbeg** Donegl
3 P8 **Rossbrin** Cork
33 P6 **Rosscahill** Galway
51 P3 **Rosses Point/An Ros** Sligo
52 H4 **Rossinver/Ros Inbhir** Leitrm
15 Q6 **Rosslare/Ros Láir** Wexfd
15 Q6 **Rosslare Harbour/Calafort Ros Láir** Wexfd
54 F7 **Rosslea** Ferman
3 J5 **Rossmackowen** Cork
4 G1 **Rossmore** Cork
4 H5 **Rossmore** Cork
22 B2 **Rossmore** Laois
20 B6 **Rossmore** Tippry
29 N4 **Rossmore Cross Roads** Laois
3 M3 **Rossnagrena** Cork
59 J9 **Rossnowlagh** Donegl
6 E6 **Rostellan** Cork
56 E10 **Rostrevor** Down
40 H4 **Rosturk** Mayo
42 B10 **Roundfort** Mayo
32 E6 **Roundstone/Cloch na Rón** Galway
31 M4 **Roundwood/An Tóchar** Wicklw
61 J5 **Rousky** Tyrone
25 M7 **Ruan** Clare
57 P1 **Rubane** Down
39 P3 **Rush/An Ros** Dublin
11 K9 **Rusheen** Cork
33 M5 **Rusheeny** Galway
13 L3 **Russellstown** Watfd
34 G6 **Ryehill** Galway
11 L8 **Rylane** Cork

S

39 J8 **Saggart** Dublin
66 C9 **St Columb's Cathedral** Lderry
39 L5 **St Margaret's** Dublin
22 C9 **St Mullin's** Carlow
60 D1 **Saint Johnstown/Baile Suingean** Donegl
57 K2 **Saintfield** Down
6 E6 **Saleen** Cork
8 G10 **Sallahig** Kerry
38 F9 **Sallins/Na Solláin** Kildre
6 B4 **Sallybrook** Cork
20 B2 **Sallypark** Tippry
34 B9 **Salthill/Bóthar na Trá** Galway
14 H7 **Saltmills** Wexfd
61 N8 **Sandholes** Tyrone
39 M8 **Sandyford** Dublin
39 M5 **Santry** Dublin
21 L4 **Sart Cross Roads** Kilken
57 M4 **Saul** Down
10 E2 **Scalp Bridge** Kerry
35 P2 **Scardaun** Roscom
42 C10 **Scardaune** Mayo
23 N3 **Scarnagh Cross Roads** Wexfd
26 F8 **Scarriff/An Scairbh** Clare
38 C3 **Scarriff Bridge** Meath
13 M6 **Scart Bridge** Watfd
10 C4 **Scartaglin/Scairteach an Ghlinne** Kerry
56 C5 **Scarva** Down
55 K8 **Scotch Corner** Monhan
55 Q2 **Scotch Street** Armagh

54 E10 **Scotshouse** Monhan
54 H6 **Scotstown**/*Baile an Scotaigh* Monhan
10 D5 **Scrahanfadda** Kerry
44 B8 **Scramoge** Roscom
12 B6 **Scrarour** Cork
23 K10 **Screen** Wexfd
36 H9 **Screggan** Offaly
66 H10 **Scriggan** Lderry
46 C9 **Scurlockstown** Meath
57 K5 **Seaforde** Down
56 D4 **Seapatrick** Down
13 N2 **Seskin** Tippry
60 G10 **Seskinore** Tyrone
4 E3 **Shanacrane** Cork
6 G6 **Shanagarry** Cork
25 P5 **Shanaglish** Galway
17 P5 **Shanagolden**/*Seanghualainn* Limrck
29 J7 **Shanahoe** Laois
24 H9 **Shanavogh East** Clare
6 C7 **Shanbally** Cork
35 J7 **Shanballard** Galway
35 K1 **Shanbally** Galway
13 P7 **Shanbally** Watfd
19 N3 **Shanballyedmond** Tippry
42 F10 **Shanballymore** Galway
12 A5 **Shanballymore**/*An Seanbhaile Mór* Cork
38 C3 **Shanco Bridge** Meath
26 H2 **Shangarry** Galway
39 P9 **Shankill** Dublin
4 G3 **Shanlaragh** Cork
46 G6 **Shanlis Cross Roads** Louth
17 N4 **Shannakea** Clare
18 D2 **Shannon** Clare
18 E2 **Shannon**/*Sionainn* Clare
36 C10 **Shannon Harbour**/*Caladh na Sionainne* Offaly
36 B8 **Shannonbridge**/*Droichead na Sionainne* Offaly
29 P7 **Shanragh** Laois
12 G4 **Shanrahan Cross Roads** Tippry
18 C9 **Shanrath** Limrck
46 C1 **Shantonagh** Monhan
28 C5 **Sharavogue** Offaly
46 C2 **Shercock**/*Searcóg* Cavan
13 Q2 **Sheskin** Watfd
20 B5 **Shevry** Tippry
22 H3 **Shillelagh**/*Síol Éalaigh* Wicklw
28 C6 **Shinrone**/*Suí an Róin* Offaly
57 M3 **Shrigley** Down
16 H6 **Shrone** Kerry
19 N7 **Shronell** Tippry
16 H6 **Shronowen** Kerry
34 B3 **Shrule**/*Sruthair* Mayo
4 E4 **Sillahertane** Cork
55 Q10 **Silver Bridge** Armagh
55 K6 **Silver Stream** Monhan
27 K10 **Silvermines**/*Béal Átha Gabhann* Tippry
60 D4 **Sion Mills** Tyrone
63 N7 **Six Road Ends** Down
18 F1 **Sixmilebridge**/*Droichead Abhainn Ó gCearnaigh* Clare
61 J9 **Sixmilecross** Tyrone
4 B4 **Skahanagh** Cork
6 C3 **Skahanagh North** Cork
6 C3 **Skahanagh South** Cork
4 C7 **Skeagh** Cork
36 H3 **Skeagh Beg** Wmeath
26 C3 **Skehanagh** Galway
34 H5 **Skehanagh** Galway
12 E4 **Skeheen** Cork
11 Q4 **Skenakilla Cross Roads** Cork
39 P1 **Skerries**/*Na Sceirí* Dublin
4 D8 **Skibbereen**/*An Sciobairín* Cork
38 H1 **Skreen** Meath
51 M4 **Skreen** Sligo
3 N8 **Skull**/*An Scoil* Cork
14 G9 **Slade** Watfd
46 H9 **Slane**/*Baile Shláine* Meath
35 L2 **Slievemurray** Galway
4 H2 **Slieveowen** Cork
14 E6 **Slieveroe** Kilken
5 Q2 **Sligga Bridge** Cork
52 C6 **Sligo**/*Sligeach* Sligo
52 C6 **Sligo Abbey** Sligo
46 H6 **Smarmore** Louth
8 C3 **Smerwick** Kerry
54 G7 **Smithborough** Monhan
21 P2 **Smithstown** Kilken
2 H1 **Sneem**/*An tSnaidhm* Kerry
52 D9 **Sooey** Sligo
9 M1 **Spa** Kerry
25 N8 **Spancehill** Clare
24 F9 **Spanish Point**/*Rinn na Spáinneach* Clare
61 K4 **Sperrin** Tyrone
33 N9 **Spiddle**/*An Spidéal* Galway
29 M8 **Spink Bridge** Laois
36 H6 **Spittaltown** Wmeath
66 C9 **Spring Town** Lderry
31 M3 **Sraghmore** Wicklw

48 F5 **Srah** Mayo
41 N9 **Srah**/*An tSraith* Mayo
28 F5 **Srahanboy** Laois
42 B5 **Sraheens** Mayo
40 E4 **Sraheens Bridge** Mayo
48 H6 **Srahmore** Mayo
48 H8 **Srahnamanragh Bridge** Mayo
49 K2 **Sranataggle** Mayo
13 J6 **Sruh** Watfd
47 J3 **Stabannan** Louth
46 G9 **Stackallan** Meath
62 C5 **Staffordstown** Antrim
47 M10 **Stamullin** Meath
38 E7 **Staplestown** Kildre
38 M9 **Stepaside** Dublin
61 Q8 **Stewartstown** Tyrone
39 M8 **Stillorgan** Dublin
54 F8 **Stone Bridge** Monhan
48 H2 **Stonefield** Mayo
19 J5 **Stonepark** Limrck
62 G8 **Stonyford** Antrim
21 N8 **Stonyford**/*Áth Stiúin* Kilken
63 L8 **Stormont** Down
60 D3 **Strabane** Tyrone
8 H2 **Stradbally** Kerry
13 Q7 **Stradbally**/*An tSráidbhaile* Watfd
29 N5 **Stradbally**/*An tSráidbhaile* Laois
42 B4 **Strade** Mayo
45 N3 **Stradone**/*Sraith an Domhain* Cavan
38 G8 **Straffan**/*Teach Srafáin* Kildre
22 H6 **Strahart** Wexfd
63 J4 **Straid** Antrim
17 N9 **Strand** Limrck
51 P3 **Strandhill**/*An Leathros* Sligo
57 N4 **Strangford** Down
67 Q6 **Stranocum** Antrim
59 P3 **Stranorlar**/*Srath an Urláir* Donegl
30 F6 **Stratford**/*Áth na Sráide* Wicklw
36 H5 **Streamstown** Wmeath
45 J9 **Street** Wmeath
20 F2 **Strogue Cross Roads** Tippry
43 Q7 **Strokestown**/*Béal na mBuillí* Roscom
43 Q7 **Strokestown Park** Roscom
66 H4 **Stroove** Donegl
11 M8 **Stuake** Cork
5 Q5 **Summer Cove** Cork
38 E4 **Summerhill**/*Cnoc an Línsigh* Meath
30 D3 **Suncroft** Kildre
29 N8 **Swan** Laois
54 H9 **Swan's Cross Roads** Monhan
53 N8 **Swanlinbar**/*An Muileann Iarainn* Cavan
61 Q1 **Swatragh** Lderry
42 D4 **Swinford**/*Béal Átha na Muice* Mayo
39 M4 **Swords**/*Sord* Dublin

T

35 P6 **Taghmaconnell** Roscom
15 L5 **Taghmon**/*Teach Munna* Wexfd
36 G1 **Taghshinny** Longfd
15 Q6 **Tagoat** Wexfd
3 J1 **Tahilla** Kerry
39 K8 **Tallaght** Dublin
46 H4 **Tallanstown** Louth
12 G8 **Tallow**/*Tulach an Iarainn* Watfd
12 H8 **Tallowbridge** Watfd
53 Q5 **Tamlaght** Ferman
61 R1 **Tamlaght O'Crilly** Lderry
55 N1 **Tamnamore** Tyrone
56 B4 **Tandragee** Armagh
36 E3 **Tang** Wmeath
18 H9 **Tankardstown** Limrck
13 K4 **Tar Bridge** Tippry
38 G2 **Tara** Meath
36 H7 **Tara** Offaly
17 K5 **Tarbert**/*Tairbeart* Kerry
17 K3 **Tarmon** Clare
11 L1 **Tarrant's Cross Roads** Cork
55 N6 **Tassagh** Armagh
10 G3 **Taur** Cork
65 M5 **Tawny** Donegl
42 F4 **Tawnyinah** Mayo
52 G8 **Tawnylea** Leitrm
27 P2 **Taylor's Cross** Offaly
3 P5 **Tedagh** Cork
54 H6 **Tedavnet** Monhan
58 C7 **Teelin**/*Tieleann* Donegl
54 B9 **Teemore** Ferman
8 G2 **Teer** Kerry
8 E10 **Teeranearagh** Kerry
8 C4 **Teeravane** Kerry
4 H1 **Teerelton** Cork
25 M10 **Teermaclane** Clare
33 K3 **Teernakill Bridge** Galway
8 H8 **Teeromoyle** Kerry
46 C5 **Teevurcher** Meath
51 L4 **Templeboy** Sligo
19 Q1 **Templederry** Tippry

13 N1 **Templeetney** Tippry
20 E2 **Templemore**/*An Teampall Mór* Tippry
3 L1 **Templenoe** Kerry
37 L6 **Templeoran** Wmeath
14 B3 **Templeorum** Kilken
62 G5 **Templepatrick** Antrim
22 F7 **Templeshanbo** Wexfd
20 F2 **Templetouhy**/*Teampall Tuaithe* Tippry
14 H8 **Templetown** Wexfd
8 B4 **Templeusque** Cork
54 C4 **Temo** Ferman
15 N7 **Tenacre Cross Roads** Wexfd
65 L8 **Termon** Donegl
44 D8 **Termonbarry** Roscom
47 L7 **Termonfeckin**/*Tearmann Feichín* Louth
27 L4 **Terryglass**/*Tír Dhá Ghlas* Tippry
37 N2 **Tevrin** Wmeath
62 B7 **The Battery** Tyrone
47 M2 **The Bush** Louth
21 Q3 **The Butts** Carlow
21 D10 **The Cross** Lderry
62 E7 **The Diamond** Antrim
62 A7 **The Diamond** Tyrone
N3 **The Downs** Wmeath
68 B7 **The Drones** Antrim
39 M2 **The Five Roads** Dublin
24 H9 **The Hand Cross Roads** Clare
23 K7 **The Harrow** Wexfd
15 K3 **The Leap** Kerry
R6 **The Loup** Lderry
36 E3 **The Pigeons** Wmeath
27 N5 **The Pike** Tippry
6 H2 **The Pike** Watfd
13 P7 **The Pike** Watfd
N8 **The Rock** Tyrone
22 C10 **The Rower** Kilken
G1 **The Sheddings** Antrim
61 M4 **The Six Towns** Lderry
57 J4 **The Spa** Down
14 B4 **The Sweep** Kilken
J1 **The Temple** Down
19 K10 **Thomastown** Limrck
46 D7 **Thomastown** Meath
20 B9 **Thomastown** Tippry
21 P8 **Thomastown**/*Baile Mhic Andáin* Kilken
54 H7 **Three Mile House** Monhan
21 M4 **Threecastles** Kilken
31 L8 **Threewells** Wicklw
20 E5 **Thurles**/*Durlas* Tippry
43 K5 **Tibohine** Roscom
16 B8 **Tiduff** Kerry
13 M2 **Tikincor** Watfd
38 D7 **Timahoe** Kildre
29 M6 **Timahoe**/*Tigh Mochua* Laois
5 L6 **Timoleague**/*Tigh Molaige* Cork
30 E6 **Timolin** Kildre
23 J2 **Tinahely**/*Tigh na hÉille* Wicklw
36 F7 **Tinamuck** Offaly
23 J8 **Tinnacross Cross Roads** Wexfd
15 M3 **Tinnakilla** Wexfd
22 C2 **Tinryland** Carlow
47 J7 **Tinure Cross Roads** Louth
19 P7 **Tipperary**/*Tiobraid Árann* Tippry
61 P2 **Tirkane** Lderry
5 L6 **Tirnanean** Cork
55 J6 **Tirnaneill** Monhan
25 P4 **Tirneevin** Galway
36 G6 **Tober** Offaly
30 F5 **Toberbeg** Wicklw
51 M8 **Tobercurry**/*Tobar an Choire* Sligo
26 D2 **Toberelatan** Galway
61 P3 **Tobermore** Lderry
11 J2 **Tobernaclougha Cross Roads** Cork
34 B2 **Tobernadarry** Mayo
52 C9 **Toberscanavan** Sligo
19 P5 **Toem** Tippry
4 F3 **Togher** Cork
47 L6 **Togher** Louth
38 D4 **Togher** Meath
37 N7 **Togher** Offaly
31 J4 **Togher** Wicklw
16 D9 **Togherbane** Kerry
15 N7 **Tomhaggard** Wexfd
34 B8 **Tonabrocky** Galway
41 M8 **Tonlegee** Mayo
40 F3 **Tonregee** Mayo
45 Q3 **Tonyduff** Cavan
4 G3 **Toom** Cork
23 J4 **Toomaghera** Clare
41 N10 **Toomakeady**/*Tuar Mhic Éadaigh* Mayo
35 K3 **Toomard** Galway
32 F5 **Toombeola** Galway
62 B4 **Toome** Antrim
4 H1 **Tooms** Cork
27 N9 **Toomyvara**/*Tuaim Uí Mheára* Tippry
19 N2 **Toor** Tippry
13 L5 **Tooraneena** Watfd
17 M6 **Tooraree** Limrck
11 R6 **Tooreen** Cork
19 N2 **Tooreenbrien Bridge** Tippry

10 E4 **Tooreencahill** Kerry
10 H2 **Tooreendermot** Cork
12 A8 **Toorgarriff** Cork
3 M8 **Toormore** Cork
17 N10 **Toornafulla** Limrck
14 K6 **Torque** Wmeath
66 C9 **Tower Museum** Lderry
14 D7 **Towergare** Watfd
6 D7 **Trabolgan** Cork
6 B8 **Tracton** Cork
3 L5 **Trafrask** Cork
9 N2 **Tralee**/*Trá Lí* Kerry
14 D8 **Tramore**/*Trá Mhór* Watfd
34 H3 **Trasternagh** Galway
2 G5 **Travara Bridge** Cork
4 B5 **Trawlebane** Cork
33 M1 **Trean** Mayo
65 L9 **Treantagh** Donegl
45 M1 **Treehoo Cross Roads** Cavan
9 J2 **Trench Bridge** Kerry
43 J8 **Trien** Roscom
54 B2 **Trillick** Tyrone
38 E2 **Trim**/*Baile Átha Troim* Meath
38 E2 **Trim Castle** Meath
35 L7 **Trust** Galway
34 E3 **Tuam**/*Tuaim* Galway
26 F8 **Tuamgraney**/*Tuaim Gréine* Clare
25 P6 **Tubber** Galway
12 H3 **Tubbrid** Tippry
21 J4 **Tubbrid** Kilken
26 C8 **Tulla**/*An Tulach* Clare
4 E2 **Tullagh** Cork
25 J10 **Tullaghaboy** Clare
52 E2 **Tullaghan** Leitrm
48 G7 **Tullaghanduff** Mayo
21 Q10 **Tullagher** Kilken
21 L10 **Tullaghought** Kilken
21 P7 **Tullaherin** Kilken
9 K10 **Tullakeel** Kerry
37 J8 **Tullamore**/*Tulach Mhór* Offaly
9 J2 **Tullaree** Kerry
21 K5 **Tullaroan** Kilken
25 L9 **Tullassa** Clare
16 D4 **Tullig** Clare
9 L5 **Tullig** Kerry
16 Q9 **Tullig** Kerry
22 F2 **Tullow**/*An Tulach* Carlow
32 E1 **Tully Cross** Galway
33 L9 **Tully**/*An Tulaigh* Galway
47 J8 **Tullyallen** Louth
15 L6 **Tullycanna** Wexfd
52 F8 **Tullycoly** Leitrm
61 P8 **Tullyhogue** Tyrone
11 K1 **Tullylease** Cork
45 P1 **Tullyvin** Cavan
42 F9 **Tulrohaun** Mayo
43 N7 **Tulsk**/*Tuilsce* Roscom
37 N2 **Turin** Wmeath
41 Q5 **Turlough** Mayo
25 L3 **Turlough** Clare
34 E6 **Turloughmore** Galway
4 E1 **Turnaspidogy** Cork
11 Q3 **Turnpike Cross** Cork
44 C10 **Turreen** Longfd
15 P6 **Twelveacre Cross Roads** Wexfd
20 D6 **Twoford Bridges** Tippry
29 K2 **Twomile Bridge** Laois
20 F5 **Twomileborris** Tippry
27 J2 **Tynagh** Galway
55 L5 **Tynan** Armagh
61 P10 **Tyrone Crystal** Tyrone
37 L6 **Tyrrellspass**/*Bealach an Tirialaigh* Wmeath

U

60 F7 **Ulster American Folk Park** Tyrone
4 F8 **Unionhall**/*Bréantrá* Cork
62 F9 **Upper Ballinderry** Antrim
20 B4 **Upperchurch** Tippry
61 Q2 **Upperlands** Lderry
5 M3 **Upton** Cork
2 G5 **Urhin** Cork
42 G6 **Urlaur** Mayo
20 H4 **Urlingford**/*Áth na nUrlainn* Kilken

V

30 H3 **Valleymount** Wicklw
8 D4 **Ventry** Kerry
29 P4 **Vicarstown** Laois
60 E4 **Victoria Bridge** Tyrone
13 K8 **Villierstown**/*An Baile Nua* Watfd
45 Q6 **Virginia**/*Achadh an Iúir* Cavan

W

37 N9 **Walsh Island** Offaly
6 E3 **Walshtown** Cork
38 H1 **Walterstown** Meath

39 L4 **Ward** Dublin
56 D2 **Waringstown** Down
5 P2 **Warner's Cross Roads** Cork
56 D10 **Warrenpoint** Down
30 G1 **Watch House Cross Roads** Kildre
22 G4 **Watch House Village** Wexfd
5 P1 **Waterfall** Cork
14 E8 **Waterford** Watfd
14 E6 **Waterford**/*Port Láirge* Watfd
14 D6 **Waterford Crystal** Watfd
6 C3 **Watergrasshill**/*Cnocán na Biolraí* Cork
2 E1 **Waterville**/*An Coireán* Kerry
59 N3 **Welchtown** Donegl
15 K6 **Wellingtonbridge**/*Droichead Eoin* Wexfd
5 J6 **West Cork Model Railway Village** Cork
64 F3 **West Town**/*Baile Thiar* Donegl
41 K7 **Westport**/*Cathair na Mart* Mayo
41 K7 **Westport Quay** Mayo
14 D9 **Westtown** Watfd
15 N4 **Wexford**/*Loch Garman* Wexfd
30 D1 **Wheelam Cross Roads** Kildre
9 M4 **White Gate Cross Roads** Kerry
4 A4 **White's Cross** Cork
63 K6 **Whiteabbey** Antrim
11 Q8 **Whitechurch** Cork
13 L7 **Whitechurch** Watfd
14 G5 **Whitechurch** Wexfd
55 Q7 **Whitecross** Armagh
26 H7 **Whitegate**/*An Geata Bán* Clare
6 D7 **Whitegate**/*An Geata Bán* Cork
44 D8 **Whitehall** Roscom
45 M10 **Whitehall** Wmeath
63 M4 **Whitehead** Antrim
47 N2 **Whites Town** Louth
62 D3 **Whitesides Corner** Antrim
31 Q6 **Wicklow**/*Cill Mhantáin* Wicklw
46 F8 **Wilkinstown**/*Baile Uilcín* Meath
25 K7 **Willbrook** Clare
43 J10 **Williamstown** Galway
21 L10 **Windgap**/*Bearna na Gaoithe* Kilken
38 C7 **Windmill Cross Roads** Kildre
29 N8 **Wolfhill** Laois
63 K5 **Woodburn** Antrim
31 M9 **Woodenbridge** Wicklw
26 D10 **Woodfield Bridge** Clare
26 H4 **Woodford**/*An Chráig* Galway
35 K7 **Woodlawn**/*Móta* Galway
14 F7 **Woodstown** Watfd

Y

46 G9 **Yellow Furze** Meath
7 K4 **Youghal**/*Eochaill* Cork
27 J8 **Youghal** Tippry